Visual Attention and Consciousness

Consciousness is perhaps one of the greatest mysteries in the universe. This ambitious book begins with a philosophical approach to consciousness, examining some key questions such as what is meant by the term "conscious," and how this applies to vision.

The book then explores the major visual phenomena related to attention and conscious experience—including filling-in processes, aftereffects, multi-stability, forms of divided attention, models of visual attention, priming effects, types of attentional blindness, as well as various visual disorders. For each phenomenon, the biological and cognitive level research is reviewed. Themes touched upon throughout are the relation between consciousness and attention, automatic vs. willful processes, singularity vs. multiplicity, and looking without seeing.

The book concludes with an evolutionary approach, describing possible functions that visual consciousness may serve and how those may affect the way we see.

The systematic review of key topics and the multitude of perspectives make this book an ideal primary or ancillary text for graduate courses in perception, vision, consciousness, or philosophy of mind.

Jay Friedenberg is Professor and Chair of Psychology at Manhattan College. He has previously written textbooks on artificial intelligence, dynamical systems and cognitive science, and has published articles on center estimation, symmetry perception and the perceived aesthetics of geometric forms.

Visual Attention and Consciousness

Jay Friedenberg

Psychology Press
Taylor & Francis Group

NEW YORK AND LONDON

First published 2013
by Psychology Press
711 Third Avenue, New York, NY 10017

Simultaneously published in the UK
by Psychology Press
27 Church Road, Hove, East Sussex BN3 2FA

Psychology Press is an imprint of the Taylor & Francis Group, an informa business

Library of Congress Cataloging in Publication Data
A catalog record for this book has been requested

ISBN: 978–1–84872–905–6 (hbk)
ISBN: 978–1–84872–619–2 (pbk)
ISBN: 978–0–203–07385–8 (ebk)

Typeset in Times by Swales & Willis, Exeter, Devon

Visit the Taylor and Francis Web site at
http://www.taylorandfrancis.com/

and the Psychology Press Web site at
http://www.psypress.com

SUSTAINABLE
FORESTRY
INITIATIVE

Certified Sourcing
www.sfiprogram.org
SFI-00555
The SFI label applies to the text stock.

Printed and bound in the United States of America by
Walsworth Publishing Company, Marceline, MO.

Contents

Acknowledgements

I would like to acknowledge the efforts of my research assistant Elena Rotundo for her speed and diligence in completing the reference list, author index, and subject index.

1 Introduction

THEMES AND CHAPTER ORGANIZATION

We cover a lot of ground in this book, surveying the empirical literature on many different aspects of visual attention and consciousness. In order to organize all this information and show how it is inter-related we divide the subject up into seven main themes. We devote one or two chapters to developing each of these themes, a preview of which is given below. Each chapter section that describes a unique perceptual phenomenon begins with an everyday example followed by a definition. We then discuss the perceptual, cognitive, and neuroscience research on the topic and how it relates to visual attention and consciousness.

THEME 1: CONSCIOUSNESS AND ATTENTION

We start by introducing the concept of consciousness. There are many different types of conscious experience so we briefly present different proposed categorization schemes. Our focus will be entirely on perceptual consciousness, specifically visual conscious experience. We then introduce attention and describe how it differs from consciousness. Attention and consciousness are closely related but recent work shows that they are not the same. It is possible to be conscious of something while not paying attention to it and to pay attention to something while not being conscious of it. Following this we present several classic thought experiments on consciousness and frame the major philosophical issues. The scientific approach to studying this phenomenon advocates a monist materialist stance that should attempt to bridge the explanatory gap between objective and subjective measures of awareness. Consciousness is best studied using both older reductionist and newer emergent approaches.

Because much of what we will discuss centers on underlying brain areas, we will introduce some of the anatomical and physiological underpinnings of vision before getting into a detailed description of the literature. The brain areas underlying conscious and unconscious vision are discussed along with the idea of the neuronal correlates of consciousness and the theory of neural synchrony. We then sketch out the structural and functional basis of visual attention along with biological models and some of the problems encountered in doing this type of research. In Chapter 7 we present different varieties of attention including preattentive and attentive, exogenous and endogenous, and object- and space-based forms.

THEME 2: AUTOMATIC MECHANISMS

Our visual world is actively constructed and a lot of what we experience is the result of lower level automatic processes. We aren't aware of our blind spot even though there are no photoreceptors in this part of the retina to provide information about what is located there. We don't notice the world "jumping" whenever we make an eye movement because of saccadic suppression. The visual system fills in this region so that we aren't even aware that we are missing anything. There are also more complex types of filling in that occur. In perceptual completion, we build up the hidden parts of objects that are occluded so that they seem complete even though we glimpse only a part of them.

It is easy to fatigue the visual system if we look at something for too long. Under these conditions we often experience aftereffects. We examine three different types of aftereffects for color, motion, and tilt in which we seem to "bounce back" and be aware of stimuli that are the opposite of what we've been staring at. These experiments demonstrate that opponency and mutual inhibition are an important part of how we see. Another instance of opposing effects in perception comes from binocular rivalry, figure ground, and ambiguous figures. In these cases the stimulus remains constant but we alternate back and forth between two different perceptions, each fighting to dominate our awareness.

THEME 3: SINGULARITY AND MULTIPLICITY

Is consciousness a single thing or are there many different streams of it? This question has occupied philosophers for millennia. Only in recent years has science been able to give us a better answer. It is possible to focus on a single thing at a time. This is known as selective attention. We survey the many models of selective attention that have been proposed to explain how it is we choose to have one thing enter awareness. We then contrast this with what is also true: our ability to split or divide our attention such that we can take in many different things at once.

Anatomically our visual system channels information into two separate pathways. One is the dorsal stream that feeds into the parietal lobes. This "where" stream allows us to identify the location of objects and how we should act toward them. The other is the ventral stream that feeds into the temporal lobe. This "what" stream enables us to identify and recognize objects. The two cerebral hemispheres are another major anatomical division of labor. Although it is a simplification, our left hemisphere is specialized in most people for linguistic skill while the right tends to favor spatial skills. Each hemisphere appears to have its own distinct consciousness. In split-brain patients, the two hemispheres can fight for control of awareness.

THEME 4: FORCED SEEING

In this section we first examine the case where we can't miss seeing something: where stimuli grab our attention and force themselves into our conscious awareness even if we don't want them to. In one condition of the Stroop effect it is impossible to state the color of a word while ignoring its name. One explanation for this is that reading is such a well-practiced skill that the visual system automatically processes a word's meaning. Similarly, in the flanker task we are asked to identify a central letter or stimulus while ignoring distractors that lie on either side. Even when focused on the target, we can't help but process these distractors, suggesting that whatever falls inside a "window" of attention is processed automatically.

Saliency maps are a convenient way of representing where in the visual field our attention goes. Luminance, color, and orientation changes have all been proposed as regions that will capture attention and that have been incorporated into computational models to predict eye movements. In attention orienting, stimuli cause us to orient our eyes and head toward some stimulus of significance. Examples include moving objects, emotional faces, and gaze direction.

THEME 5: LOOKING WITHOUT SEEING

Next we examine cases where you can be looking at something but not see it. In priming and masking experiments researchers present a stimulus such as a word very quickly. Observers report no conscious awareness of having seen the word but it influences their behavior nonetheless, indicating that it has been processed at an unconscious level. In the attentional blink and repetition blindness phenomena we miss a second target because we are still busy processing a target that came before it. In change blindness we miss seeing even obvious changes to two scenes when they are alternated. Inattentional blindness occurs when we fail to see an object or event when we are staring right at it, demonstrating that attention is not always centered at the point of fixation.

THEME 6: DAMAGED BRAINS

Apart from measuring intact brains, there is also much to be gained by looking at deficits incurred as the result of brain damage. There are a large number of different visual disorders, each with very modality-specific effects. In Chapter 11 we cover the large number of different object processing disorders, known as visual agnosias. We look at case studies, symptoms, and explanations for different agnosias that include difficulties perceiving color, motion, objects, faces, and even a deficit in realizing one has a deficit. In Chapter 12 we summarize other fascinating consciousness deficits such as scotomas, blindsight, and problems in allocating attention correctly as is the case in neglect, extinction, and Balint's syndrome.

THEME 7: EVOUTIONARY INFLUENCES

We end the the book by looking at evolutionary themes. Why is there a need for conscious vision? What role does attention play in the survival of the organism? There are various proposals for why such awareness is important. We will examine these and conclude with a very general theory of consciousness and how it may operate in the brain as dynamic pattern of activation. We compare the various models that have been proposed to account for conscious vision and make suggestions for how they may be integrated. The future of consciousness research is bright—increases in technology and new methods will undoubtedly bring us closer to understanding this phenomenon.

WHAT IS CONSCIOUSNESS?

Consciousness is perhaps one of the greatest mysteries in the universe. How is it that we are aware of ourselves? Why is it that we have minds? The universe seems as if it could just as easily exist without out any sort of consciousness. From a scientific standpoint the universe could work just as well without it. Many complex physical processes operate just fine without any type of awareness. Physics, chemistry, biology, and other sciences seem adequate to describe many natural phenomena such as the movement of tides, cell physiology, and plant life. So why can't science provide us with a complete explanation of consciousness? We will examine these questions but first need to lay down some groundwork.

Obviously any starting point in the study of consciousness must begin with a definition. What is consciousness? The answer is not so easy. In fact, a recent book on the topic has been written without providing any definition (Blackmore, 2012). It might help then to start by describing what philosophers have said about it. Nagel (1974) provides us with an intriguing argument. He asks us to think about a bat using echolocation to navigate and pursue insects while flying around. The bat emits a pulse of sound. When the sound hits an object it bounces back an echo. The bat then analyzes the echo to determine the distance and other properties of the object. Nagel argues that "there is something that it is like" to be a bat using echolocation. Just as we hear a sound and interpret its meaning, the bat interprets its echoes in some sort of meaningful way. It seems reasonable to suppose that the bat has an experience or is aware of the sound. It is this experience or awareness that we wish to understand. However, because this understanding is derived from being a bat, we will never be able to share the experience.

Consciousness is a subjective experience. Although we may be able to better understand what it is like to be another human hearing a Beethoven symphony, smelling a rose or seeing a Monet painting, we can never be sure that we are actually having the exact same experience ourselves.

In other words, consciousness is a subjective phenomenon. You and only you can know what it is like to hear a symphony. When it comes to studying consciousness scientifically this poses a big problem. Science is an objective endeavor. As such, it can only provide us with objective descriptions. It can tell us which neurons in the brain are active and at what times but it can't explain what it is like to be the person whose brain is acting in that way. At best, science can provide a complete mapping of objective to subjective phenomena, it can tell us what is going on in the brain whenever we have an experience, but it can't explain the subjective quality of experience, known as its qualia.

This objective/subjective difference is known as the explanatory gap. It seems as if there will always be a gap between what can be described objectively and what can be experienced subjectively, between having a brain and having a mind, and between our "inner" world and the "outer" world. This gap is what makes consciousness such a puzzle and has intrigued philosophers and scientists from the very beginning. Jackson (1982) poses this difference using a thought experiment. He asks us to think about a neuroscientist named Mary. Mary lives in the future and as a neuroscientist she understands everything there is to know about color vision. But Mary has been brought up in a black and white room and has viewed the world only through a black and white TV monitor. One day we take Mary out of her room and have her experience the world in full color for the first time. Will Mary be amazed at the color red or will she simply acknowledge that she always knew it would look this way? According to Jackson, Mary will learn something new. There will be some additional information generated by this experience that cannot be explained by science, the qualia, or subjective feel of seeing the color red.

Another way to think about consciousness is the "zombie" thought experiment. Imagine somebody who physically and behaviorally is indistinguishable from you. They walk, talk, carry on a conversation, and do everything the way you do. The only difference is that your zombie is unconscious (Moody, 1994). If such a zombie were possible, then we would have to admit that consciousness is not necessary. Some have suggested that it might even be optional, like getting leather seats when buying a new car. In this case, we would have to believe that consciousness makes no difference, and we can get along just fine without it. The question we would need to answer then is why we have consciousness at all and what purpose it serves. This issue is addressed in Chapter 13. On the other hand, if you determine that these sorts of zombies are not possible, then the question becomes how consciousness comes about in people like us.

VARIETIES OF CONSCIOUSNESS

Consciousness is difficult to understand in part because there are so many different types. There are broad categories of consciousness that differ from each other qualitatively. For instance, global brain activity varies dramatically when awake compared to when we are in different stages of sleep. There are also major differences between being conscious and unconscious. Physicians use a categorization scheme to describe levels of nonconscious states. A shallow form of consciousness is called a minimally conscious state, while a deeper comatose condition is a vegetative state, deeper than this and a patient is said to be in a coma. We must also consider the case where an individual can be under the influence of some drug such as marijuana or LSD and the way this state differs from being sober.

Many early psychologists had their own particular categories of conscious states. The psychoanalytic psychologist Sigmund Freud proposed the unconscious, preconscious, and conscious. William James differentiated between dynamic and static forms of thought that he labeled as transitive and substantive, respectfully (James, 1890). The philosopher Ned Block more recently has a four-fold classification of conscious states, two of which we will discuss here and two that we will discuss later (Block, 1995). He states that we have a monitoring consciousness, which is that part of our mind that can think about other parts of our mind. This "thinking about thinking" is also referred to as metacognition. We also seem to have a self-consciousness that is our awareness of our self as having a mind and a body that is separate from others and from the environment. The neuroscientist Antonio Damasio believes that our self-consciousness is formed from signals about our bodily states that are sent to our brain (Damasio, 2000).

Another classification scheme we can use is based on the source, type, and mode of consciousness (Table 1.1). If we are attending to stimuli in the environment as when we are looking at a palm tree, then the source of information is external. If we are forming a visual image of a palm tree with our eyes closed, then the informational source is internal. Type of consciousness can be considered as falling into three main categories: perception, cognition, and emotion. If we are attending to visual, auditory, olfactory, gustatory, or tactile information then these correspond to a perceptual mode. One might also argue for vestibular and proprioceptive senses which are both internal perceptual sources, as well as for perception of temperature and pain. Awareness of thoughts we can label as cognitive and awareness of emotions as emotive. Again, we could argue for a number of subcategories here. Awareness of a memory vs. awareness of language are two cognitive possibilities. Happiness, sadness, and grief are examples of emotional modes. Moods are also sometimes considered to be in a class by themselves as they are of lower intensity and longer duration than emotions.

In all of the examples listed above there are probably different patterns of brain activity that underlie the experience as well as qualitative or quantitative differences in the corresponding subjective states. A long-term goal for cognitive science is to classify these types and to map the objective measures to the subjective ones. This is a broad approach. Just as important, perhaps

TABLE 1.1

One Way to Classify Conscious Experience is by its Source, Type, and Mode (Mode refers to different types of information or processes within a source)

		Example
Source		
	External (outside world)	Seeing a palm tree
	Internal (inside world)	Imagining a palm tree
Type		
Perception	Visual	Your friend's face
	Auditory	A Mozart sonata
	Olfactory	The smell of coffee
	Gustatory	The taste of apple pie
	Tactile	The feel of leather
Cognition	Memory	Last year's summer vacation
	Language	Listening to a psychology lecture
	Problem Solving	Calculating a tip
Emotion	Happy	Getting married
	Sad	Your father's death
	Fearful	Seeing a snake
	Anger	Someone steals your money
	Surprise	A surprise birthday party
	Disgust	Rotting garbage

more so, is to investigate a specific form of consciousness in as much detail as possible. That is the approach of this book. Here, we look at perceptual consciousness, specifically visual consciousness, and even more specifically the different manifestations of visual consciousness including perception of objects, color, and motion.

Perceptual awareness means being aware of something and being able to report its presence, either verbally or by some prearranged signal (Frith, Perry, & Lumer, 1999). The verbal report process is not perfect. Reports about our inner experiences can be lies. It is entirely possible to deliberate misreport the contents of our awareness. These lies could take the form of "white" lies told to satisfy the researcher or "denial" lies told to avoid being embarrassed by poor performance or a failure to understand instructions. In the vast majority of cases we can safely assume that participants in such studies are telling the truth.

According to the illusion of complete perception we feel that we are aware of everything in the visual scene. An example of visual search can be used to demonstrate this (Coren, Ward, & Enns, 2004). When we look out, say into a crowd of people and attempt to locate our friend Jim, it feels as if we are "taking it all in," but clearly we are not, since we cannot identify our friend immediately. When we do only then can we say that he enters our conscious awareness. Our brain thus fools us into thinking that we are aware of what is "out there" in a glance when we really aren't.

VARIETIES OF CONSCIOUS VISION

Stoerig (1996) distinguishes between three levels of conscious vision. First we have phenomenal vision corresponding to awareness of specific qualia. These are really sensations rather than perceptions. They are low level and include awareness of color, movement, and perhaps oriented line segments. These units are the features or stimulus dimensions that are combined at higher levels to produce more integrated percepts. Patients with damage to the lateral geniculate nucleus (LGN) of the thalamus or to striate cortex lack this awareness.

Figure–ground segregation and feature binding constitute the second level of conscious vision. At this level, regions of the visual field are resolved into different depth planes. More complex features are formed from more basic primitives and parts or entire objects get represented. Patients with apperceptive agnosia lack this level of awareness (see Chapter 11 for more on the different types of agnosia). They have suffered damage to extrastriate areas, as in the temporal lobe. Other areas associated with these symptoms include the fusiform face area for prosopagnosics, the lateral occipital complex and the parahippocampal place area. We refer the reader to Chapter 2 on neural underpinnings for an introduction to the areas underlying visual function.

The third level involves recognition and identification of objects and scenes. Semantics or meaning derived from information in memory comes into play here as there needs to be some sort of matching between stimulus input and stored information. This level corresponds to associative agnosics who can reproduce objects well by drawing when asked to but cannot produce the names associated with them. Damage to visual memory areas in the temporal lobes and the limbic system are present here.

VARIETIES OF UNCONSCIOUS VISION

We can also identify four levels of unconscious vision (Stoerig, 1996). The first is characterized by a neuroendocrine response. Those who are totally blind have damage to retinofugal projections excluding the pathway to the hypothalamus. They are incapable of perceiving any light whatsoever but still inhibit melatonin release under bright light conditions (Czeisler et al., 1995). Retinal outputs to the hypothalamus are still able to regulate pineal gland activity in such individuals.

A second level is reflexive vision. These patients demonstrate the pupillary light reflex; their pupils will constrict in response to increased light on the retina and dilate with a lessening of this light. They also have the photic blink reflex, and optokinetic nystagmus, this last being the ability of the eye to track a moving object without movement of the head. These reactions exist in people who are in a comatose state and in those lacking ganglion cell projections to the LGN that then feed to primary visual cortex. They do, however, have intact retinal efferents to collicular and other areas known to mediate optic reflexes. These individuals are also incapable of perceiving any light.

Stage three is in patients with destruction of primary visual cortex (area V1) or of the connections that feed to it. In these blindsight patients there is no conscious perception in the blind areas of their visual field. However, as noted in greater detail later, these patients do demonstrate residual visual capacities. A stimulus presented to the blind portion of their visual field affects a response to a subsequent stimulus in the sighted portion (Cowey & Stoerig, 2003). When stimuli are presented directly to the visual field defect they can respond with above-chance performance. In these circumstances a patient can to some degree identify whether an object was present, what type of object it may have been, or where it was located. A more detailed summary of blindsight abilities is described in the damaged brain section.

VISUAL ZOMBIES

Koch (2004) lists another class of unconscious phenomena, what he calls visual "zombie agents." These are not the philosopher's zombies in which an entire person is duplicated without consciousness. Instead, they are specialized sensory-motor processes that carry out automatic visual functions in the absence of awareness. These sorts of zombies are putatively operating in our visual system continually all the time.

One function zombie agents carry out are eye movements (saccades) to a visual target. In one experiment subjects sat in a dark room and at the start of a trial fixated a central light (Goodale, Pelisson, & Prablanc, 1986). Then, a light appeared in the periphery. Normally, we quickly and automatically move our eyes to the general location of a target and then initiate a second corrective movement that places our gaze more precisely on the target item. On some trials in this study the light was moved during the observer's initial saccade. Normally we are not aware of the "jump" in the visual world that occurs during an eye movement, a term dubbed saccadic suppression. Even though these participants weren't consciously aware of the light's position after this second movement, they still automatically and quickly adjusted, saccading a second time to position the gaze near the new location.

According to Koch, these eye movement controllers in the visual system are an example of a visual zombie. They perform the crucial role of always putting our eyes at a proper location. It makes sense that this process should be unconscious. If we had to voluntarily and effortfully determine where to look next each time we wouldn't have much attention left to perform other more important tasks. Other examples of visual zombie agents include those that maintain our balance using optic flow, the movement of objects and surfaces in directions opposite to our own. Milner and Goodale (1995) postulate many more such agents that govern hand gripping, pointing, and foot placement. Instead of zombies, however, they refer to them as on-line systems. These authors argue that there are really two visual systems. The vision-for-action system is unconscious and governs rapid responses to stimuli of the sort we have just described. The vision-for-perception system is conscious and acts more slowly. Its job is to classify, recognize, and identify objects.

WHAT IS ATTENTION?

This book is about visual consciousness and visual attention. Our everyday intuition tells us that that these two are the same. After all, it seems as if we are conscious of what we attend to. From a scientific standpoint, however, they can be dissociated. It is therefore worth describing what attention is and how it relates to consciousness.

Attention can be conceptualized as a form of mental activity or energy that is distributed among alternative information sources. These informational sources can be stimuli from the outside world as is the case in perception, or they can be internal mental content such as thoughts and memories. When attention is allocated to a source that source becomes prioritized and the processing of information from that source is usually facilitated. Visual attention simply means attention that is allocated to and used to process visual items.

Visual attention has been conceptualized in terms of opposites. It is believed to be focused yet divided, selective yet integrative, covert and overt, endogenous and exogenous, object-based and space-based, and capable of being narrowed into a spotlight or widened into a floodlight. These dichotomies and the research that supports them are discussed in the varieties of attention chapter.

ATTENTION AND CONSCIOUSNESS

What is the real difference between attention and consciousness? To begin we need to know that attention serves two different functions. Baars (2007) argues that these are selection and integration. Attention is selective in that it allows us to choose only some of the information that the senses make available to us. Otherwise we would be overwhelmed and not be able to make sense of anything. But attention also integrates in that we can use it to link different pieces of information together. We can select that one banana on the produce shelf that looks the best but also cross that item off our grocery list by integrating what we see with other information in memory.

The common-sense distinction between attention and consciousness is that attention selects first and now that we have selected something we can be conscious of it. Attention thus implies selecting one event over another, while conscious events are those we are now aware of and can report verbally in an accurate manner. We can think of this a cycle. We attend to something, are consciously aware of it—this awareness makes us think of something else that causes us to move our attention again. This new selection causes us to have a conscious experience of a new event and so on. We can think of visual attention as producing a constant stream of stimulus-based inputs from the outside world that compete against and influence an inner stream of conscious contents (Fox et al., 2005; Mazoyer, Zago, & Mellet, 2001).

There is a brain-based difference here as well. Conscious sensory stimuli cause activation in the frontal and parietal lobes whereas unconscious stimuli elicit mostly localized activity in visual areas (Baars, 2002; Dehaene et al., 2001). Baars (2007) conjectures that frontal lobes initially do the selecting but their activation then begins to die out. Once the selected information is conscious, there is now a reactivation of the frontal areas by posterior visual and parietal areas. These two regions may then sustain each other's activity through a continuous feedback loop (see Figure 1.1).

Another distinction between attention and consciousness has to do with processing vs. post-processing. Miller (1962) was one of the first to advocate that we are conscious of the results of a mental process but not of the process itself. If we apply this to vision we find that we are usually aware of the results of an attentional selection process but not the actual act of selection. For example, when we are looking around a room we may notice the objects in it such as a sofa, chair, or desk, but we do not typically notice our eye movements or attentional shifts from one of these objects to the next. We are also not explicitly and immediately aware that a sofa is a piece of furniture, but some part of our brain has to be active in order for us to recognize, categorize, or compare it against another object.

It makes sense that we only need to be aware of "the important stuff." If information is important, we need to think about it and use that information as the basis of performing some action.

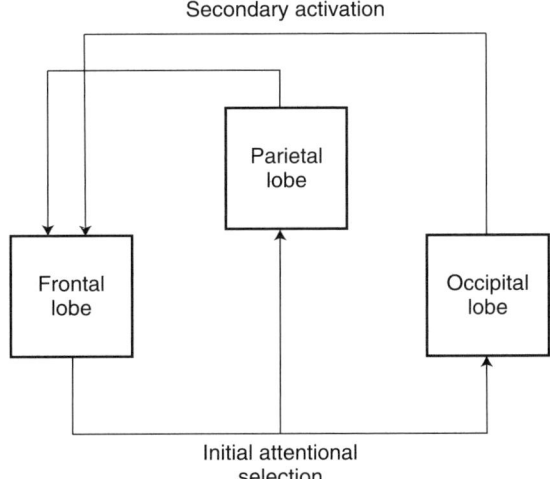

FIGURE 1.1   Part of the cyclical activity between anterior and posterior brain areas that may occur during conscious visual awareness (after Baars, 2007).

Thus, consciousness seems to be the end result of some selection processes. Selection in many cases can take place automatically and unconsciously but the results of selection are given priority access to consciousness so that decision making, planning, and action can then be carried out.

DISSOCIATING TOP-DOWN ATTENTION AND CONSCIOUSNESS

Tsuchiya and Koch (2009) elaborate further on the dissociation between top-down/exogenous attention and consciousness. They argue that events can be attended without being consciously perceived and that an event can be consciously perceived without being attended to. Based on a review of the literature they create a two-by-two table that separates top-down attention from consciousness. This is depicted in Table 1.2. In the lower-right corner of the table are events that require top-down attention and give rise to conscious experience. For instance voluntary attention is necessary in order to perceive novel, unexpected, or unfamiliar stimuli, as is the case for

TABLE 1.2
A Four-fold Classification of Percepts and Behaviors (after Tsuchiya & Koch, 2009)

	May not give rise to consciousness	Gives rise to consciousness
	Formation of afterimages	Pop-out
	Rapid vision (<120 ms)	Iconic memory
Top-down attention is not required	Zombie behaviors Accommodation reflex Pupillary reflex	Gist Animal/gender detection in dual tasks Partial reportability
Top-down attention is required	Priming Adaptation Processing of objects Visual search Thoughts	Working memory Detection/discrimination of unexpected 　and unfamiliar stimuli Full reportability

inattentional blindness (Mack & Rock, 1998). In the upper-left side of the table are cases where no top-down attention occurs and where there are no salient stimuli to capture attention either. Under these conditions (i.e., "spacing out," daydreaming) there may be no overt visual consciousness but implicit perception that exerts behavioral influence is possible.

When focusing on one area of the visual field, we still perceive many aspects of what is outside that area. The gist of a visual scene remains under such conditions. If a photograph that covers the entire background of an unattended region is presented unexpectedly for 30 ms, participants can accurately report a summary of what was there (Fei-Fei, Iyer, Koch, & Perona, 2007). These situations and others correspond to awareness without attention, as depicted in the upper-right quadrant of Table 1.2. There is also the situation where participants can pay attention to a location for some time and not see object attributes at that location. Priming studies for invisible words suppressed by masking occurs only when attention is paid to the prime-target pair (Naccache, Blandin, & Dehaene, 2002). This corresponds to the remaining lower-left quadrant in Table 1.2.

Paradoxically, attention can even interfere with conscious awareness. Olivers and Nieuwenhuis (2005) found that observers were actually better at detecting the first and second targets in an attentional blink task when they were asked to concurrently perform a secondary auditory task that directed their attention away from the letter stream. Low spatial frequency patterns under in the ground portion of a display can also be discriminated better without spatial attention (Wong & Weisstein, 1982, 1983; Yeshurun & Carrasco, 1998).

The philosopher Ned Block proposes two types of consciousness (Block, 1996, 2005). Phenomenal consciousness (P) is the subjective feeling or experience of a stimulus, similar to qualia. The feeling of the color red would differ from that of the color green. Access consciousness (A) on the other hand are the processes that access this information in order to perform some goal such as stating what one has seen or making a behavioral response. In this context P is consciousness without top-down attention (the upper-right quadrant in Table 1.2), while A consciousness is consciousness with attention (the lower-right portion of Table 1.2).

Crick and Koch (1995) have a neural theory that can account for the difference between consciousness with and without attention. Attended stimuli in the visual field boost the activity of neurons representing them in the ventral stream, including areas V4 and IT, relative to responses for non-attended events (Braun, Koch, & Davis, 2001; Desimone & Duncan, 1995). Through long-range connections these neurons engage in a reverberating circuit with frontal areas, including dorsolateral prefrontal cortex. The result of this cyclical self-sustaining activity, in their view, is conscious awareness of what one is seeing, i.e., access level (A) consciousness. Neurons that don't engage in this neural "coalition" may be prone to fire less quickly and to die out sooner over time, even though they may engage in other more local coalitions. In the Crick and Koch view, these neurons may have enough sustained activity to generate phenomenal (P) consciousness. This view and the neural events that accompany it are described in more detail in the section on neural synchrony in Chapter 2.

FRAMING THE PROBLEM

If we are to study consciousness scientifically, then we must come up with an empirically testable understanding of it. Part of the difficulty in doing this lies in the lack of a generally accepted definition of the term as we have just discussed. Also problematic are more basic metaphysical and epistemological issues. These concern our understanding of what constitutes reality and how we can understand it. It is to these topics that we turn our attention to next.

According to monism there is just one type of universe and it is physical or material in nature. This physical world contains the actual objects and events we experience through our senses.

This physical universe also contains our bodies and brains. In dualism there are two types of universe. One is physical and material as is the case in monism, but then there is another universe, one that is immaterial, not made of physical "stuff." It is this universe where mental events take place, according to the dualists. Dualism arose as an explanation for the existence of minds. It was motivated by the notion that mental phenomena seem to be different from physical ones. For example, if we look at an apple we have an internal perceptual or conceptual experience of the apple that seems fundamentally distinct from the real apple that is "out there." Our mental representation of the apple in the form of a visual experience is mental in nature and so is postulated as existing in a separate realm from the physical by the dualists.

Chalmers (1996) makes a distinction between the easy and hard problems of consciousness. The easy problems are to explain the functioning of the brain and how it performs its basic tasks such as pattern recognition, memory, and language. This can all be understood in terms of information processing without any recourse to consciousness. The hard problem, however, is to explain how and why we have qualitative phenomenal experiences at all. From this perspective we can ask questions such as: Why does chocolate taste the way it does? How are we able to have different forms of awareness corresponding to things like taste, touch, and smell? The easy problems can all conceivably be solved with the progress of technology and science. The hard problems may never be solved.

Another dichotomy that is hard to resolve concerns how to understand complex systems like the brain. By reductionism a whole can be explained by an understanding of its parts (Silberstein, 2002). In this account we can explain everything there is to know about the brain by understanding everything there is to know about neurons or about synaptic chemistry. In the emergent perspective we need to figure out more than the parts to explain the whole. In this case a complete understanding of the brain would necessitate an understanding of not just neurons but of how neurons interact with each other, or how the brain and body as a whole interact with the environment. The ways in which parts interact in emergent systems is rule governed and the rules are invariant even though the parts may change over time (Holland, 1998).

A SCIENTIFIC APPROACH TO THE STUDY OF CONSCIOUSNESS

In this section we explicate a scientific view of consciousness adopted in this book. It consists of a response to each of the major issues outlined above. To start, we need to ask the question of whether consciousness exists at all. To answer this we have to say yes. At the very least we need to acknowledge that there is a subjective component to certain brain events. There probably is something that it is like to be a bat or other creatures. However, because these are subjective phenomena, they can't be explained scientifically from a first person perspective. They can only be explained scientifically from an objective, third person perspective. As scientists we need to accept the fact that we cannot provide answers to these questions: they are untestable assertions that fall outside the scope of science, like the question of whether or not God exists.

What science can do is provide an increasingly complete explanation of the neural mechanisms that underlie different forms of conscious experience. We can specify what patterns of neural activation correspond to seeing red, feeling happy, or thinking about summer vacations. This means we will have objective data from brain imaging and other techniques that must be correlated with subjective measures such as verbal report and behavioral responses. There is a debate about what constitutes an appropriate subjective estimate. For example introspection may give us accurate depictions for certain mental events but not for others. But we have to accept these measures and continue to use and refine them. They have proven to be useful thus far and have served as the primary dependent variables in most psychology experiments. Examples include rating scales, response time, sensitivity in the form of d-prime from signal detection experiments, and the like. On the objective side there will no doubt be improvements to functional magnetic resonance imaging (fMRI), magnetoencephalography, transcranial magnetic stimulation (TMS), and computational simulations, as well as the introduction of new technologies such as the knife-edge scanning microscope.

So as scientists we can admit there is an explanatory gap but work to narrow it by studies examining the correspondence between the two. The gap may be equivalent to the Grand Canyon now, but future research may bring it to a crack a few inches across. It is not inconceivable that in the future we will be able to explain and predict neural responses to many stimuli, internal and external. That is, we could measure how the brain will react to an environmental stimulus as in object recognition or to an internal stimulus, as in how one thought or image may lead to another. This will no doubt be difficult due to the complexity of the subject, but not impossible. Other hurdles that must be overcome include the explanation of why the same person reacts differently to the same stimulus on two different occasions or why two different people react differently to the same stimulus. In fact, it is the study of just these sorts of differences that should yield clues to brain function.

Mary, the neuroscientist in Jackson's thought experiment, probably would have a different experience when let out of her room. However, if we were measuring her experience during the change, we could elucidate more about it. We couldn't explain what it was like for Mary to see red, but we could explain what it was like for her brain undergoing the change. In other words, we would have a better understanding of the linkage between the subjective and the objective in that particular circumstance.

In regards to the zombie thought experiment, it wouldn't be possible to have a zombie that could be exactly like us in every way and not be conscious. Consciousness is an integral part of our constitution. If it were eliminated what is left over wouldn't be able to walk like us, talk like us or do anything like us. This argument is a bit like taking the battery out of a toy doll and still expecting the doll to talk and move around. Other critics have taken similar views. Patricia Churchland (1996) refers to the argument as "feeble" while Daniel Dennett (1991) calls it "bogus." Although the human version of the zombie may not be possible, an artificial person who can perform all human feats but not be conscious is more likely (Friedenberg, 2008).

The standard scientific take on the monist/dualist debate is clear. There is only one universe and it is physical, this view going by the name of physicalism or materialism. There is no evidence of any non-physical universe or that thoughts are anything other than brain activity so by Occam's razor we default to the simpler monist perspective. The burden of proof is on the dualists. When questioned on what their alternate mental realm might be like, or what the relationship between these two universes are like they are (un)remarkably silent. Please note that the scientific search for the correlation between objective and subjective measures is a search for relationships in the physical world. This is different than the supposed explanations for causality between the mental and the physical realms. Examples of these have been given by philosophers and include views like classical dualism, parallelism, epiphenomenalism, and interactionism (Kitzis, 2002).

Reductionism has been the dominant view in science for some time. Only recently has the emergent perspective started to gain popularity (the Gestalt psychologists can be considered an exception to this). Recent years have seen an expansion of the emergent view as manifested in dynamical systems theory and network science. For overviews of these fields see Kelso (1995) and Lewis (2009). These perspectives are interactionist in nature as they focus on the relationships between parts to explain system-level behavior. There is much promise in store for the application of these techniques to the study of mind. Application of dynamical concepts such as state spaces, attractor basins, oscillatory models, small world networks, and the like have already made significant inroads (Friedenberg, 2009).

2 Neural Underpinnings

STRUCTURAL ORGANIZATION OF THE VISUAL SYSTEM

Throughout this book we describe research that refers to many different brain areas. These regions are often abbreviated and because there are so many of them it is helpful to provide a brief sketch of each now, listing their name, location, and function. Figure 2.1 shows an overhead view of early processing in the visual system with each of the major structures included. Figure 2.2 shows information flow starting with primary visual cortex and extending forward to other cortical regions.

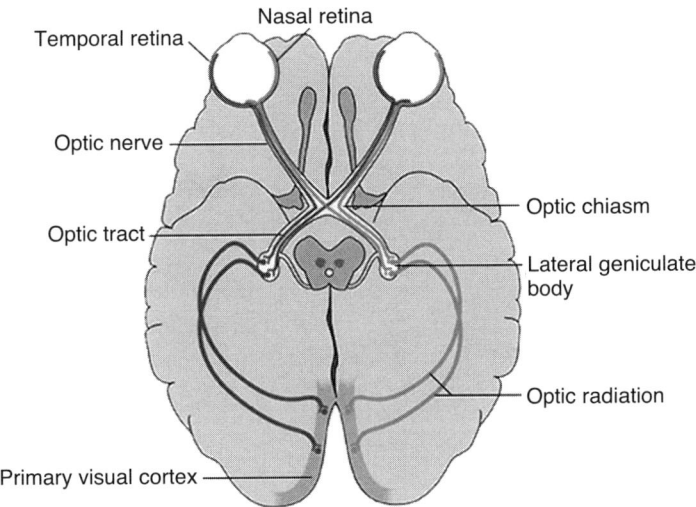

FIGURE 2.1   An overview showing the anatomy of initial information processing in the human visual system.

1. The retina is a layer of photoreceptors located in the back of the eye. Ganglion cells in one of these layers respond to spots of light or dark. Axons from these cells exit the eye through the optic nerve and after crossing over at the optic chiasm project to the thalamus.
2. Retinal cells synapse with neurons in the LGN of the thalamus.
3. Thalamic axons project backward to the striate cortex, also known as striate or primary visual cortex. Cells in area V1 here code for a variety of different features including line orientation, spatial frequency, and color.
4. Area V2 receives many feedforward connections from area V1. V2 neurons also appear to be modulated by more complex visual properties such as the orientation of illusory contours and figure–ground areas. V2 neurons send forward connections to areas V2, V3, V4, and V5.
5. Area V3 is forward of V2 and has been implicated in representing the entire visual field and global motion perception. There is both a dorsal and a ventral region.

6. Area V4 is located anterior to V2 and receives connections from it. This region receives attentional modulation. Neurons here code for color and for object features. They also appear to code for stimulus salience.

7. The middle temporal region, area MT, plays a major role in the perception of motion. Neurons here respond selectively to direction and speed of motion. It receives inputs from V1, V2, and dorsal V3.

8. Inferior temporal cortex or area IT contains neurons that code for large features and entire objects. It constitutes part of the ventral stream responsible for object recognition.

9. The fusiform gyrus, located on the posterior portion of the temporal lobe, contains neurons that respond selectively to faces. This area is also known as the fusiform face area, or FFA. Damage to this region results in the inability to identify faces.

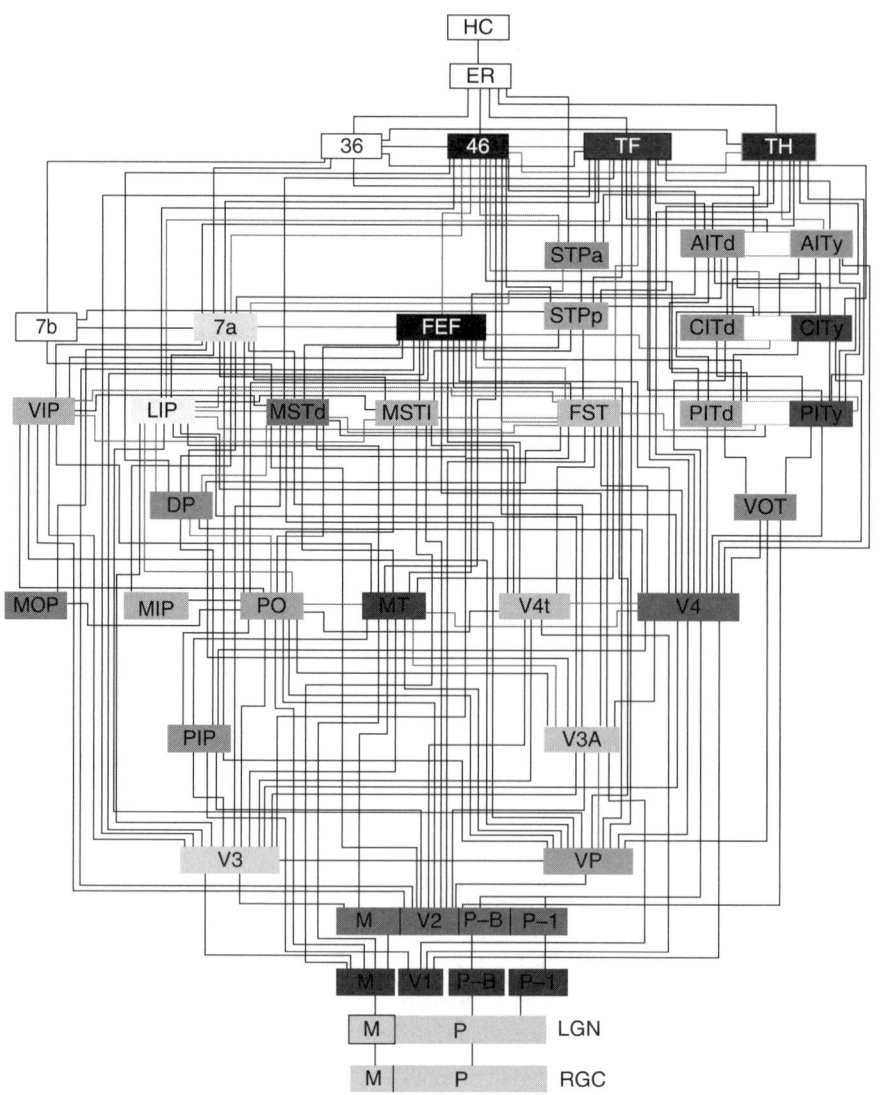

FIGURE 2.2 Schematic diagram of cortical pathways in the visual system. Most connections are reciprocal (after Kellman & Shipley, 1991).

THE NEURONAL BASIS OF CONSCIOUS AND UNCONSCIOUS VISION

THE NEURONAL CORRELATES OF CONSCIOUSNESS

Christof Koch, in his book *The Quest for Consciousness* (2004), devotes a lot of time to explaining what he calls the Neuronal Correlates of Conscious, or NCC. He refers to it as "the minimal set of neuronal events and mechanisms jointly sufficient for a specific conscious percept." There is supposed to be a direct correspondence between the NCC, which can be measured objectively, and a specific subjective experience that we can have. Note that he is stating a *specific* conscious experience, such as seeing our pet dog, and not a more general one such as being awake. Any change in a subjective state must be associated with a change in a neuronal state. However, the opposite of this may be the case: two different neuronal states could lead to the same conscious experience.

Koch believes that consciousness has an evolutionary purpose, i.e., it is not just some side effect or unintended consequence of brain function. As such, the NCC must have some influence on behavior. This means that activity in consciousness neurons will affect activity in motor neurons that produce our actions. It also means that the NCC should receive inputs from sensory areas. So the NCC is not isolated from other brain areas. It is part of a perceptual-motor loop that takes in information from the outside world and controls motor actions that effect events that happen there.

Is the NCC identical to a percept? If it were then once we explain the NCC we have a complete understanding of the physical basis that undergirds a specific conscious experience. According to the philosophical view of physicalism the NCC equals the percept and there is nothing more to explain. However, Koch is open on this view. He states that the relationship between physical and mental phenomena may be more complex.

Koch discriminates between enabling and specific factors for consciousness. An enabling factor is a background condition that must be met in order for any consciousness to happen at all, whereas a specific factor is necessary to have a particular form of conscious experience. Enabling conditions provide for the *quality* of being conscious while the specific factors provide the *content*. To use a computer analogy, it might be useful to think of the enabling conditions as the operating system that is always running in the background when a computer or smartphone is turned on. Specific factors would then correspond to individual software programs or applications that run on the operating system.

According to Koch the reticular activating formation (RAF) is the main enabling factor. Look ahead to the brain areas that subsume attentional function for more on the RAF. This structure originates in the brain stem but has widespread cholinergic projections to other parts of the brain. Activity here causes arousal and alertness. When it is sufficiently damaged an animal falls into a stupor or comatose-like state. Moods and emotional states based partly on feedback we receive from our bodies, what is called extended consciousness, may also constitute one of the enabling factors (Damasio, 1999).

For focused perceptual consciousness, in which a person is aware of something, rather than just being aware, Koch says there must be a coalition of neurons that are working together in a coordinated way. For instance, in order to be able to see an object may require synchronous activity between cells in the inferior temporal lobe (area IT) and the prefrontal cortex. The cells that appear to participate in these coalitions exist in the cortical sensory areas, the frontal lobes and the thalamus.

At a microscopic level it is probably the case that more than one neuron in a given location participates in the NCC. Since much of the cortex is layered, several cells each in a different layer but in one circumscribed area might be active members of a coalition. A distributed code, both locally and globally is the most robust against damage.

The neuronal coalition for color perception will differ from that of motion perception in that it will involve greater activity in area V4, the region that underlies color vision. Likewise, the coalition for motion perception will differ from that of color perception in that it will involve greater area MT activity, the cortical region specialized for motion perception. However, it is likely there will be some degree of overlap between two coalitions, most likely in the frontal areas that synchronize with posterior visual areas.

How far can we take this specificity? Instead of saying that a specialized region of the brain is necessary for a particular percept, why not postulate that a group of neurons or even one neuron is responsible? There may be individual consciousness neurons that code for one type of awareness, just as individual molecules or neurotransmitters have specific actions. At the other extreme we may find generalized consciousness neurons that participate in all conscious awareness no matter what the type. We don't have the answer to these questions yet, but probably will within the next few decades.

THE NEURONAL BASIS OF CONSCIOUS PERCEPTION

So what differences do we then see when looking specifically at conscious level perception? Presentation of low contrast gratings elicits more activity in comparison to when it is presented subliminally (Rees & Heeger, 2003). Conscious recognition of words presented visually produces an increase in activity in the ventral visual pathway and in the parietal lobe (Dehaene et al., 2001; Kjaer, Nowak, Kjaer, Lou, & Lou, 2001). Changes in brainwave activity are also observed with 40 Hz oscillations and alterations to the alpha rhythm of the parietal and occipital regions (Summerfield, Jack, & Burges, 2002; Vanni, Revonsuo, & Hari, 1997). Regions that become active in visual cortex during binocular rivalry and during changes in ambiguous stimuli have already been reviewed previously in this book, as have changes to visual areas associated with illusions such as the phantom grating and filling-in processes (Meng, Remus, & Tong, 2005; Sasaki, & Watanabe, 2004).

Studies measuring brain activation during conscious perception only demonstrate a correlation between the two. In order to establish causality we need to examine deficits resulting from brain damage or subjective experiences induced through TMS (Rees, 2009). We refer the reader to the sections on brain damage discussed elsewhere and focus here on the experimentally induced activation results.

Blind patients who have suffered retinal damage report seeing phosphenes (a ring or spot of white) when researchers stimulate their visual cortex directly using TMS. However, blind patients with cortical damage do not, implying that primary visual cortex may be necessary for conscious awareness (Cowey & Walsh, 2000). When visual striate cortex and temporal lobe visual regions are stimulated directly visual experiences are produced. This suggests these areas may be necessary but that retinal, thalamic and midbrain structures may not be. It is not entirely clear if area V1 is necessary for awareness, but when feedback from higher areas (V5 and MT) to V1 are interrupted by TMS, impaired motion perception results (Pascual-Leone & Walsh, 2001; Silvanto, Cowey, Lavie, & Walsh, 2005). This suggests that conjoint or coupled activity between striate and extrastriate cortex could be necessary.

THE NEURONAL CORRELATES OF UNCONSCIOUSNESS

Just as we can seek to find the NCC that underlie conscious experience, we can also seek to find those brain areas that are active when unconscious visual processing occurs, what is called the neuronal correlates of unconsciousness (NCU). We can conceptualize this as the necessary neural activity that is the basis for and directly influences visually guided behavior. This behavior is affected by stimuli and can be measured operationally but does not appear accessible to verbal report. These brain areas and function would be those underlying priming, masking, the attentional blink, inattentional blindness, and the like.

How do we tell apart NCC from NCU? There are two major approaches. The first is to look at accidental brain lesions in humans and deliberately induced lesions in animal subjects. We can then map deficits onto regions by noting which symptoms seem to go along with which areas. This is the approach described in the damaged brain chapters and it has been useful in terms of revealing the component areas of conscious vision; those areas corresponding to form, color, motion, and other features of coherent object perception. The second approach is to experimentally inactivate brain areas through the use of TMS. Lesion studies are permanent while TMS or electrical stimulation techniques are transient.

The Neuronal Basis of Unconscious Perception

Rees (2009) reviews the literature on brain activity associated with and without conscious awareness. There are a substantial number of studies now that show many visual areas activated by unconscious stimuli. Studies in which words are presented but then masked are not consciously perceived by are able to prime subsequent responses nonetheless. This shows that at the very least they have been processed to the semantic level, which would imply the IT area and perhaps even farther up the dorsal pathway. Other studies show activation in striate cortex, area MT, word-selective areas and object-selective areas in both the dorsal and the ventral streams (Dehaene et al., 2001; Fang & He, 2005; Haynes, Driver, & Rees, 2005; Moutoussis & Zeki, 2002). In the section on priming in Chapter 9 we have already seen that emotional faces not consciously perceived can affect responding,

The research summarized above shows that nearly all parts of the brain normally activated during conscious visual perception can also be activated during unconscious perception. This means that we cannot single out any one area or set of areas that correspond exclusively to visual awareness or to the lack of it. Any differences must therefore be the result of different patterns of activation.

NEURAL SYNCHRONY

Neural Synchronization and the Binding Problem

One intriguing hypothesis about the neural states underlying consciousness involves neural synchronization (Engel & Singer, 2001; Singer, 1999). This is the widespread synchronous firing or oscillation of neurons throughout different cortical areas. An issue in synchronization is how a grouped cell assembly representing an object distinguishes itself from other ongoing neural activity. This is important because when perceiving a particular object or scene, other visual information that is present must be suppressed. Focusing on one object but ignoring another or attending to one location of visual space at the expense of another implies that the cell assembly must increase its saliency somehow. Singer and Kreiman (2009) mention a few possibilities for how this might occur. First, cells that are not part of the group can be inhibited. Second, the amplitude of the selected cells can be increased. Third, the grouped cells can fire at the same rate. They also mention that any such grouped cell assembly in order to stand out must be maintained for some time and that this puts a limit on how quickly one assembly can follow another. In conscious terms this means there should be a "speed limit" on the number of things we can be aware of one after another.

Faced with a vast flood of information from visual inputs the visual system adopts a "divide and conquer" strategy. It breaks the input into separate streams, each operating in parallel on the image. Different parts of the cortex became specialized to process specific aspects of a visual object or scene. In the ventral stream, area V4 processes color, while area IT in the temporal lobe processes shape and form. In the dorsal stream, area MT processes motion while parietal areas deal with location.

When these neurons coding for different aspects of a stimulus synchronize, they could effectively link or unify each of these features into a coherent whole. This corresponds to our subjective experience: we don't perceive a fragmented reality consisting of parts but instead a unified one, with entire objects and surfaces. As an example, imagine looking at a red Ferrari sports car that drives past you. We don't perceive the color, shape, and motion of the car separately. Each of these features is unified into a single object that we recognize as a particular type of car with a specific color moving in a specific direction.

This issue of how these different pieces of information get linked into a coherent object representation is called the binding problem (Goldstein, 2010). Neural synchrony is one solution to the binding problem. By having color neurons, shape neurons, and motion neurons oscillate in phase with each other and with frontal lobe regions, the "pieces" get combined and are now accessible as a unitary whole to conscious visual awareness.

EVIDENCE IN SUPPORT OF NEURAL SYNCHRONY

There are several lines of evidence to support the neural synchrony conjecture. First, studies in comparative cognition show that conscious processing in mammals increased along with expansion of the cortex. These more recent areas are located farther "upstream" from lower level sensory areas and communicate with each other and with downstream inputs, supporting the notion that these additional regions are what underlie awareness (Krubitzer, 1998). This makes the frontal areas a prime candidate for the "pacemaker" or "coordination center" that links up with posterior visual centers to synchronize their activity.

There are two ways neurons might code for objects. In the first, we have "grandmother" cells, whereby converging inputs representing lower level features are combined hierarchically into single cells that represent feature combinations or entire objects. In this way, we might have oriented line detectors that combine to form angle detectors that combine to form features like a nose, eyes, or mouth. These might in turn converge on cells that code for entire faces, such as your grandmother's face. We can think of this as a local form of object perception, since it relies primarily on localized neurons or groups of neurons.

We see this convergent architecture in the visual system and it has several advantages. It allows for rapid processing and is suited for frequently occurring features such as those found in objects you might recognize over and over again in everyday life. It also does not require any additional brain areas. Those neurons representing higher level representations by themselves are also responsible for their access to conscious awareness. Studies do show that neurons active during the first few tens of milliseconds can mediate awareness, as is described in the section on masking elsewhere in this book (Rolls, 2006).

Singer and Kreiman (2009) however, thinks it is unlikely that activity in these cells codes for conscious awareness. He states that it is expensive in terms of the number of required neurons and not suited to dealing with the vast number of feature combinations that exist with each new object we can encounter. His proposed second way of neural coding is in the collective activity of a constellation of neurons, each representing different features. In this account a single cell standing for red can participate in the representation of a red Ferrari or a red apple. This produces a "savings" in neuron numbers. Synchronized oscillations between coalitions of such cells in widespread visual areas would then constitute the basis for object representations. We can therefore think of this as a global form of object perception.

If local coding were the basis of consciousness, then we would expect local lesions to interfere with conscious perception of that particular subsystem. Damage to color neurons would result in an inability to see color, damage to motion areas would result in an inability to perceive motion, and so on. However, we would not expect local damage to impact on the overall perception of conscious awareness. This is in fact the case as is demonstrated by different types of agnosias. Damage to area MT, for instance, produces deficits in motion perception, an inability to judge when to stop pouring water into a glass for example, but does not impair the patient's general consciousness.

THE PHYSIOLOGICAL BASIS OF NEURAL SYNCHRONIZATION

In this section we will examine experiments the address some of the neurological specifics of how synchrony takes place. Interestingly, it appears that synchrony is enhanced when there is a global desynchrony as measured by electroencephalogram (EEG) and also when subjects are attentive. Synchrony for specific stimuli is facilitated under these conditions (Herculano-Houzel, Munk, Neuenschwander, & Singer, 1999; Munk, Roelfsema, Konig, Engel, & Singer,1996). This global pattern may be a prerequisite background condition for synchrony to occur. Speculatively, it seems that global disorder enhances saliency of the more localized ordered cell activity.

Neural activity measured in cats while they performed an attention task shows that synchrony actually happens before execution of the response, while the animal is preparing itself. In this study, the cortical areas needed to perform a focused attention task, association, somatosensory, and motor areas, synchronized rapidly (with zero phase-lag) during the preparation phase. They then increased after the appearance of the stimulus, were maintained until task completion, and only terminated once the reward for that trial became available (Roelfsema, Engel, Konig, & Singer, 1997). Attentional mechanisms thus seem to induce some sort of expectancy effect on the relevant neurons, perhaps a coherent subthreshold modulation that enables fast synchrony.

Studies with human participants have looked at differences in brain wave activity between conditions where conscious and unconscious perception takes place. In a masking paradigm where words were visible and available to explicit verbal report (the conscious awareness condition), there were theta wave or low frequency oscillations in cortical areas that persisted until a decision was made (Melloni et al., 2007). In this awareness condition they also found a P300 evoked potential in the EEG that has been interpreted as signifying the transfer of information into working memory. They also obtained a burst of high frequency gamma wave activity in frontal and central areas before stimulus presentation. These correlated with the anticipated time of stimulus presentation. The authors interpret these bursts as the reactivation of information in working memory.

In the above study activation of working memory is taken as the neural correlate of conscious awareness. When items are placed into this store or activated there, the assumption is that the person is thinking about or aware of them. Also of note in this experiment was the time course of neural changes that took place between the conscious and unconscious conditions. The first recorded difference was not in the amplitude of the oscillations but in their phase locking or synchrony. This gamma wave phase locking occurred about 180 ms after stimulus presentation in the conscious condition and lasted for about 100 ms. It was widespread, measured both inside and between the two hemispheres.

Conscious awareness of the stimulus in this task seemed to be mediated by very brief local oscillations that then became synchronized globally, and not with any increase in power. They speculate that this short, high frequency global burst of activity is a trigger event for access to conscious awareness. Singer and Kreiman (2009) speculates that high frequency waves are used to coordinate activity between different cortical areas and that once this activity is synchronized, it can be maintained by lower frequency oscillations.

THE NEURONAL BASIS OF ATTENTION

BRAIN AREAS THAT SUBSUME ATTENTIONAL FUNCTION

Attention plays an important role in many different cognitive phenomena as well as vision. This may be why there are at least six distinct brain structures implicated in attentional effects (Posner & Petersen, 1990). Many of these structures are functionally interconnected and collectively form an attentional neural network. Figure 2.3 provides an overview of their locations. We provide a list of the structures below along with a brief description of their function.

1. The reticular activating system (RAS) controls the brain's overall arousal and alertness levels. Nuclei are located in the hindbrain but have widespread connections to many areas of the cortex. Activation of the RAS is associated with the ability to sustain attention over time.
2. The superior colliculus is located in the midbrain. Its function seems to be the shifting of visual attention from one object or location in the visual field to another. It is considered to be part of the system that controls eye movements.
3. The thalamus relays incoming sensory information to the cortex. It also serves as a "gatekeeper" for cortical excitation as well, relaying excitatory inputs from the RAS to various cortical regions.
4. The parietal lobe seems to be responsible for the allocation of attentional resources, for example, to different spatial locations. It is also implicated in feature binding.

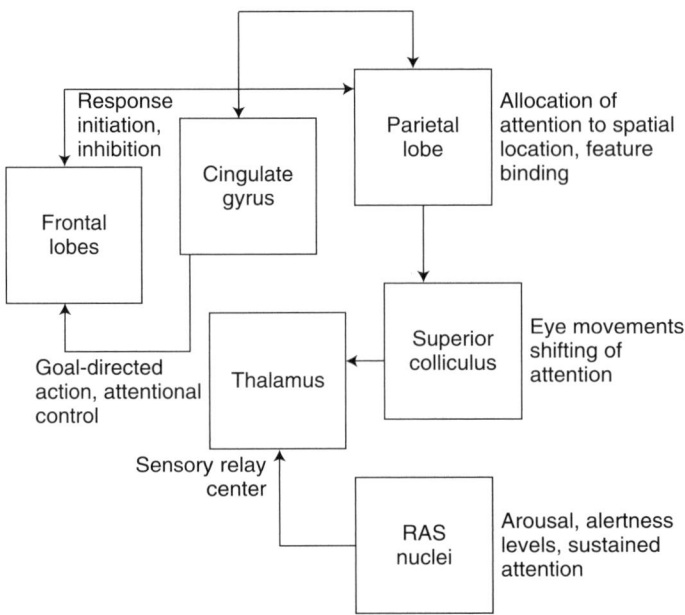

FIGURE 2.3   Different parts of the brain that make up the attention network and some of the direct and indirect pathways that connect them.

5. The cingulate cortex initiates a response on the basis of what is attended, especially in cases where the response entails the inhibition of an alternative response.

6. The frontal lobes play a role in goal-directed action, executive function, and problem solving. They are the source of feedback signals to posterior visual areas and are believed to exert top-down attentional control over incoming visual information.

THE ANATOMICAL BASIS OF VISUAL ATTENTION

It is generally acknowledged that there is no single center for visual attention in the brain. There is no area that "lights up" whenever an object is being attended to. Brain imaging studies have instead shown that there are multiple different attention areas throughout the brain. Some of these areas seem to play unique roles, while others may have multiple roles. Any given act of attention therefore shows up as an inter-play between these regions as they work together. These structures collectively are known as a functional network (Fuster, 2003). When describing functional networks for visual attention, a differentiation is made between target and source areas. A target area is typically modulated by a source area. Signals originating from the frontal areas typically feed back to modify activity in the posterior occipital areas. In this case we can say the frontal regions are the source and the occipital areas the target.

Examination of monkey cortex has revealed a highly connected set of modules or processing areas, over thirty in total (Felleman & van Essen, 1991). About half of these modules have a self-contained topographical mapping of the visual field. Most demonstrate specificity of response, they respond only to a particular stimulus feature. For example, area IT neurons respond to specific views of faces, hands and other complete objects. Neurons in area MT respond to speed and direction of motion and many area V4 neurons are driven by color.

Many of the connections between these modules are two-way, meaning that each area can drive the other. In response to a visual stimulus, there is a wave of activity that travels upward in the system, known as a feedforward pathway. Following this, there are messages that then travel back down the system, in a feedback manner. Numerous reciprocal activation loops between modules are also probably present as a normal part of visual perception. The modules operate in a highly parallel manner, with activity ongoing in adjacent areas simultaneously. There is also a hierarchical organization present. Neurons with small receptive fields respond early on but converge in successive layers to neurons with larger receptive fields. In area V1 for example, neurons respond selectively to oriented line segments, these converge to form angle and moving angle detectors, which converge with yet others to form representations for complex features and whole objects.

MEASURES OF BRAIN PHYSIOLOGY IN ATTENTION TASKS

One question we can ask concerning attention is whether objects compete with each other for access to awareness. Kastner, De Weerd, Desimone, and Underleider (1998) investigated this. In one condition of their study they flashed complicated visual patterns at four separate locations on a computer screen one at a time, each for 250 ms. In the second condition all four patterns were shown at the same time, also for 250 ms followed by a 750 ms blank screen. If we factor time into account the stimuli in both conditions were presented for equivalent periods. If there are competitive interactions for attentional access, they should occur in the simultaneous condition only. Using fMRI measures, this is indeed what they found. There was less pronounced neural activation in visual areas in the simultaneous compared to the sequential condition. What is more, this competition was seen only in those areas whose neurons contained large enough receptive fields to allow more than one object in. There was no effect in V1 cells whose receptive fields are small.

There was suppression in area V4 neurons and in temporal cortex though, whose receptive field sizes are larger.

Even in cases where there is no competition, we would expect increased neural activation to visual areas that are attended compared to those that are not. We have already described studies that demonstrated a response enhancement or gain control effect with single neurons, but a study by Mangun, Hillyard, and Luck (1993) demonstrates that this effect is found for larger brain areas as well. They presented rectangles in random order to different screen locations while asking observers to covertly orient attention to one of these locations. There was a greater evoked potential in the hemisphere contralateral to the covert attention side. Positron emission tomography (PET) imaging studies show the same result. Heinze et al. (1994) presented stimuli in either one half of the display or the other. Greater activation was found in the hemisphere contralateral to the attended side.

As the visual system has a retinotopic organization, if we attend to a particular location in the visual field we might expect to see increased activation in the attended areas only. This is indeed the case. Using fMRI, Brefczynski and DeYoe (1999) presented a set of objects to participants but asked them to orient their attention to just one of them. Activation was increased, but only in the attended locations. The effect was found for both striate and extrastriate cortex. In another study attentional effects were found also in the LGN, which is lower down in the processing stream than what might be expected. These results can be interpreted according to the attentional spotlight metaphor of visual attention, in which we can move our attentional focus from one location to another in much the same way a spotlight is moved across a scene.

Where in the brain does the "command" to focus attention originate? If attention originates in areas outside the visual system then we would expect to see activation in those areas first. If this were true, these areas could then be seen as controlling where visual attention goes. They would be attentional source regions that subsequently activate perceptual target regions. Studies of this sort consistently show activation of lateral prefrontal and posterior parietal cortex. These seem to be the areas that control what is called endogenous or top-down attention, in which a person voluntarily wills focus to a location (Corbetta, Miezin, Shulman, & Petersen, 1993). This fronto-parietal control is not limited to spatial forms of attention however. It has also been found to control attention based on stimulus features, time intervals, and in rapid serial visual presentations (Coull & Nobre, 1998; Giesbrecht, Woldorff, Song, & Mangun, 2003; Marois, Chun, & Gore, 2000; Wojciulik & Kanwisher, 1999).

Corbetta et al. (2000) suggest that there more to this story. There may be two fronto-parietal systems, one for exogenous (driven by external stimulus factors) and another for endogenous (driven by internal commands) shifts of attention. Endogenous shifts in the dorsal system that regulates perception-for-action are said to include the superior frontal cortex and the intraparietal sulcus in both hemispheres. Shifts of an exogenous nature in the ventral system that regulates perception-for-recognition would activate the temporo-parietal junction and the inferior frontal gyrus in the right hemisphere only. There also appears to be a prefrontal area found to be active in both systems that could govern each (Fox, Corbetta, Snyder, Vincent, & Raichle, 2006).

NEURAL MODELS OF ATTENTION

Banich (2004) outlines several types of neural attention models. We will describe two of these. In component process models, distinct brain areas each have a unique function. In these models if brain area A performances function X then no other area can perform X. One downside to these models is that they are sensitive to damage. If area A is damaged, then function X can never be performed. That is, no other brain area will be able to take over its function.

In distributed network models, the areas can be characterized as having some operational overlap. In this case, brain area A can perform functions X and Y, while brain area B may be able to perform functions Y and Z. These models are better able to handle damage. If damage occurs to area A, then X may be lost forever if no other area can do it. However, function Y will persist as it can be taken over by area B.

Posner, Inhoff, Friedrich, and Cohen (1987) propose that each of the multiple brain areas responsible for the control of attention performs a distinct operation. Their model describes the changes that occur in visual selective attention, where attention is shifted from one spatial location to another. They propose that the parietal lobes are used to release attention from a specific location. The superior colliculus then moves attention to a new location. Finally, the thalamus engages the attention and focuses it on the new location. Much of the evidence to support this model comes from research using the Posner cueing paradigm which we describe in greater detail elsewhere.

To illustrate this model, imagine that you are paying attention to your friend Harry because he is currently talking to you. Harry is to your left. Your other friend Tom now interjects to say something. Tom is to your right. In this situation, your parietal lobe would first activate to stop your focus on Harry. Following this, your superior colliculus would move your spatial attention to the right in the direction of Tom. Lastly, your thalamus would now refocus your attention on Tom.

Mesulam (1981) proposes an alternative neural model of attention. The model encompasses four brain areas. To begin, the posterior parietal cortex provides a representation of the space in which attention will be directed. Another structure, the cingulate gyrus, plays a motivational role. It determines what should be paid attention to and what should be ignored. Third, the frontal cortex helps execute motor programs for attention-related actions. These actions include gazing at certain regions in the visual field, scanning across the visual field, or reaching out to grasp an object. Finally, reticular structures generate arousal and vigilance levels.

Here is an example that will illustrate how all these areas might work together. Imagine that Jessica is at a donut store. She missed dinner the night before and so is very hungry. Her posterior parietal cortex contains a sensory representation of the donuts on a shelf in front of her. This representation includes the locations of chocolate donuts to her left and jelly-filled donuts to her right. In this scenario, her cingulate cortex directs her attention to items of significance, meaning that she will pay more attention to the donuts than to the shelf on which they are sitting. Her frontal cortex, supervising motor actions, will direct her hand to point out which ones she wants to buy. Underlying all this are arousal levels that have been determined by her reticular system. If Jessica had a good night's rest, her arousal and vigilance ought to be at high levels.

ATTENTION AND SINGLE NEURONS

Much of our discussion thus far has been on large-scale changes that occur in the brain as a result of attention or consciousness. Researchers have also examined the kinds of changes that take place within individual neurons. Wolfe, Kluender and Levi (2010) outline three main ways a neuron can respond to attention. Figure 2.4 shows a typical V1 neuron that is selectively tuned to a vertical line before any attentional influences, so that it fires maximally when a vertical line is placed inside its receptive field. A receptive field is the retinal area that feeds to the cell and influences its responding. In the absence of any attentional focusing cell will fire the most in response to vertical lines but then more and more slowly as the orientation of the line is changed away from vertical.

So let us imagine that a person is now selectively attending to a vertical line that is inside this cell's receptive field. They are focused on this line only and trying to exclude lines of other

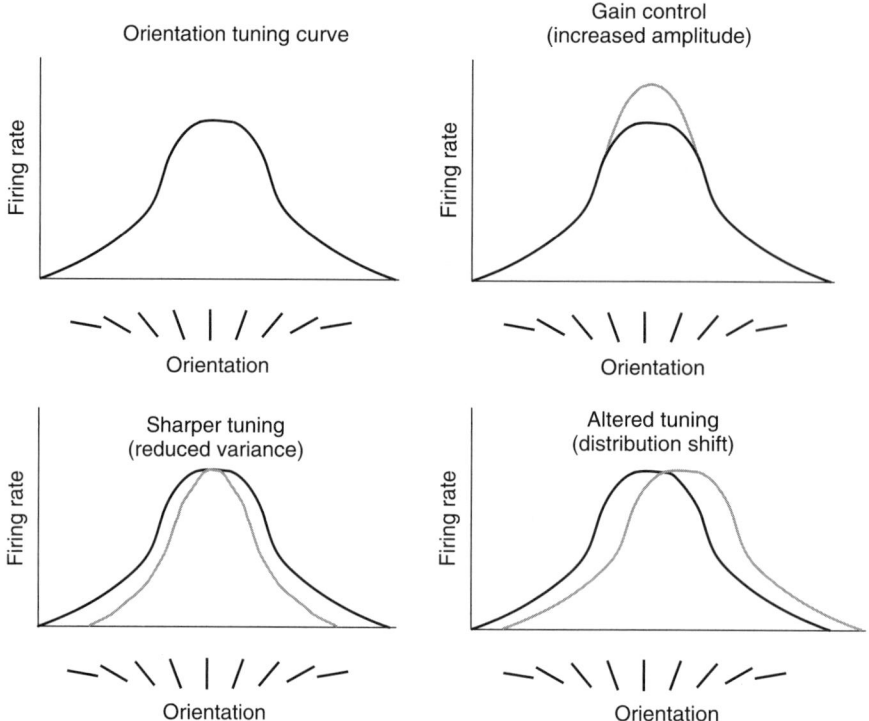

FIGURE 2.4   Three possible ways attention may change the orientation tuning properties of cells in the visual system.

orientations that may be present in the visual scene. As a result of this focus, they will be able to respond faster and more accurately to the vertical line. For instance if this were a visual search task and the participant were asked to identify a vertical line as the target, they would do so more efficiently.

One effect of attention we might see in this neuron is response enhancement. This would produce a higher peak in the orientation tuning curve, meaning the cell is firing faster than it used to. An increased amplitude in response, either at the single neuron level or at the population level, is referred to as gain control. EEG studies done in the 1950s and 1960s found that the amplitude of sensory evoked potentials increased when attention was focused on an object (Hillyard, Vogel, & Luck, 1999). Similar results were obtained using PET and fMRI studies.

Another change we might see with attention is sharper tuning, whereby the variance of the cell's response diminishes. If this were the case, the distribution of firing would be more narrowly focused around the vertical, so that if it responded weakly to a 45 degree line before the focus, it might respond even more weakly or not at all to it after attentional focus. This means the neuron is better able to "ignore" lines of similar orientation. Both response enhancement and sharper tuning have been found (Lu & Dosher, 1998; Treu & Trujillo, 1999).

Another possible response is altered tuning. Attention could conceivably switch one cell's preference for one orientation to another. Evidence for altered tuning has been found for receptive fields. When monkeys are trained to shift their focus from one area to another in a display, the receptive field for a given neuron has been found to shift along with it (Womelsdorf, Fries, Mitra, & Desimone, 2006). It is probably the case that visual system cells demonstrate all three types of response described here and that they work interactively with one another For example, a response enhancement in one cell might cause other neurons to sharpen or alter their tuning (Wolfe et al., 2010).

PROBLEMS WITH STUDYING THE NEURAL BASIS OF CONSCIOUSNESS

There are five major difficulties in studying the neural basis of consciousness. Stoerig (2002) describes these in greater detail. We outline them here. To start, consciousness can be considered a global state or a trait. If it is a state, then it is in effect a default condition of normal mental function and would be expected to correspond to a large volume of brain activity. If it were a trait, then it corresponds to specific identifiable experience and may be associated with particular brain regions. This is a problem secondarily because it means that both global and local areas are concurrently active at any given time and it becomes difficult to disassociate the two.

A third issue is that if we accept Block's view of phenomenal and access consciousness then it means there are at least two regions corresponding to qualia on the one hand and verbal report-ability on the other. This means it may be possible to perceive some visual aspect of a stimulus but not report it or vice versa and thus have difficulty telling which region is responsible for what. Another instance of this "one or many" problem is being able to differentiate between an overall awareness of an object vs. awareness for each of its component attributes, especially if there are multiple loci coding for each.

Fourth, we know that vision is a somewhat sequential process. Where in this stream does consciousness reside? It would be a bit far-fetched to say the color perception takes place only in retinal cone cells, yet that is certainly a necessary first step. This brings up the issue of dependencies in processing, where one area may do most of the required computation, yet relies on inputs from other areas. A final issue related to stages in processing has to do with the transition from unconscious to consciousness vision. We currently have no clear area where or when this happens. This points to the importance of studying not just "centers" of conscious awareness but its temporal aspects as well.

3 Under Construction

Although much of perception seems effortless, there is quite a bit of ongoing processing "behind the scenes" that allows us to experience the world the way we do. In other words, our conscious experience is built. This construction is necessary because the visual inputs in some cases underspecify the experience. For example, we all have a blind spot where the optic nerve leaves the eye. Because there are no photoreceptors there, we literally should not be able to perceive anything at those locations in the visual field, and yet we do. That is because the visual system is able to take existing visible information and use it to seamlessly fill in the unspecified parts.

Saccadic suppression is another example of constructed vision. Whenever we move our eyes rapidly from one point to another the perceived world jumps. We should experience this as a streaked blur, as if we kept our eyes open and moved our head in one direction very rapidly. Yet this never happens. That is because the visual system suppresses perception during this movement. This means that a significant percentage of what the eye receives never gets transmitted to the brain in a way that can be consciously interpreted.

Illusory contours are also built by the visual system. These are lines that are not present in the stimulus: they exist only in our mind. This is because the information present in the stimulus is set up in such a way that under normal circumstances there *should* be a line there. In the Pac-Man pattern for instance, edges are aligned with each other at the same orientation but with spaces or gaps between them. The visual system doesn't need to see the entire line to know one might be there. It can interpolate based on the information that is present and build one, filling in the gaps between the edges. This is efficient from a computational point of view, as there is no need to perceive and process the line in its entirety. The brain is not a draftsman, diligently copying everything that it sees. Instead, it is much more like a detective, who must piece together a case based on clues and incomplete information.

In this chapter we will examine two additional effects that show construction over areas larger than points or lines. In these cases, entire two-dimensional areas get filled in. Under the right conditions, a stationary figure in peripheral vision will be seen as taking on the texture or color of the background behind it. In effect, these types of object will phenomenally disappear. They are "erased" from conscious experience, perhaps because they are redundant and not practically useful for vision. Finally, we will look at the case of perceptual completion, in which objects that are partially occluded or hidden by other objects are still perceived as whole. Completion processes are necessary in that we "know" objects don't go out of existence when they are partially covered up. The visual brain makes an assumption that they are still there because in reality they usually are.

One of the larger debates in perceptual science is between "computationalists" and those in the ecological perception movement. Computationalists argue that visual stimuli are impoverished and that much of perception must therefore be constructed. According to this view extensive computation must take place in order to produce a coherent visual experience. The ecological perception movement argues that most or all of the information necessary to perceive coherently is in the stimulus or in the way the organism interacts with its environment. In the ecological view, vision is direct and immediate so that little computation is necessary. We won't take sides in this argument, other than to say that this debate probably hinges on how computation is defined. If some computations are either "hard-wired" or genetic in origin or well learned due to practice and experience, then they may happen so quickly and automatically that they require few processing resources. If this is the case then they may not qualify as computations in the customary sense.

THE BLIND SPOT

The retina consists of several different layers of cells including photoreceptors, bipolars, and ganglion cells. Because these are cells, like every other cell in the body they need arteries to supply them with oxygenated blood and veins to take away the deoxygenated blood. Also, in order for a message to be sent from the retina, the ganglion cell axons that form the optic nerve need some way to exit. The arteries, veins, and optic nerve all travel through a region on the retina called the optic disc. Because of this there are no photoreceptors located there and we are effectively "blind" in each eye at this location. This area is referred to as the blind spot.

If we are blind in those spots, then how come we don't notice it? Why don't we walk around seeing two black circles in our visual field? The answer is that the visual system fills in these areas based on the surrounding image. In other words, we construct a portion of the world in the absence of any actual information about what's there. This phenomenon shows that vision is an active process. The brain goes beyond the information given to it by the eyes. Our conscious experience of the world is therefore more than just a reproduction or simple translation of inputs from sensory receptors.

Exactly how big is the blind spot? Spillman, Otte, Hamburger, and Magnussen (2006) examined this question. They presented stimulus frames of different widths around the spot. Complete filling-in was obtained for frame widths of 0.05 degrees visual angle for color and for 0.20 degrees for texture. Incomplete filling-in occurred when the frames did not line up around the blind spot border because of a saccade. These results show that local cortical processes around the outside border of the spot are responsible for the filling-in process.

Araragi and Sunaga (2009) presented a line on only one side of the blind spot. If the line were outside of the border its proximal end was perceived as ending there. If, however, the line was inside the border the end was perceived as terminating on the opposite side. Using a moving line presented below the spot, they were able to determine that, on average, filling-in happened at 2.84 degrees visual angle.

What is the shape of the blind spot? Araragi and Nakamizo (2003) presented a pair of lines on either side of the blind spot and allowed observers to vary their length until the two appeared joined. They varied the orientation of the line and found that the minimum length of the line to produce a perceptual filling-in increased going from horizontal to vertical. They suggest that this difference is due to the elliptical shape of receptive fields in binocular neurons that process information from this portion of the retina. These fields are apparently longer vertically than horizontally and so completion requires a shorter length at that orientation.

Another question that comes up is exactly where in the brain filling-in happens. Komatsu, Kinoshita, and Murakami (2002) recorded the activity of cells in area V1 of a monkey during a visual fixation task. Neurons in layer 6 of this area fired in response to the presence of large objects in the blind spot. These neurons have very large receptive fields that extend outward from the blind spot. The authors conclude that these cells probably encode information that is used as part of the perceptual filling-in process. These results replicate much of the findings of an earlier study (Komatsu, Kinoshita, & Murakami, 2000).

SACCADIC SUPPRESSION

Take a look at the world around you. Although you may not notice, your eyes are constantly moving, stopping briefly at different locations before moving on again. The stopping points are known as fixations and the movements are known as saccades. We can think of each fixation as a "snapshot" or photograph of the world at one moment in time and the saccades as the positioning of a camera for another shot. If we were consciously aware of the motion induced by the eye movement during the saccade, the world would be seen as swooping by. Not only would this be disconcerting, it would interfere with perceptual processing of the fixated object or scene. The visual system effectively "shuts down" during the movement to prevent this. The process is known as saccadic suppression.

The result of all this is that the brain doesn't receive a continuous "video" of the world. It must construct this from each of the pictures it receives one after the other. In effect our visual system builds up a coherent continuous percept of reality (a "home movie") even though it receives something more akin to individual pictures separated in space and time (a "photo" album).

ILLUSORY CONTOURS

Look at Figure 3.1. In the figure on the top are three black Pac-Man like figures. These are arranged so that their inner contours form the vertices of an equilateral triangle (Kanizsa, 1955, 1979). On the bottom is an arrangement of four such Pac-Man figures, this time arranged at the corners of a square. What is compelling about each of these figures is that we see the triangle and square even though they are not entirely there! Only a small amount of contour is visible, yet our visual system seems to extend the contours so that they meet, forming completely bounded shapes. Most of the contour that we see in these figures has no luminance difference across the edge, so the contours are perceived in the absence of any actual physical stimulus. We also see not just the outer boundary lines, but also a complete surface. These phenomena are called illusory contours. They have also been referred to as illusory surfaces.

There are several features of these stimuli. Illusory surfaces look brighter (or depending on the illusion, darker) than their background. They also stand out from their background in depth. One illusory rectangle can also appear to be superimposed on top of another, with a clear separation in depth. Some theories of illusory contours emphasize cognitive or top-down factors such as reasoning or past experience (Gregory, 1972; Hochberg, 1978; Rock & Anson, 1979). Others place the mechanism at early visual processing (Davis & Driver, 1994; Grossberg & Mingolla, 1985; Peterhans & von der Heydt, 1989). Although research has focused mostly on the static form of these illusions there is also a motion-based version (Gyulai, 2007).

Much of the recent work on illusory contours has examined the brain mechanisms that underlie the effect. The majority of findings suggest that the processing of real and illusory contours share the same cortical mechanisms (Vogels & Orban, 1987). Both actual and illusory contours have been found to activate primary visual cortex neurons (Lee & Nguyen, 2001; Sheth, Sharma, Rao, & Sur, 1996). However, in some brain areas, differential activation is seen. For instance, illusory contours induce different activity in area 17 than do actual contours (Ramsden, Hung, & Roe, 2001). It is believed that both early prestriate and later prestriate areas are involved in illusory contour perception (Larsson et al., 1999; Montaser-Kouhsari, Landy, Heeger, & Larsson, 2007). We describe some of this research in greater detail next.

Maertens and Pollmann (2005) used fMRI to record changes in activity level in area V1 while observers performed a discrimination task involving Kanizsa illusory squares. They found that the same areas used to perceive real contours were also activated during the learning of the illusory stimuli. What is more, the effects lasted over a period of 10 months, and were specific to the location in the visual field where the patterns were presented. Larson et al. (1999) obtained similar results using PET imaging for areas V1 and V2. Only one area, the right fusiform gyrus, was activated more strongly by illusory contours than real contours in their study.

Brighina et al. (2003) studied the effect of repetitive transcranial magnetic stimulation (rTMS) on illusory contour perception. Application of rTMS produces lasting inhibition of cortical activity. In this study they applied the procedure over the left and right occipital cortex of eight subjects and then had them perform a regularity/irregularity judgment regarding Kanizsa squares

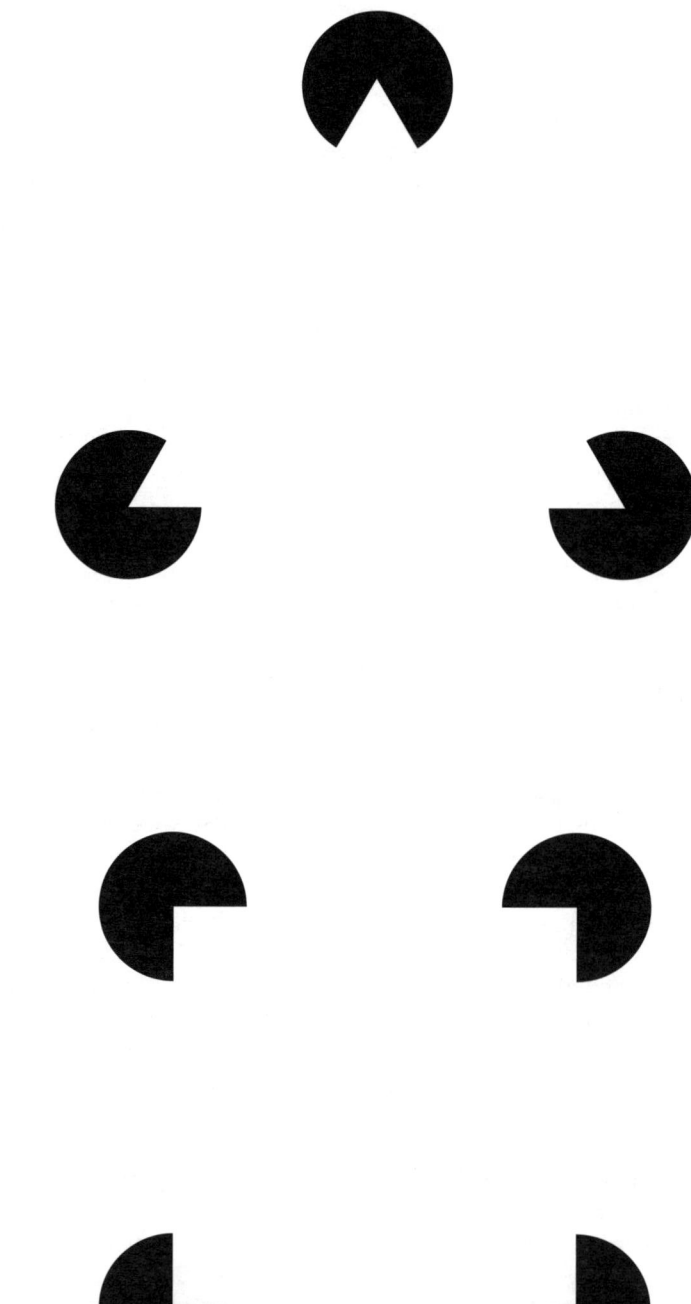

FIGURE 3.1   Demonstrations of illusory contours (after Kanizsa, 1979).

in both a pretest and posttest condition. Compared to controls these participants took significantly longer to perceive the illusory contours. The effect was specific to right side extrastriate occipital cortex only.

The work we have reviewed so far implicates both primary (striate) and secondary (extrastriate) occipital cortex in the perception of illusory contours. Primary areas contain orientation selective neurons that code for physically present lines, so it is not much of a surprise that such neurons may also code for illusory lines. But what role do the higher visual areas play? Sary et al. (2008) set out to answer this question. They used single cell recording techniques to measure neuron activity in monkey inferotemporal cortex in response to Kanizsa figures and various control stimuli. Inferotemporal cortex is responsible for recognition of global shape structure. They found that these neurons were responsive to illusory contours but had longer onset latencies. They took longer to respond in comparison to neurons coding for real contours. They speculate that these neurons may be the source of feedback information to early visual areas. It could be that more global object properties such as the shape of the Pac-Man figures are represented here and then fed back to primary visual cortex, where they could help construct an illusory contour (the feedback mechanism is discussed below).

Two possible neural mechanisms for the formation of illusory contours have been proposed (Sary et al., 2008). In the lateral account the physically present contours activate facil-itator cells because the line endings and orientation in their receptive fields match those in the stimulus. These facilitator cells then turn on other cells with similar orientation selectivity and whose receptive fields are located in-between them (Kapadia, Westhimer, & Gilbert, 1999; Kasamtsu, Polat, Pettet, & Norcia, 2001; Polat, Mizobe, Pettet, Kasamatsu, & Norcia, 1998). All of this can take place using lateral connections between cells in the primary visual areas. In the feedback account, cells in higher visual regions that have large enough receptive fields can take in one or more inducers in the stimulus. This information can then be fed back to the primary regions and used to interpolate a line or a corner. For instance, neurons that represent two Pac-Man figures can send this information to areas V1 and V2, where an illusory line can be constructed between them (Bullier & Henry, 1979; Givre, Schroeder, & Arezzo, 1994). Of course, these two mechanisms may both be used simultaneously to construct a percept (Oliva & Schyns, 1997).

FILLING-IN

If the blind spot demonstration fails to convince you that the brain can cover up blank areas in the visual field, perhaps this demonstration will. Ramachandran (1993) asks us first to turn on our TV and set it to a channel where it is not picking up any station. This results in a pattern of "snow" or white noise across the screen. In the middle of the screen stick a small circular gummed label with a tiny black dot in the center. Then, seven or eight degrees of visual angle from this dot, place a one centimeter square piece of gray paper. Now step back and view the display from about three feet away. If you fixate on the central dot for several seconds you will soon see the gray square disappear, to be replaced by the surrounding snow!

This demonstration and the blind spot phenomenon are both examples of the more general perceptual effect known as filling-in. In this process the visual system interpolates information across a region of the visual field, literally adding content about the surround to that region. This occurs even though the real stimulus properties for that region do not possess that content, i.e., the effect happens in the absence of an actual stimulus. In addition to the blind spot, there are pathological scotomas, or patches of blindness due to brain damage, that also get filled-in (Sergent, 1988). Filling-in of retinal images also occurs during artificial retinal stabilization, when an image is continually projected to the same location (Gerrits, de Haan, & Vendrik, 1966).

More recently researchers have studied filling-in by presenting a shape that is either gray or colored on a background texture. This pattern is shown some distance away from a fixation point, usually in the peripheral visual field. Participants are instructed to gaze at the fixation point. After several seconds, the shape appears to be filled-in by the surrounding background pattern (De Weerd, Desimone, & Ungerleider, 1998; Ramachandran, Gregory, & Aiken, 1993; Spillmann & Kurtenbach, 1992). This is the effect demonstrated by the artificial scotoma in the previous exercise.

The speed with which a figure gets filled-in depends on a variety of factors. Images that are more effectively stabilized get filled-in faster (Martinez-Conde, Macknik, & Hubel, 2004). Other factors include the size and length of boundaries enclosing the figure, the relative size of figure and background, and figure salience (Sakaguchi, 2001; Stuerzel & Spillmann, 2001; Weichman & Harris, 2001). The border between figure and background is particularly important (Paradiso & Nakayama, 1991).

De Weerd, Smith, and Greenberg (2006) were able to enhance the filling-in process by instructing participants to selectively attend to the shape, color, or location of the presented figure. They were able to predict the distribution of reaction times to filling-in as a multiplicative factor of the reaction times for unattended figures. Notice that this is another case of higher order cognitive control over what has traditionally been considered to be a low level stimulus-driven perceptual process. This was also true for amodal completion.

Meng, Remus, and Tong (2005) were able to produce a moving filling-in effect. They presented moving gratings to peripheral vision of human subjects, separated by a gap of seven degrees of visual angle. In conditions where the orientation of the two gratings was aligned, the subjects reported seeing a "visual phantom" of the real grating filling the gap between them. The phantoms occurred regardless of whether visual attention was directed toward the gratings or toward a letter presented at a central fixation point. They conclude that the effect requires presentation of the inducing gratings in conjunction with some form of visual attention and that visual attention can modulate the effect.

What neural mechanism underlies the filling-in effect? According to one account, it involves the process of disinhibition (Grossberg, 1987; Neumann, Pessoa, & Hansen, 2001). In normal vision it is assumed that the border representation around a figure actively inhibits the spread of features from the surrounding region into the figure. Image stabilization on the retina weakens this inhibitory signal; it inhibits the inhibition, which amounts to disinhibition. The spread of surface features such as texture, color, brightness, or motion from the surround is now free to enter the figure and fill it up.

In the visual phantoms study by Meng et al. (2005), fMRI recordings showed activity in areas V1 and V2 corresponding to the spatial locations of the gap where the phantoms appeared. They speculate that there is a propagation of neural activity into this gap area from the surrounding regions, perhaps through long-range horizontal connections between neighboring columns with similar orientation preferences. Their imaging data implicate early visual cortex as the locus for the effect, as there was relatively little neural activity in areas V3a and V4v.

Mendola, Conner, Sharma, Bahekar, and Lemieux (2006) presented a colorless disc with a higher luminance than the background to several participants, who indicated the presence or absence of filling-in by making a keypress. Using fMRI, they discovered lowered activation in contralateral areas V1 and V2 with increased activation in areas V3 and V4, intraparietal sulcus, posterior superior temporal sulcus, and the ventral occipital-temporal region. This pattern of brain activity was similar for presentations in the upper or lower visual field and resembled that for other bistable stimuli such as in binocular rivalry. They posit that the filling-in process calls on higher level cognitive functions that may then feed back to alter activity in earlier visual areas. Notice that this explanation differs from that in the previous paragraph, which involved early areas only. It is possible that both early and late mechanisms may be at work. For a comprehensive review of how filling-in may happen, see Komatsu (2006).

PERCEPTUAL COMPLETION

Once more take a look at the room around you or the natural environment if you are outdoors. You may see a desk that interrupts your view of a chair, or perhaps a tree that is partially covered by a bush. Yet in both of these instances you have little difficulty "completing" your view of the covered object. Even though you can't see part of it, the object seems whole. You don't, for example, perceive the covered object as disappearing or assuming some strange shape once it is out of view. In the real world then, we rarely view objects in their entirety. Most of the time the surface of one object, known as an occluder, is in front of and hides part of another. The visual system seems to fill in or complete the missing object so that we perceive it as continuing behind the occluder. This process is known as amodal completion (Kanizsa, 1975; Michotte, Thines, Costall, & Butterworth, 1991).

How does the visual system do this? One way to start is to examine the way that contours or edges relate to each other when they pass under an occluder. Kellman and Shipley (1991) refer to this as the concept of relatability. In an experiment these researchers presented participants with a rectangle that occluded a portion of a line (see Figure 3.2). In one condition, the two ends can be connected by a simple curve with a single bend in it. In another condition the simplest line that connects them is an S-curve with two bends in it. The majority of participants perceived the line as a single continuous object only when they were relatable by a curve with a single bend. In the other condition, the preferred perceptual outcome was that there were two separate lines, that is, two objects that did not connect with each other behind the rectangle.

The example given above is two-dimensional. Most of the objects we encounter are three-dimensional. In these cases, there are other principles that can explain completion. Figure 3.3 shows two boxes. Note that there are several types of junction, or place where the objects meet. The Y and arrow junctions almost always occur as corners or places where two or more surfaces come together in a single object. In these cases, there is no occlusion. T-junctions, however, almost always happen when one surface occludes another and so would signal the location where surfaces from two different objects meet. These junctions are called nonaccidental features because they are very unlikely to happen by accident or chance.

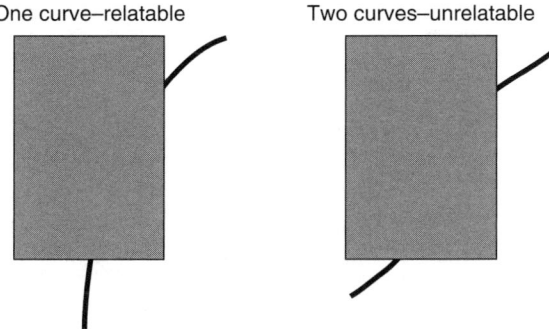

FIGURE 3.2   Observers perceive the two ends of the line occluded behind the rectangle as being part of the same object when they can be related by a curve with a single bend. If the two ends are related by a curve with two bends they are not perceived as being part of the same object.

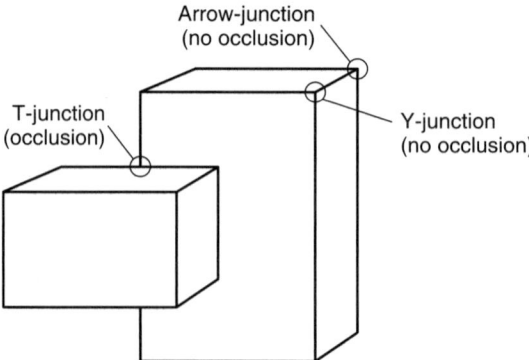

FIGURE 3.3 Arrow and Y-junctions most often occur at corners of single objects that are not blocked by other objects. T-junctions, however, typically occur at intersections where one object is occluding another.

There are two general categories of amodal completion. In global completion, the entire completed shape is a simple as possible. In local completion the completion itself is a simple as possible. Figure 3.4 shows examples of each. Van Lier, van der Helm, and Leeuwenberg (1995) presented figures like this to participants and determined their preferred outcomes using drawing and simultaneous matching tasks. The authors create a model to explain the results. In their model, the two possible interpretations compete with each other for dominance with the "best"

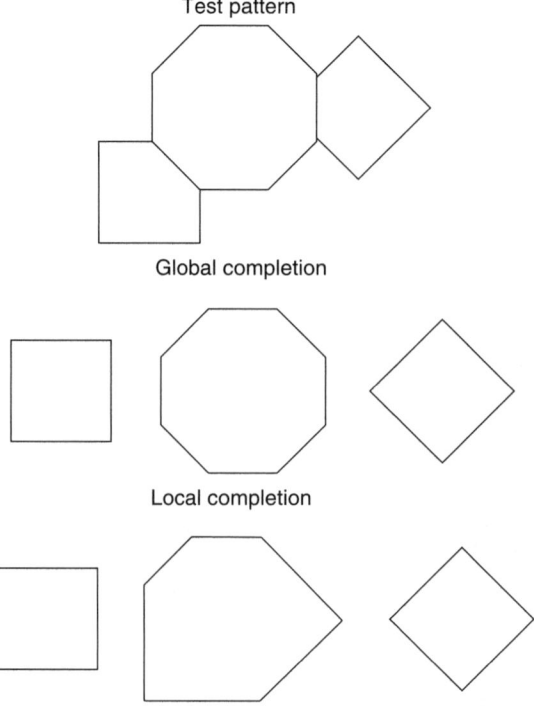

FIGURE 3.4 A pattern with its global and local completion alternatives (after Kanizsa, 1985).

interpretation winning out. They discuss the factors that affect global goodness. These are pattern orientation, relative orientation of edges, familiarity, coincidence and local configurations. The goodness of a local configuration according to the authors is primarily the number of occluded or virtual parts.

Amodal completion is believed to occur early in visual processing and may even operate concurrently with or prior to perceptual grouping (Davis & Driver, 1998; Palmer, Neff, & Beck, 1996; Rensink & Enns, 1998). This idea seems reasonable, as the Gestalt principle of good continuation certainly seems a likely mechanism for contour completion. The fact that completion is a low level visual process is again supported by studies showing that it is unaffected by cognitive factors like the observer's knowledge or experience (Kanizsa & Gerbino, 1982). A number of experiments support the notion that stimulus properties alone can account for the effect (Kellman, Guttman, & Wickens, 2001; Takeichi, Nakazawa, Murakami, & Shimojo, 1995).

However, Lee and Vecera (2005) provide some evidence to the contrary. In their study they measured degree of amodal completion while manipulating cognitive load. In one condition, participants had to maintain four items in working visual short-term memory. Amodal completion was halted for these participants. In comparison, when there was no cognitive load and no items had to be retained, amodal completion occurred as normal. They conclude that amodal completion is not independent of higher order cognitive factors such as attention and memory.

4 I'm Getting Tired of This

Aftereffects are an interesting feature of the visual system. By this we mean that overexposure to one type of stimulus often results in the perception of its opposite. For example, if we stare at one colored shape for an extended time and then look away at a blank surface, we will see the shape filled by its opposite color. This is known as a color aftereffect. Motion aftereffects occur when we stare for long enough at a portion of the visual field that is consistently moving in one direction. In this case we then look away and see motion in the opposite direction. For instance, if we were to look at traffic speeding to the left on a freeway, we would then afterwards perceive rightward motion. There are also tilt aftereffects where we perceive a line tilted in a direction opposite to the orientation of several previously viewed line segments.

One of the explanations for aftereffects involves the concept of opponent neural adaptation. In this view single neurons or groups of neurons code for one aspect of a stimulus. These neurons have mutually inhibitory interactions with neurons coding for the opposite aspect of the stimulus. By this account continual exposure to one aspect of the stimulus fatigues these neurons. They in turn lose the ability to inhibit their opposites. These opposing neurons then gain increased strength due to the decreased inhibition and are able to suppress their rivals more powerfully. This process is described in greater detail below.

The research on aftereffects shows that there is more going on than just neural opponency. Color aftereffects for example can be made contingent upon other features such as orientation. This implies that there are connections between areas coding for such features, i.e., there must be a connection between the parts of the brain that code for color and orientation. It is also uncertain to what extent aftereffects are learned, how long the effect should persist, and whether or not attention is required. Color aftereffects seem to be handled by preattentive processes while motion aftereffects are more easily affected by conscious voluntary control over attention.

COLOR AFTEREFFECTS

If you stare at a color pattern long enough and then look away at a white surface, you may be surprised to see the same pattern but in different colors. For example, in the American flag illusion staring at a flag with green and black stripes and with black stars against a yellow background produces an afterimage of the flag in its original colors. This demonstration of an afterimage reveals an important aspect of color vision, known as color opponency. There are cells in the retina and the LGN of the thalamus that have opponent effects, meaning they code for opposite wavelengths. The two primary ones are red–green and blue–yellow (there is also black–white). If these cells are stimulated for an extended period of time as happens in this demonstration, then these cells lose their ability to respond and instead we see an enhanced response by that color's opposite. If red is adapted and fatigued there is a corresponding increase in the activity of the green cells and vice versa. Under these conditions we see the opponent color, so if we stare at red we see green and if we stare at blue we see yellow.

McCollough (1965) was the first to discover that color aftereffects can be contingent on other visual features such as line orientation. The basic methodological procedure for this is to have observers look at for instance, a pattern of green vertical stripes and red horizontal stripes. This is the adaptation period and can last for seconds or minutes. Following adaptation a checkered pattern containing neutral black and white vertical and horizontal elements is shown. Observers will now report seeing the vertical areas as reddish and the horizontal areas as greenish. This phenomenon has since been dubbed the McCollough Effect (ME). Although orientation has been used most often in the literature, contingent color effects have been found for other stimulus features such as spatial frequency (Skowbo, Timney, Gentry, & Morant, 1975).

One topic of debate in the research on this topic has been whether the ME is specific to a class of stimuli such as orientation and spatial frequency or whether it is a more general associative learning process. If it is a classical or associative learning phenomenon, then all manner of stimuli when paired with colors should produce aftereffects. This interpretation has been supported by demonstrations showing Pavlovian-type conditioning results like generalization, extinction, and spontaneous recovery (Allan & Siegel, 1986; Brand, Holding, & James, 1987). However, Siegel, Allan, and Eissenberg (1992) report that only a limited class of stimuli will elicit color aftereffects. They used square, cross, and triangle forms and found these were able to elicit the ME. Even a non-patterned stimulus, the lightness of a frame surrounding a colored area, produced ME effects.

If the ME were a perceptual effect then it should only last for a limited time. Reported durations in some studies put this at no more than 24 hours. That is because feature-specific neurons such as those for line orientation in the primary visual areas eventually recover. If the effect were learned, it could be expected to last longer than this, on the order of days or weeks as we see with classical conditioning studies. Stromeyer and Mansfield (1970) found the ME to persist for as long as six weeks. Siegel et al. (1992) found a 24 hour duration for the effect with the frame stimuli. Subsequent criticisms of this finding are that the color aftereffect should go away if observers are instructed to use eye movements to scan the adaptation and testing forms (Broerse & Grimbeek, 1994). However, these objections have been subsequently refuted (Siegel, Allan, & Eissenberg, 1994). Overall the results support the notion that the ME is an associatively learned process. However, a specific perceptual mechanism cannot be ruled out.

Color aftereffects raise the question of which features are preattentive or attentive. In Chapter 7 on varieties of visual attention we discuss feature integration theory (Treisman & Gelade, 1980). In this view color and form are separate stimulus attributes. They are represented in separate feature maps and get conjoined only through an act of effortful attention. In the ME, however, orientation and color conjoin easily and are assumed to reflect features present in preattentive vision (Houck & Hoffman, 1986). Is attention therefore necessary for this contingency? Houck and Hoffman (1986) set out to explore this issue. They presented gratings with different color and orientation combinations both inside and outside the focus of attention. They obtained the ME whether the stimuli were attended or not. This implies that color and orientation are preattentive. However, these same authors, using a visual search task, found that these two features were separable. They conclude that different experimental procedures may be revealing different aspects of preattentive processing.

How long does it take us to become consciously aware of color? If it were a fast preattentive process, color might be processed by early cortical mechanisms before we even had a chance to be conscious of them. If this were the case, then we might only become aware of color after additional processing by extrastriate visual areas has occurred. Previous research varies with respect to the minimum presentation time necessary to produce conscious visual experience of color. These estimates run from 15 Hz (33 ms per frame), to 18.8 Hz, to 30 Hz (Gur & Snodderly, 1997; Holcombe & Cavanagh, 2001; Kelly, 1983; Wisowaty, 1981).

Vul and MacLeod (2006) used the ME to probe when conscious awareness of color takes place. On each trial they presented a sequence of four alternating color-orientation gratings followed by a neutral test stimulus. For example, on a given trial an observer might see a red vertical grating followed by a horizontal green grating. This alternation would then occur once more followed by the test stimulus containing vertical and horizontal black and white lines. The strength of the aftereffect was measured as the color contrast between the two sides of the test stimulus necessary to cancel the aftereffect colors. The main parameter varied was the frame duration, or how long each of the frames was visible.

The results showed a ME at frame durations as short as 10–20 ms. This is significantly faster than the duration necessary for conscious color perception. The neurons that track the conjunction of color and orientation thus do not seem on their own to give rise to conscious awareness. It may be that conscious experience arises only when these early striate neurons send their outputs farther upstream to extrastriate cortical areas. The exact pathways and mechanisms by which this might occur are now mostly speculative.

MOTION AFTEREFFECTS

The next time you watch a movie wait until the end when the credits scroll up the screen. Instead of reading them, fixate your eyes on the center of the screen and stare at it for about one minute. If you now look away at a stationary object like a wall you will see the object or surface moving in the opposite direction. In this case the wall will appear to be moving downward (Blake & Sekuler, 2006). If you want more of a real-world example, look at the center of a waterfall for a minute and then look away. This time you will see upward motion. This latter example is known as the waterfall illusion (Addams, 1834). The more general term for this effect is the motion aftereffect (MAE) and it holds not just for translational motion but also for expansive/contractive and rotational motion as well (Mather & Harris, 1998).

Chaudhuri (1990) found a reduction in the MAE when the observer's attention was diverted away from a linear motion-adapting stimulus. This demonstrates that at least some attention is necessary for the effect and that when this attention is diverted elsewhere, the aftereffect-inducing stimulus is not encoded or processed. Houghton, Macken, and Jones (2003) explored the nature of this diversion. They diverted a subject's attention away from a moving sinusoidal grating in several different ways that all involved cognitive or higher-order functioning (such as searching for a string of digits) and were not based on visual attention. In each case there was a reduction in the MAE. These results demonstrate that the MAE, previously believed to be an automatic process, is in fact not immune to cognitive functioning (Allport, 1993; Pashler, 1998). Here we see another instance of how a supposedly fast, automatic, and bottom-up perceptual process such as motion perception is perhaps not so fast, automatic, or bottom-up as we may believe. These data imply that motion perception is not functionally isolated from cognitive factors, i.e., it is not a module that is insulated from top-down influences like instructional set, language, and memory.

Another example of the top-down influence on the MAE comes from the observation of static images. Winawer, Huk, and Boroditsky (2008) presented photographs with an implied direction of motion. For example, they showed a picture of a cheetah running or of a human athlete sprinting to the left or right. Observers who adapted by viewing these photos experienced the MAE in the direction opposite that of the implied motion. This result is significant because there was no actual movement in the stimuli to trigger motion-sensitive neurons. The implied static motion by itself was sufficient to activate the same direction-selective circuits that underlie perception of real motion.

If observers adapt to two random dot fields moving in different directions, the resulting MAE is in the direction opposite the average of the two field's motion vectors (Riggs & Day, 1980; Verstraten, Fredericksen, & van de Grind, 1994). So if upward and rightward motion were viewed, the resulting MAE would be downward and to the left (270 degrees). Alais and Blake (1999) showed random dot patterns where the majority of the dots were moving in one coherent direction. They then took 25 percent of these dots and moved them in another direction. In one condition subjects were asked to pay attention to this secondary motion when it occurred. For these people, the direction of the MAE was shifted by about 20 degrees, equivalent to a 70 percent correlation of the secondary dot direction.

Another study demonstrates even more powerfully the role attention has to play in motion perception. Bonneh, Cooperman, and Sagi (2001) presented an array of random dots over a salient visible object, such as a yellow circle. In tasks where participants are asked to pay attention to the object and the dots are set in motion the object is reported to completely disappear for several seconds and then reappear. This effect is referred to as "motion-induced blindness." It is not clear what causes this, although a number of factors such as binocular suppression and masking have been ruled out. One explanation is that the movement automatically captures attention, drawing it away from the object and preventing it from entering conscious awareness (Carter & Pettigrew, 2003). In this sense the motion may be considered as a stimulus which induces automatic attentional orienting that cannot be suppressed.

Regarding the neural basis of motion perception, it has been long known that area MT in the visual pathway is the first major center where motion information gets processed. Tootell et al. (1995) had participants view expanding or contracting rings for 40 seconds while fixating at their center. A subsequent stationary ring was seen to contract or expand for 20 seconds. The fMRI recordings showed an increase in the change of activity in area MT after termination of the moving rings that slowly faded away over a period of 20 seconds. This result is what we would expect if some neurons adapted to the original motion but then became fatigued, allowing activity in opposite direction motion neurons to become stronger. Subsequent research supports the notion that cells in area MT that code selectively for one direction of motion have opponent characteristics with neurons representing the opposite direction (Culham et al., 1999; He, Cohen, & Hu, 1998).

TILT AFTEREFFECTS

The tilt aftereffect (TAE) is an error in judging the orientation of a line after adaptation to a line-like stimulus at another orientation. For example, the classic effect involves looking at a single adaptation line at different orientations in separate conditions and then judging the orientation of a single test line (original work by Gibson & Radner, 1937). Under these conditions, a vertical line appears displaced in a counterclockwise direction after exposure to lines tilted between vertical and 45 degrees clockwise. In comparison, a vertical line appears displaced in a clockwise direction after viewing lines tilted between 45 and 90 degrees visual angle. The counterclockwise tilt is called the expansion or direct effect because the perceived tilt and adapting line orientation are in opposite directions. The clockwise tilt is called the contraction or indirect effect because the perceived tilt orientation follows the orientation of the adapting line. Figure 4.1 depicts an example of the direct effect.

Adapt   Test   Perceive

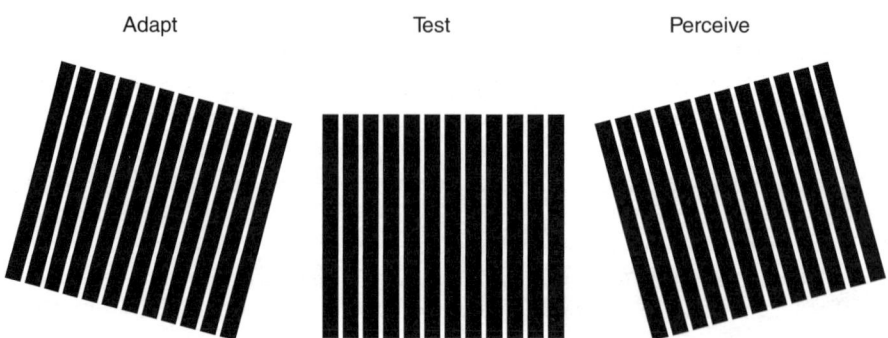

FIGURE 4.1   A demonstration of the direct tilt aftereffect using spatial frequency gratings. Stare at the center of the adaptation grating for at least 30 seconds, moving your eyes around slightly to avoid afterimages. Then stare at the vertical lines. They should now appear tilted slightly counterclockwise as indicated in the perceive grating.

Another similar effect similar to the TAE is called the rod and frame illusion. For the inducing stimulus there are two salient directions corresponding to the pair of sides in the rectangular frame. If the frame were vertical, these would be the two parallel vertical lines and the two parallel horizontal lines. In the procedure a line inside the frame is adjusted to the perceived vertical. If the frame is tilted between 0 and 75 degrees, then according to the major axes hypothesis the rod appears tilted away from the frame axis closest to true vertical (Beh, Wenderoth, & Purcell, 1971). Figure 4.2 shows what this is like visually.

Joung, van der Zwan, and Latimer (2000) utilized bilaterally symmetrical dot patterns, each of which is characterized by a single axis of reflectional symmetry. The axis separates the two corresponding sides of the pattern but is not visible. They presented these dot patterns at 15 and 75 degrees and then had observers adjust the perceived orientation of subsequent reflected dot patterns. They obtained results identical to those for the TAE. These effects were large in this experiment but smaller when the adapting stimulus was the symmetrical dot pattern and the test stimulus was a grating. In a later study, symmetrical dot patterns with two or four reflectional axes of were used. These were compared with line stimuli, without any dots but with axes physically present at the same orientations (Joung & Latimer, 2003). In each case the results were similar. The data imply that the neural mechanisms for symmetry detection and judgment of line contour orientation might be shared.

As the research on symmetric dot patterns shows, physically present contours are not the only class of stimulus that can produce TAE phenomena. Effects have been found for color contours that are non-luminance defined, random-dot stereograms, and even illusory contours (Berkley, Debruyn, & Orban, 1994; Cavanagh, 1989; Elsner, 1978; Paradiso, Shimojo, & Nakayama, 1989; Tolhurst & Thompson, 1975; Tyler, 1975).

Over the years a number of explanations for the TAE have been proposed. Many of these have emphasized some sort of neural mechanism involving lateral inhibition, satiation or neural fatigue (Carpenter & Blakemore, 1973; Coltheart, 1971; Kohler & Wallach, 1944). More recently, Bednar and Miikkulainen (2000) have proposed a very detailed self-organizing model of the primary visual cortex that can account for the indirect effect. Their model not only explains the TAE but also the long-range lateral connections in the cortex and how this brain area can reorganize following retinal and cortical lesions.

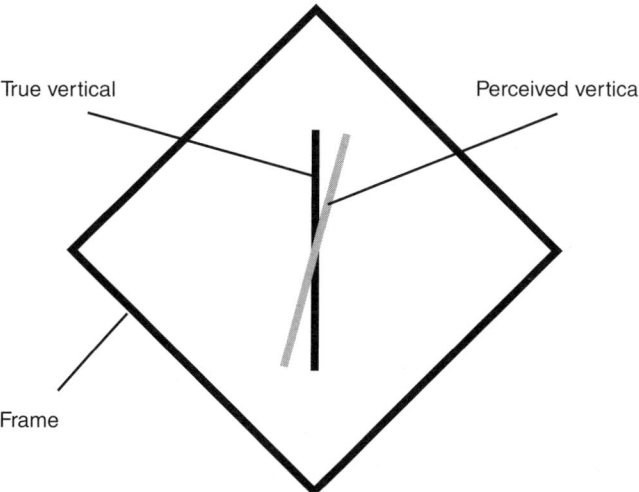

FIGURE 4.2   In the rod and frame effect a vertical line inside a tilted frame is adjusted to the perceived vertical. In this case the perceived vertical is seen tilted away from the frame axis closest to the true vertical.

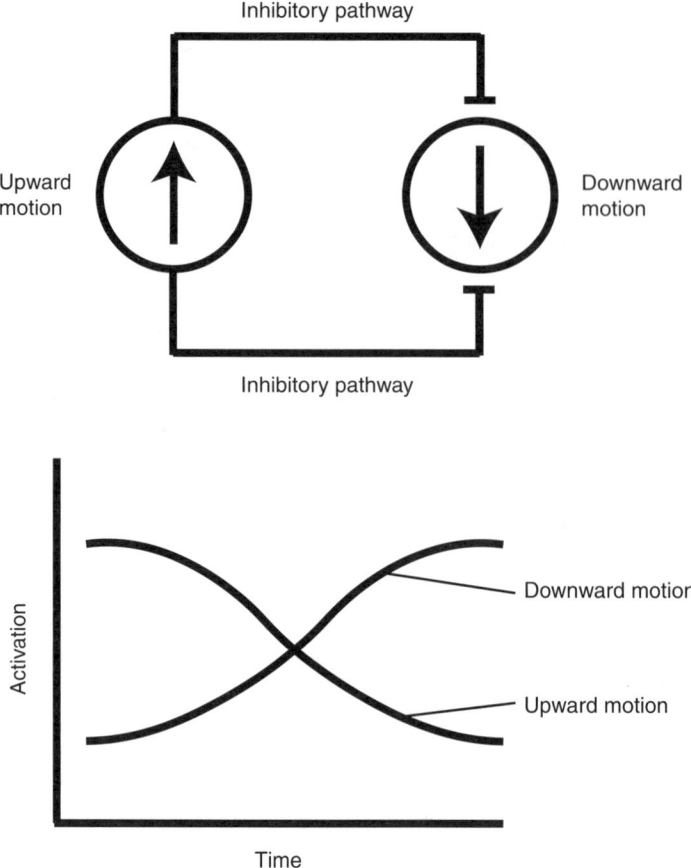

FIGURE 4.3 According to opponent process theory, neurons coding for opposite features are mutually inhibitory. In this example, upward motion coding neurons, if over-stimulated, eventually lose their ability to inhibit downward coding neurons. The result is increased activation of the opposing feature. The activation level of these features changes over time as shown in the graph.

All of the phenomena described in this chapter, including color, motion, and tilt aftereffects have been described according to neural adaptation (Noguchi, Inui, & Kakigi, 2004). Generally speaking, these explanations posit the presence of feature detectors that are tuned selectively for different aspects of the stimulus. For color these would be neurons coding for opponent colors such as red, green, blue, and yellow. For motion, they are neurons representing different directions of motion, such as up, down, left, and right. For tilt, the neurons would stand for different line orientations such as vertical or horizontal.

In some of these views, a mutually inhibitory architecture is proposed in which opposite feature types each suppress one another. So, if one class of neurons coded for upward motion, these neurons would inhibit other neurons coding for downward motion and vice versa. When one of these types in fatigued through adaptation, it loses its ability to inhibit its counterpart. This decrease in inhibition results in temporarily increased activity in the counterpart as well as increased inhibition of the original. The result is perception of the opposite feature as the aftereffect until the original receptors recover and a balance is once more maintained. Figure 4.3 shows a simple generic circuit that can produce these effects.

5 Same but Different

In this chapter we examine cases where two different aspects of the same stimulus each compete for conscious awareness. In binocular rivalry two different images are presented to each eye. Surprisingly, the brain does not fuse these two images into a single percept. Instead each image is perceived separately, one after the other. Rivalry is a great technique to use in the study of visual consciousness because one can isolate what brain areas are active when each image is perceived. Stimulus aspects and instructions can both influence which image is dominant in rivalry, suggesting that awareness is governed both by early preattentive mechanisms and later more conscious ones.

Figure–ground assignment, in which one area in the visual field is determined to belong to an object and another to the background, has traditionally been considered to happen very early in visual processing. This assumption was based on the perfectly logical idea that areas need to be determined as figures before attention can be directed toward them or before they can be recognized. However, research shows that these processes are more likely to run in parallel and mutually disambiguate each other. There is evidence to suggest that preattentive and attentive processes are both involved in the figure–ground assignment process.

In multi-stable figures, an ambiguous stimulus is presented to observers. The figure can be perceived in two or more different ways. With extended viewing participants report seeing first one alternative and then another and will typically alternate back and forth between these two possibilities over time. Studies using ambiguous figures such as the Necker cube have demonstrated that attention drives eye movement. When a new percept enters consciousness, eye movements are then directed to a location consistent with this new interpretation. As is the case with figure–ground assignment, both bottom-up and top-down factors appear to exert an influence on what alternative is perceived.

BINOCULAR RIVALRY

Having two eyes helps us to determine depth perception, or how far away objects are from us. Each eye sees a slightly different view of the world. The brain uses these differences, known as binocular disparity, to compute distance information. A simple way to demonstrate this is by holding a finger out in front of your face at arm's length. Look at it first with your left eye only, then with your right. You will see your finger jumping back and forth. Now slowly move your finger closer. The alternations increase, indicating that the images each eye sees get larger the less the distance. So the greater the disparity, the closer an object is. The ability of the visual system to compute depth from such differences is called stereopsis.

We now address the interesting question of what happens when two completely different images, not the same image from different views, are presented to each eye. Figure 5.1 depicts two orientation gratings. The one on the left is vertical while the one the right is horizontal. Under controlled conditions we can present the vertical grating to the right eye only and the horizontal grating to the left eye only. What would you see? If the brain fuses the two images into one, you might predict seeing a single grating with both vertical and horizontal stripes, i.e., a square grating. This is not the case. Instead you see either one of the oriented gratings or the other but not both together. Participants presented with these stimuli report seeing one of the two gratings for a few seconds, followed by the other grating, where the two continue to alternate back and forth. Each percept seems to vie for conscious awareness, with neither winning out. This phenomenon is binocular rivalry, abbreviated as BR (Alais & Blake, 2005).

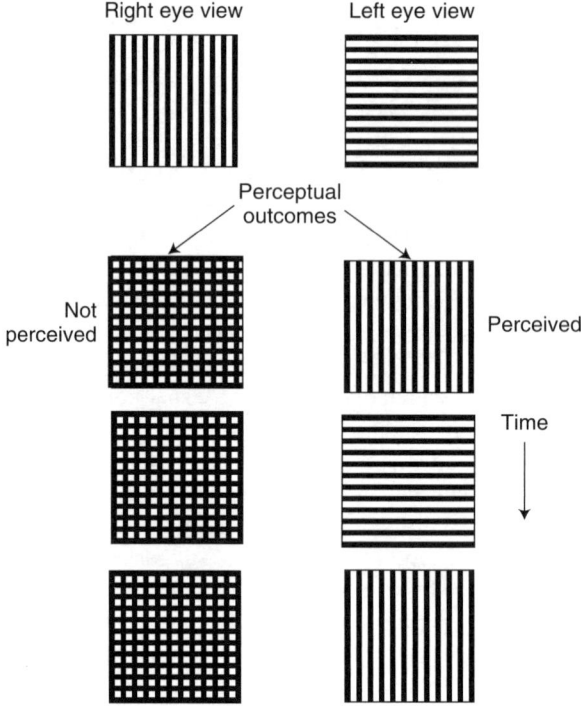

Right eye view   Left eye view

Perceptual
outcomes

Not
perceived   Perceived

Time

FIGURE 5.1   If the vertical grating was presented to the right eye and the horizontal grating to the left eye, what would you see? The perceptual outcome is not the fused combination of the two patterns as might be expected, but instead an alternation between each. This phenomenon is known as binocular rivalry.

What is the role of attention in BR? If it were under late-stage voluntary attentional control, observers might be able to shift their perception back and forth between the two images, forcing themselves to see the left or right eye view at will. If instead preattentive early-stage mechanisms modulated the process then the alternations might occur more or less at random or be sensitive to stimulus changes. As is sometimes the case in science, the answer is not so clear. Evidence exists to support both views.

A number of early BR studies focused on stimulus characteristics. If grating contrast for an orientation pattern in one eye is enhanced, it tends to dominate and suppress the alternate eye perception (Fahle, 1983). This study also found that vertical patterns dominate over horizontal ones and that obliquely oriented patterns were almost as dominant as vertical ones. Thomas (1980) found that the rate of alternation increased as the relative orientation difference between two gratings in either eye increased, up to a 90 degree difference. Walker and Powell (1979) found that phase, spatial frequency, and contrast affected BR. However, other work suggests that under certain conditions factors like spatial frequency and color may not play a role (Blake & Lema, 1978; Kitterle & Thomas, 1980).

The fact that competition in BR is influenced by stimulus parameters as mentioned above suggests the rivalry occurs early on (Blake, 1989). One way this might occur is through inhibitory connections between channels devoted to each eye. Indeed, neuroimaging does show this sort of activity both in the primary visual cortex, area V1, and even earlier than that in the LGN (Haynes, Deichmann, & Rees, 2005; Tong & Engel, 2001). But competition also seems to happen at higher levels between more fully formed stimulus representations that may fight for access to conscious experience. For example, eye alternations are slower than what would be predicted by monocular competition alone (Logothetis, Leopold, & Sheinberg, 1996). Gestalt grouping principles, considered a mid-level visual process, also appear to influence dominance between the eyes (Alais, O'Shea, Mesana-Alais, & Wilson, 2000).

Other studies have examined whether observers have any sort of conscious voluntary control over alternation. Under instructions, it is possible to keep one target image dominant for a period of time and to slow down or speed up the alternation rate, but to a limited degree (Meng & Tong, 2004; van Ee, 2005). Paffen, Alais, and Verstraten (2006) had participants perform a distractor task of variable difficulty while measuring BR. The greater the attentional load demanded by the task, the fewer the reported alternations. They conclude that attention speeds rivalry, but may have more limited control over the rivalry process itself. Based on the results of these experiments it is likely that BR happens both early and late and can be influenced by stimulus characteristics as well as attentional set (Chong & Blake, 2006; Nguyen, Freeman, & Alais, 2003; Wilson, 2003).

We can next turn to the neural basis of BR. What brain areas are active during BR and which ones may be responsible for conscious awareness of one percept over another? Polonsky, Blake, Braun, and Heeger (2000) measured cortical activity in the primary visual cortex (area V1) while inducing perception of one image over another using contrast. They found increased activation not just in V1, but in nearby visual areas (V2, V3, V4v and V3a) when participants perceived the dominant pattern.

In an fMRI study Sterzer and Rees (2008) presented different faces to each eye to produce rivalry and then removed the faces for variable intervals. They found activity in the fusiform face area persisted after removal and concluded that these brain areas specific to the stimulus are responsible for percept maintenance during the delay, what they refer to as a perceptual "memory." However, they also obtained activation in frontal and parietal areas during the delay and speculate that these regions may be responsible for conscious awareness of the percept.

Wunderlich, Schneider, and Kastner (2005) investigated early prestriate visual areas and BR. They varied the contrast of grating stimuli to induce a transition from one monocular image to another while measuring LGN activity. There was greater activation in the LGN when a high contrast grating was perceived and less activation when a low contrast grating was perceived. Apparently, visual awareness of one pattern or the other may be mediated far earlier in the visual pathway than has been previously surmised.

These studies paint a very broad picture, since they implicate activity throughout the entire visual system and brain, from the thalamus to frontal and parietal regions. One way to simplify this situation is to assume that stimulus factors such as contrast may preferentially drive lower level mechanisms such as the LGN and area V1. Top-down factors such as instructions, attentional focus, and complete conscious awareness seem to be driven more by activity in higher level visual pathways such as the temporal lobes and other more distant regions such as the parietal and frontal lobes.

FIGURE–GROUND

The term figure in perception refers to a distinct shape with clearly defined edges. Figures are usually objects like people, chairs, books, etc. They are usually "thinglike" and more memorable. Ground on the other hand is what is left over after a figure is perceived. The sky, a wall, or another object can all serve as background to a given object. For example, if you are looking at a chair in a classroom, the chair itself would constitute the figure while the floor and other chairs behind it become the ground. Figure–ground relationships denote differences in depth. The object is seen as closer while the ground is seen as farther away. Ground is also perceived as continuing behind an object, since an object partially occludes its background. Contours that separate regions group differently depending on how the regions around them are perceived. A contour is perceived as "belonging" to the figural area adjacent to it.

Figure–ground segmentation is the process by which the visual system organizes a visual scene into figures and their backgrounds. Usually this happens quickly and effortlessly, without any uncertainty as to which regions are figure and which are ground. Sometimes, though we may encounter a situation where figure and ground are ambiguous, meaning the two types of region reverse from time to time, the figure becoming the ground and vice versa. One of these situations is shown in Figure 5.2. This is the famous vase/faces figure (Rubin, 1915/1958). It can be organized into two possible interpretations. If the middle portion is perceived as figure and the outer portions as ground, then one sees a vase surrounded by space on either side. If, however, the outer portions are perceived as figure and the inner section as ground then it appears as two faces looking at each other with space in-between.

A number of factors influence figure-ground segmentation (Goldstein, 2010; Wolfe et al., 2010). Usually, areas that are symmetric, smaller, convex, at vertical or horizontal orientations, that surround other areas, that are parallel and that have meaning are perceived as figure. Examples of these different situations are depicted in Figure 5.3. Recent evidence suggests that areas near the bottom of a display are additionally perceived as figure (Vecerra, Vogel, & Woodman, 2002).

Some researchers argue that figure–ground segmentation happens preattentively, breaking up a scene into parts that can then be focused on for further processing (Marr, 1982; Treisman, 1986). Logically this makes sense because once regions have been tagged as figures, the visual system then knows which parts can be grouped, speeding recognition of all objects in the scene. Others, however, propose that fixation or the locus of visual attention can influence segmentation (Hochberg, 1971; Sejnowski & Hinton, 1987). An instance of this could come from visual search

FIGURE 5.2   Rubin's famous face vase figure demonstrates that figure and ground can compete for access to visual awareness.

FIGURE 5.3   Areas that are symmetric, small, convex, or parallel or are perceived as figure.

where knowledge of the target could influence where segmentation should occur, facilitating target identification. Recent work suggests that both of these processes are possible.

Kimchi and Peterson (2008) employed overlapped displays to determine if grouping is preattentive. Participants in their experiment saw two displays one right after the other. Each display was a figure–ground pattern where regions could group to form figure and ground based on convexity. On top of this pattern was another small matrix pattern made up of black and white squares. Participants were asked to judge if an element in the matrix pattern changed and whether there was a figure–ground change. The reasoning in this study was that if attention was drawn away from the convexity patterns in the matrix task, there would be none or very little left over for figure-ground segmentation. If segmentation occurred, then it had to have occurred preattentively. This is in fact what they found.

Vecera, Flevaris, and Filapek (2004) used cues to direct attention to different regions of a figure–ground stimulus. The precued region was perceived as figure and the shared contour between that region and its neighbor was perceived as belonging to the figure. When the cue directed attention outside the figure–ground stimulus, it had no effect on assignment of figure or contour ownership. Based on these results it appears that exogenous spatial attention can serve as a cue for segmentation processes. The authors conclude that figure–ground assignment and exogenous attention can happen simultaneously, perhaps mutually constraining each other in a recurrent, interactive fashion.

Given that the brain in general and the visual system specifically exhibit massive parallelism, it should come as little surprise that figure–ground segmentation, attention, and pattern recognition all run alongside one another. This allows one process to help another, especially if there is an ambiguity. For instance if a region doesn't resolve well as a figure based on stimulus factors such as symmetry and convexity, then focal attention could be directed toward it. This would accelerate pattern recognition, allowing similarity and meaningfulness to fix the problem.

The research summarized above should make us pause to reconsider what processes are "high level" and "low level" and whether they happen early or late. An alternate way to address this issue is to examine those brain areas involved in figure–ground segregation and visual attention. If the area for one of these abilities gets activated first, this would lend credence to its having precedence over the other.

Qiu, Sugihara, and von der Heydt (2007) measured activity in the visual cortex of monkeys while they performed figure–ground related tasks. Their results show that selective attention and figure–ground organization rely on a shared population of cells in area V2. A portion of the cells they studied were active in response to figure–ground segregation only without attentional selectivity. Another portion were selective to attention only without segregation, but about 40 percent showed both influences. They argue that there are separate mechanisms for each of these processes that remain independent until they interact with each other at this stage. So it appears that these processes run in parallel until at least V2, where they may pool resources, share information and otherwise influence one another.

Likova and Tyler (2008) used human fMRI imaging to study the cortical regions involved in figure–ground discrimination. Their model can account for why figures are so salient perceptually, since they are the areas that "own" contours, appear closer in depth and have a determinate shape. In comparison, the ground is weaker perceptually since it has no contour, appears farther away, and lacks any definite shape.

In their model retinotopic representations of the stimulus occur at areas V1 and V2. This information is then transmitted to V3. Area V3 uses this information to compute stimulus aspects such as the regions between borders. It then sends this information to area MT, where figure and ground are determined based on Gestalt principles such as relative size and enclosedness. Of particular interest here is a background suppression signal sent from MT to V1/V2, where the regions corresponding to ground in the current stimulus are in effect turned off, making the remaining figural region more salient. This process model is intriguing because it suggests that figural regions become salient not through additional activation, but by subtraction of surrounding area activations. As it stands, it is currently the most detailed model of neural figure–ground mechanisms.

MULTI-STABILITY

An ambiguous figure is one that can be seen in more than one way. The perception of these figures fluctuates between several alternate interpretations even though the stimulus itself remains constant. If there are only two possible interpretations, it is referred to as a reversible figure. Figures that have been commonly used to study this phenomenon include the Necker cube, the vase/faces, the duck/rabbit, the lady/hag, the lady/saxophone player and apparent motion displays. Figure 5.4 shows some examples. In general, we can refer to this perceptual ambiguity as multi-stability, since there is no single stable experience.

In one sense, multi-stability is actually part of a much larger issue in perception, that of constancy. This refers to our brain's ability to perceive objects as staying the same despite

FIGURE 5.4 Examples of bistable figures that can be perceived in more than one way.

changes in their appearance. Every time the image of an object is projected on the retina, it is ambiguous and subject to multiple interpretations. After some amount of experience, however, the visual system seems to become very good at determining what the object is, despite the fact that it may have never been viewed from the same perspective, seen at a given orientation, under particular lighting conditions, etc. So multi-stable perception can be considered as a failure of object constancy. It is actually a case of our visual system being fooled by a carefully constructed stimulus, one that would very rarely occur in the real world. Even so, they are interesting to look at and can be used as a tool to study conscious experience.

Much of the research examining multi-stability in static forms has been done using the Necker cube. When viewing the cube, there is always a preferred initial percept, which for most people is with the lower face forward (Brown, 1955). Individual observers then demonstrate a consistent reversal rate, averaging across subjects at about 16 reversals per minute (Orbach, Zucker, & Olson, 1966). However, people do differ considerably in how quickly this happens, with some "slow" and some "fast" observers (Washburn, Mallat, & Naylor, 1931).

Kornmeier and Bach (2004) summarize two of the predominant theories on why reversals occur. According to the passive satiation view, a neural representation for one of the percepts becomes fatigued after prolonged activation, inducing a switch to the alternate representation, which has had time to recover and is now stronger (Babich & Standing, 1981; Long & Toppino, 1981; Long, Toppino, & Kostenbauder, 1983). This is a bottom-up theory since adaptation to the stimulus is driving the change. In the other explanation, attention and centralized decision-making processes are thought to play a more central role. Evidence in support of this comes from studies showing effects of learning and cognitive state (Hochberg & Peterson, 1987; Peterson & Hochberg, 1983, Reisberg & O'Shaughnessy, 1984).

Einhauser, Martin, and Konig (2004) studied eye movements and perceptual switching with the Necker cube. They used an eye tracker to record fixations under free-viewing conditions and found that eye movements both precede and follow switches. After perceptual switching, most eye saccades change to a position consistent with the new percept. But after eye location is at this location, a switch back to the other percept begins. They speculate that eye position provides a feedback signal that suppresses the current percept.

Why should this happen? One might predict focal attention to strengthen rather than weaken a current percept, especially when the eyes are fixated on a location consistent with it. What we see here instead seems to be a case of visual attention guiding fixation rather than the other way around. Once an alternate percept is reached, perhaps through a covert attentional shift, the eyes are then instructed to follow. These results suggest that we can pay attention to where we are looking, but we can also allocate attention to where we are not. In these instances it makes sense to move the eyes to the new percept in order to further strengthen it. The weakening of the current percept by a feedback signal may be a necessary prelude to this process.

We can now turn to the neural basis of the effect. Kornmeier and Bach (2004) presented subjects with three versions of the Necker cube. There was an ambiguous version without any bias and two versions where one of the two possible outcomes was biased through the use of depth cues. They were interested in whether the neural response for the unbiased and biased versions would differ. The first case is an example of endogenous attention because the reversal happens spontaneously to a neutral stimulus. The latter case is an example of exogenous attention because the change is driven by a change in the stimulus itself.

EEG signals were found to originate from occipital and parietal areas 160 ms after stimulus presentation in the endogenous case. Signals from these very same areas, only 50 ms earlier were found for the exogenous conditions. The authors conclude that perceptual disambiguation, whether endogenous or exogenous, happens early on in perceptual processing, in the primary visual areas, the same areas that underlie normal object perception. However, other studies additionally show frontal lobes activity during Necker cube reversals (Struber, Basar-Eroglu, Miener, & Stadler, 2001).

Kornmeier and Bach (2004) further speculate that each of the cube representations is coded for in the brain by neural networks, each with a different pattern of connection strengths. These networks correspond to different attractor states. Slight internal perturbations such as noise or shifts in attention as well as external changes in the stimulus can cause the state of the dynamical system to move as a trajectory through the neural state space to the opposing attractor. Friedenberg (2009) provides a more extensive discussion on dynamical systems and perception.

6 One or Many?

Our visual world seems unitary. That is, it seems like we are a single person looking out and perceiving everything as a single scene. But when we examine the brain, this perception becomes puzzling. That is because of the brain's parallel processing of visual attributes in different streams. Why don't we perceive an object's color as a separate experience, given that a separate part of the brain processes it? Furthermore as we will soon see, the visual system splits into two different streams, one specializing in object identity, the other in object location. Given this, we might ask why we don't consciously experience identity and location also as two separate attributes. Finally, we know that the brain consists of a left and a right hemisphere. Information from the eyes from each half of the visual field is sent to only one hemisphere. Still, we perceive spatial extent as continuous. In this section we will examine these "splits" and their relation to attention and conscious perception.

Zeki (1998) postulates the existence of parallel visual conscious experiences corresponding to different processing streams, what he calls "micro-consciousness nodes." Other researchers argue that there should be a "convergence zone" where each of these streams come together to yield holistic perception (Pribram, 1999; Vogeley, Kurthen, Falkai, & Maier, 1999). The dorso-lateral prefrontal cortex seems a good candidate for such a location as it receives inputs from a number of different brain areas. The "what" and "where" pathways indeed do converge on prefrontal area 46 (Van Essen, Anderson, & Felleman, 1992). The frontal lobes in general are associated with executive functions such as planning, sequencing of events and goal attainment, so it would make sense that they receive visual information in order determine what behavior to engage in next.

Frontal regions have pathways that lead back to visual areas, so the connections here are two-way. As discussed elsewhere, these pathways are those along which feedback and reentrant activity could occur, thus allowing frontal cortex to modulate incoming sensory information. Attention may be the means by which this happens. Posner (1994) states that frontal attentional processes can amplify the first feedforward signals they receive from posterior areas, making these inputs salient and thereby increasing our conscious awareness of them. They could do this not only the first time, but on subsequent iterations, for example when disambiguating a weak or degraded representation.

Gazzaniga and Miller (2009) argue that consciousness is an emergent property that comes out of hundreds or even thousands of specialized modules. Each module performs a very specific operation for a particular type of information and mediates one aspect of a conscious experience (Logothetis, 1998). These modules are not restricted to the visual domain but can mediate all other types of consciousness as well. They are widely distributed throughout the brain. In their scheme, some of these circuits are connected to others, but none are connected to a majority of the others.

These modules are always competing for attention. Only some of them win and it is these that determine our conscious experience at any given moment in time. Despite this "cacophony" of different processes, we are only aware of a single unified conscious experience. The reason for this, according to Gazzaniga and Miller, is due to the presence of another specialized module called the "evaluator," located in the left hemisphere. The job of the evaluator, which is ostensibly only present in humans, is to integrate all of the competing other sources of information and make a coherent narrative or explanation out of them. The evaluator is constantly interpreting these other thoughts, emotions, and behaviors after they happen and essentially creating a "story" that can account for them. We provide an example of how such an evaluator might function in the section on hemispheric differences below.

SELECTIVE ATTENTION

MODELS OF SELECTIVE ATTENTION

Broadbent (1958) proposed a theory to account for why we can't focus on two streams of information coming in simultaneously from the same sense. Research using listening tasks showed that we can attend to one thing well but not to two things at the same time. To Broadbent, this suggested the presence of a filter that could block out ignored information, allowing only attended information to enter awareness. The filter selects certain parts of the information—only red items for example—and allows it to pass through blocking the rest.

The selection in Broadbent's model is based on stimulus characteristics such as color or shape. In the next step, whatever information gets past the filter then undergoes pattern recognition. Following this step, information travels past any selection mechanism to a short-term memory store, where it is held for a longer period of time and made available for subsequent processing and response. Broadbent's model is referred to as an early selection model because the filter screens out information before it can be recognized. Figure 6.1 shows each of these processing stages.

Attenuation theory is similar to filter theory but with one exception (Treisman, 1964). The filter does not completely block out the unattended information. Information that is important will make it through even though it is not being attended to. Examples include your name or items associated with danger or threat. Later on in the sections on salience and orienting we will describe other examples.

Meaning or semantics is another criterion by which information can be selected. This runs contrary to early filter models that posit only stimulus characteristics as the basis for selection. Deutsch and Deutsch (1963) and Norman (1968) proposed a second selection process, based on semantic characteristics. This selection happens later in processing. Their model is thus an instance of a **late selection model**. The first stages of processing in this model are the same as earlier models. Information from the sensory store is filtered on the basis of stimulus features and then recognized. However, before being passed into short-term memory, it goes through a secondary selection process. This mechanism selects information on the basis of meaning. The selected items end up in short-term memory. Those not selected never reach this stage.

A more contemporary view is that selection can happen early or late. Michael Posner and Charles Snyder (1975) advocated the idea of a "moveable filter," one that can operate at various stages in processing according to the observer's needs. Experimental evidence backs this hypothesis. Event-related potential (ERP) recordings have found brain activity that happens both early on and later during attentional selection tasks (Hillyard, Hink, Schwent, & Picton, 1973; Luck & Hillyard, 1994).

Exactly where along this processing chain does conscious awareness occur? It is difficult to say. Clearer, the farther in the information travels the more likely it is to reach consciousness. Information that enters working memory is by default assumed to be fully conscious, since this is where effortful processing such as the rehearsal of items takes place. More limited forms of awareness are probably available earlier on however. Information at the filter level may only correspond to sensations, i.e., fleeting images of color or shape completely devoid of meaning. Information at the pattern recognition level may correspond to percepts or primitive percepts, object-level representations with little or some semantic content.

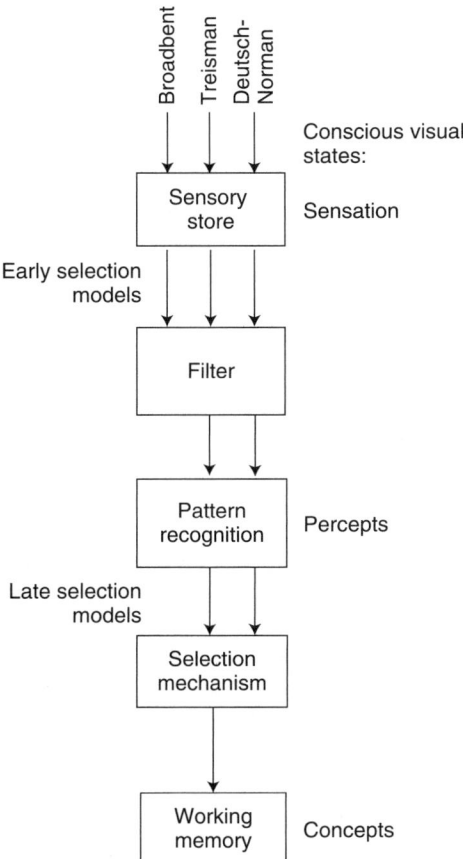

FIGURE 6.1   Different models of selective attention posit different stopping points for incoming stimulus information. According to Broadbent's filter theory, information is stopped early on at the filter level. In late selection models such as the Deutsch–Norman model, information is stopped at the later occurring selection mechanisms. In Treisman's attenuation model, certain types of information can get all the way through into working memory and conscious awareness. Possible states of visual awareness that might correspond to each processing level are shown on the left.

A PSYCHOLOGICAL THEORY OF VISUAL ATTENTION

Bundesen (1990) was the first to develop a general mechanism for attentional selection. It was motivated by suggestions in the literature of an agent or director in the mind who job is to direct attention to internal representations of stimulus items. Of course, this brings up the homunculus problem, which is the question of who now tells the director where to place attention? This problem in philosophy is known as an infinite regress. Bundeson's solution was to introduce a "horse race" model where items compete for attentional access. The item with the greatest salience or activation value over some time interval "wins" and is automatically included in awareness. The proposed mechanism does not completely do away with a "director" however. A higher-level intelligent agent is allowed who can employ top-down resources to bias one item or set of items over others based on context, knowledge, and previous instructions, etc.

   This notion of a race between elements competing for attentional awareness has also appeared in another view of attention, called the biased competition model (Desimone, 1999; Desimone &

Duncan, 1995; Duncan, 1996). Each item's representation gains activation the more biased it is. Bias can come from perceptual or attentional sources, either bottom-up saliency or top-down focus. While this theory of visual attention (TVA) is a cognitive model and couched in information-processing terms, the biased competition model is neurobiological in origin. The biased competition model employs inhibition between competing representations, a feature not seen in TVA.

TVA provides a computational account of two attention processes: filtering and pigeonholing. Filtering refers to being able to locate a target defined by some criterion such as color. Pigeonholing then categorizes the item based on its features. So for instance, if a person was instructed to locate red numbers in a display filled with green letters and numbers, the filtering process would be responsible for actually locating the items. The pigeonholing process would then be able to name or otherwise identify the item as being, say, a red number five.

The filtering process can be considered as a search, while the pigeonholing process can be considered as an object recognition task. Recall our presentation of the different selection models. In late selection models, the recognition stage happens first followed by the selection process. Every element in the field needs to be recognized, then elements are selected based on whether they belong to the target category. The downside of this approach is that it is computationally intensive. The upside is that the search process is intelligent. It can be guided by knowledge. For early selection models the selection process happens first. Features are extracted from the items and the selection is based on those features. Full recognition occurs only at the end for the selected elements. This process is less computationally intensive, so it can happen faster, but the ability to search based on more complicated feature combinations is lost.

Although it may seem that these two processes are distinct, they do not need to be. Both are decision problems and the information required to do both is the same (Bundesen & Habekost, 2008). Assuming the target and the object are both defined by sensory qualities, then in each process the goal is to determine whether these properties are present. For selection, if the feature is present its location in the visual field is noted. For recognition, if the feature is present, it is matched against a stored representation to see if it qualifies as being a particular object.

The TVA model formulated here is unique in that it views selection and recognition as "two aspects of the same process" instead of two separate processing stages. They are neither early nor late but instead happen at the same time. TVA is also formulated quantitatively. There are equations with specific parameters that can be substituted in for various experimental scenarios. It has been tested against a wide variety of different attention experiments and been able to account well for the data.

The first stage in TVA consists of sensory processing. An image of a display or visual scene is presented. From this image a representation or visual impression is formed. This will contain local color and depth for different surfaces over the entire image space. Unit formation comes next. Features are combined by the Gestalt grouping rules, here resulting in a part–whole organization. Parts of the scene, lower level units, get grouped to form larger objects or regions called higher level perceptual units. It is these units that are the elements that get selected.

In order to determine if a unit belongs to a perceptual object category it is compared against an internal representation or template drawn from memory. Templates are held in either short- or long-term visual memory. If held in short-term memory, they are considered the same as mental images. The degree of match between a perceptual unit and a template indicates how likely it is that this particular unit corresponds to the pre-determined object category. The greater the match the greater the activation strength of a particular representation and the greater the likelihood that it will be chosen as a target in a visual search task, for instance.

GLOBAL WORKSPACE THEORY

Global workspace theory or GWT (Baars, 1997) uses the metaphor of a theater to explain consciousness and selective attention (Figure 6.2). To start, there is a spotlight that shines on a stage. Like the spotlight view of visual attention a spotlight or attentional focus can be moved to point at different actors or scenes. Whatever falls under the direct illumination of this light is now the subject of primary awareness. Events caught in the fringe or halo of the light are only partially lit and as such produce only partial awareness. There is no awareness at all for things on stage that are entirely outside the fringe of the spotlight.

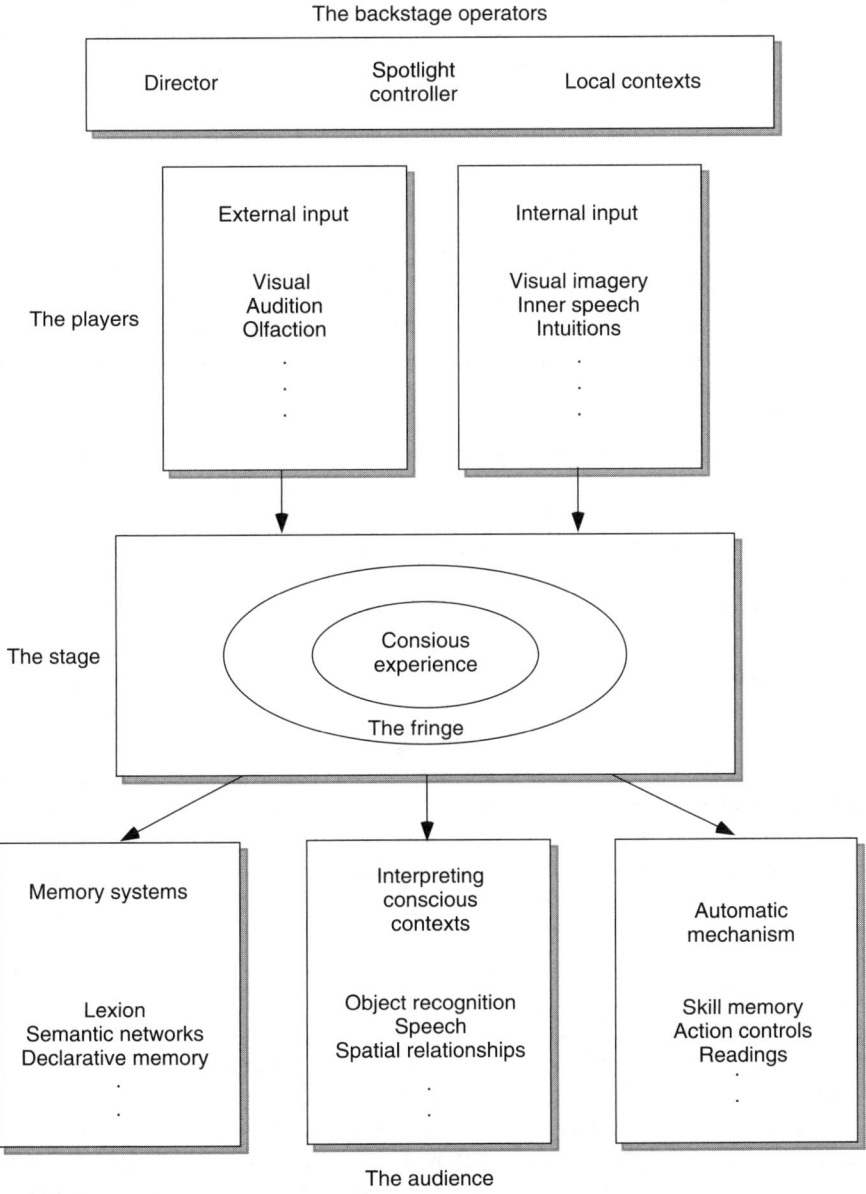

FIGURE 6.2 A depiction of Baar's (1997) global workspace theory of attention.

The contents of the spotlight are broadcast to members of the audience who are aware only of what the spotlight shows them. There are also backstage operators that influence the movement of the spotlight and what happens on stage. These are like directors and spotlight operators we might find in a real theater. In this model information competes for access to the stage in much the same way actors wait to appear for their next scene. This information can come from internal and external sources such as visual perception or imagination based on retrieval from long-term memory.

Members of the audience in GWT are equivalent to different cognitive mechanisms that receive the information and process it. Examples of such processes include pattern recognition, reading, and motor control. If the spotlight shone on a person's face, a face recognition system would now have access to the face and be able to identify who it was. If the spotlight were shown on a word, the word would now become available to a reading comprehension mechanism that could extract its meaning. The purpose of consciousness in GWT is to make relevant information available to the various cognitive processes that need it. Anything in the global workspace becomes accessible to and can be used by any of the audience members.

DIVIDED ATTENTION

In contrast to selective attention where we are focusing on one thing and ignoring others, we can now ask the opposite question: How many things can we pay attention to at the same time? This situation is referred to as divided attention. A critical related concept is capacity limitations. This means simply that there is a limit on how much information we can take in at any one moment. Some of our limitations are innate. For instance, our peripheral vision has lowered acuity relative to central foveal vision, which reduces our ability to see clearly what is going on too far away from our point of gaze. Another innate limitation is that there is only so much attention to go around, attention in this sense is a resource. If too much attention is paid to one thing, there may not be enough (or any) left over to perceive something else (Pashler, 1995).

The earlier work on divided attention involved comparing performance in two conditions, a successive condition where a smaller number of items are presented on at a time, or a simultaneous condition where a larger number of items are presented all at once. Shiffrin and Gardner (1972) did just this and found that for small numbers of alphanumeric characters, performance in both conditions was equal. This was the case for digit characters even when the task required reporting the highest digit, which ensured that the participants in the study were processing all the items to the level of identification (Pashler & Badgio, 1987). This equal performance is exactly the result one would expect if the observers were able to process all the items in the display parallel, so at least for this simple task with this number of characters we can assume that the visual system has no capacity limits.

The results are not always so rosy though. When the displays consist of two words, there is a distinct advantage for the successive condition. This is the case when the goal is to detect a particular word or to specify whether one of the words belongs to a particular category (Duncan, 1987). Note that this capacity limitation is for visual attention and not for memory. It is a limit on how much information gets into awareness, not on how many items may be held in working memory, which is known to be 7 ± 2.

Duncan (1980) presented displays in which participants had to identify items from either one of the diagonals in a 2×2 array. When there was only a single item in one of the diagonals and none in the other, performance was high, almost as good as in the successive condition. When there were two items, one in each of the diagonals, performance was poor, being much worse than that in the successive situation. Successful identification of a target in one diagonal was directly tied to performance in the other. If the observer detected an item in one of the diagonals, falsely or not, their ability to accurately recognize one in the other was impeded. Notice that this is exactly what we would expect if visual attention were a limited resource. If attention is "pulled" in one direction, there is less left over to go to the other direction.

Chapter 7 discusses parallel search when participants are asked to detect a single target among a variable number of distractors and the target varies from along a single perceptual attribute like color or size. Under these search conditions, observers are able to successfully "take in" all of the items at once, apparently because the target–distractor difference automatically draws attention to the target. This is believed to be a preattentive process and either does not involve attention or involves very fast attentional processes. However, Pashler and Badgio (1985) found search times that reflected parallel processing of multiple items to the level of identification when the task was to report the largest of several digits present. So, it seems that under certain conditions visual attention can be "spread out" or divided in this way. If we are using the attentional spotlight/zoom lens metaphor, then these effects may correspond to an increase in the diameter of the attentional aperture without a corresponding decrease in resolution.

The flanker task also discussed elsewhere has been used to determine the spatial extent of the spotlight. Eriksen and Yeh (1985) found interference from distractors when they were within one visual degree from the central target. When these distractors were moved farther away than one degree the interference disappeared, but did not continue to disappear in a gradual fashion. As a result, they concluded that the attentional spotlight has a width of about one degree. Recall also the studies that have found we can move a spotlight as well as adjust its diameter and shape. The spotlight and zoom lens metaphors for visual attention can thus account for how we divide our attention across the visual field.

Are we capable of apprehending most of a normal visual scene? After all, in the experimental examples just described there are a limited number of items located in specific regions of the visual field. Real world scenes are much more crowded with objects and occupy a larger spatial extent. In our discussion of change blindness we discovered that if even large changes are made to a scene that alternates back and forth, subjects can be remarkably unaware of them. This suggests that we don't retain a detailed representation of a scene from a fixation but only think that we do. In other words, the visual system fools us into thinking that we are aware of everything we look at when in reality we have only a vague impression of it.

A number of studies have looked at how the ability to divide attention degrades with age. Brouwer, Waterink, Van Wolfferlaar, and Rothengatter (1991) compared young people in their 20s with older people in their 60s using a simulated driving task. Both groups were asked to perform a primary task of tracking lanes and a concurrent secondary task of reporting dot patterns presented in the display. The older showed a decreased ability to successfully divide their attention in comparison to the younger group. Madden et al. (1997) measured regional cerebral blood flow (rCBF) in a young and older group of men as they performed a divided visual attention search task. The older group's performance was worse. More interestingly, when the participants had to divide their attention to multiple areas in the display there was increased rCBF in the occipitotemporal, occipitoparietal, and prefrontal cortical regions. The occipitotemporal pathway showed greater activation in the younger group.

Mcmains (2006) had participants attend to two spatially separated and masked targets separated by a distractor while recording fMRI imaging data. They found enhanced activation in striate and extrastriate brain areas corresponding to the retinotopic location of the targets, but not the distractor. So under these conditions, the visual system appears to be allocating increased resources to neural machinery that processes the exact locations where the items appeared. No such activation was seen for the area in-between, suggesting a completely split spotlight.

DORSAL AND VENTRAL PATHWAYS

Anatomical work in primates and lesion studies in people have provided evidence of two major processing pathways in the visual system. Ungerleider and Mishkin (1982) in an important experiment lesioned different areas in monkey cortex. In one condition they removed part of the temporal lobe. These animals were then given an object discrimination task in which they were shown one object and then had to choose it when it was presented later with an additional object. These monkeys with temporal lobe damage were unable to make the discrimination.

In a second condition they lesioned part of the parietal lobe. These monkeys had to choose a food reward that was closest to an object, what is called a landmark discrimination task. They had difficulty performing this task. Based on these results they concluded that the temporal region is responsible for identifying objects while the parietal region is responsible for locating objects. The ventral pathway that includes the temporal lobe has become known as the "what" pathway while the dorsal stream that includes the parietal lobe is the "where" pathway (Figure 6.3).

These two processing streams are not entirely separate, as there are several connections between them. The flow of information is not always feedforward, as there are descending feedback connections also present (Merigan & Maunsell, 1993). Shared information between the streams makes sense, as we routinely need to both identify and locate objects. For example, if you see a comb in your bathroom you would first need to recognize what it is, but then also be able to determine its position if you were to reach for and pick it up.

Goodale and Milner (1995) take issue with the "where" pathway. Rather than code for location, they suggest it codes for actions, such as saccades or reaching. Evidence from the literature suggests that there is no single representation of space in the parietal lobe. Instead, there appear to be different sensory-motor maps that carry out different types of actions (Milner & Goodale, 1995; Rizzolatti, Riggio, & Sheliga, 1994). For instance computation of saccade landing points probably takes place in the lateral intraparietal area (LIP), while endpoints for grasping are probably taking place in area 7b, also in the parietal lobe. Goodale and Milner (1992) thus state that the dorsal pathway be renamed as the "how" pathway. Jeannerod (1994) says a better distinction would be the "semantic mode" for ventral and the "pragmatic mode" for the dorsal stream.

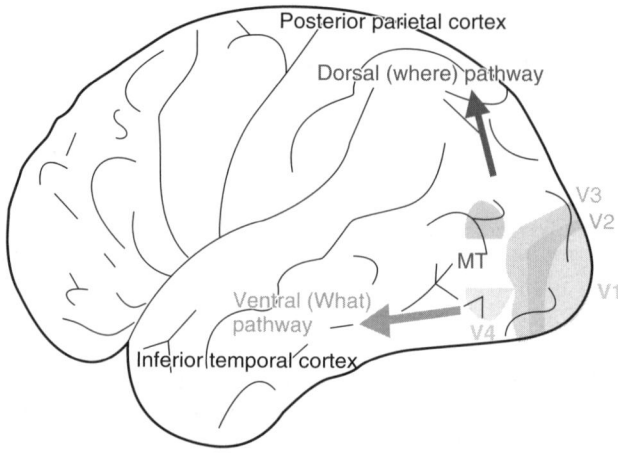

FIGURE 6.3 Visual information after leaving the occipital lobe travels in two separate directions. The dorsal pathway travels upwards toward the parietal lobe and results in our ability to identify the location of objects. The ventral pathway travels downward to the temporal lobe results in our ability to recognize objects.

Deubel, Schneider, and Paprotta (1998) argue that most of the research on attention and perception has focused on the ventral stream, while comparatively little work had been done on the dorsal stream. Tipper, Lortie, and Baylis (1992) had subjects reach toward a light that appeared in one of several locations. When another color light appeared at the same time they found a decrement in performance, but only when the secondary light was between the starting position and the target light. This is a different result than that obtained in interference tasks for target identification, where distractor proximity decreases accuracy, signifying a separate attentional system for visually guided actions.

Other work shows that dorsal and ventral streams may share a common attentional mechanism (Deubel & Schneider, 1996). To account for these results Schneider (1995) has proposed a visual attention module (VAM) that helps determine objects to identify and to act. In the VAM model the object is selected from among alternatives. The system is prioritized for recognition and is capacity limited in that it can only handle one object or feature at a time. However, attentional processing in the dorsal stream happens concurrently, calculating possible motor actions toward the object such as reaching or grabbing.

Heiner, Schneider, and Paprotta (1998) tested this supposed coupling of attention between the two streams. They had participants reach toward a cued letter location. At the same time there was a secondary task requiring discrimination of two stimuli. When the discrimination task occurred at the cued target location, performance was good. If the discrimination happened at another location, performance was poor. The results imply that both streams operate off of the same attention resources. When attention is focused at different locations for the performance of these two tasks there is less attention left over for both tasks and performance suffers.

HEMISPHERIC DIFFERENCES AND CONSCIOUSNESS

It is now well known in psychology that each of the two cerebral hemispheres are specialized for performing separate functions. The left hemisphere is dominant for language in most people and underlies speech production capability (Milner, 1962). It is also specialized for written language. The right hemisphere is superior for spatial tasks including part–whole relations, spatial relationships, apparent motion detection, mental rotation, spatial matching, mirror image discrimination, amodal completion, causal perception, and face processing (Corballis, Fendrich, Shapley, & Gazzaniga, 1999; Corballis, Funnell, & Gazzaniga, 1999; Corballis & Sergent, 1988; Forster, Corballis, & Corballis, 2000; Funnell, Corballis, & Gazzaniga, 1999; Levy, Trevarthen, & Sperry, 1972; Nebes, 1972, 1973; Roser, Fugelsang, Dunbar, Corballis, & Gazzaniga, 2005).

The corpus callosum along with the anterior commissures are pathways connecting the left and right cerebral hemispheres (see Figure 6.4). In some people with epilepsy a seizure of uncontrolled neural firing happens in one of the two hemispheres. In order to stop it from spreading to the other side of the brain, operations are sometimes performed in which these pathways are surgically cut. These individuals are then known as split-brain patients.

Split-brain procedures have also been performed on animals. Sperry (1961) did this to a number of different species including frogs, rats, cats, and monkeys. He found that each animal in essence had two independent minds. He was able to train each hemisphere of these animals to give a different response, in some cases different responses to the same stimulus, which produced conflicting behaviors. A situation similar to this has been observed in human split-brain patients. Mark (1996) recounts the story of a patient who was asked how many seizures she had. In response she raised a different number of figures on each hand. At one point her two hands even fought with each other! This is phenomenon is known as hemispheric rivalry. Fortunately in people it doesn't last longer than a few weeks after the operation.

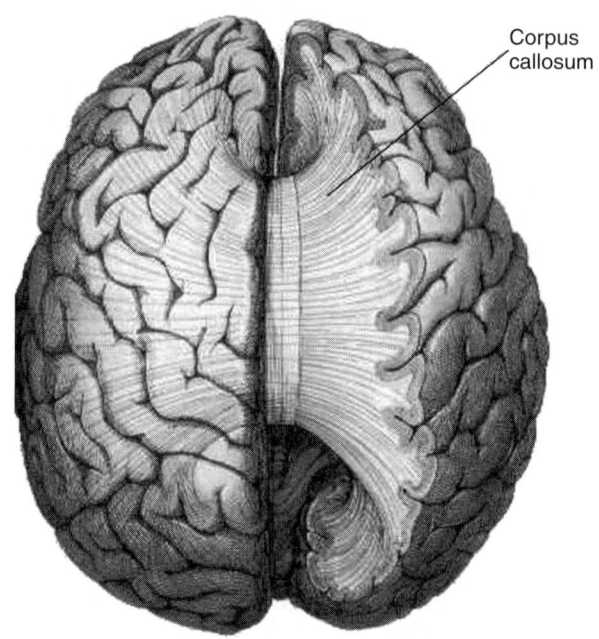

Corpus
callosum

FIGURE 6.4 The corpus callosum is a set of fibers that connect the left and right hemispheres. One hemisphere can be conscious of something the other hemisphere is not.

In split-brain patients each hemisphere can be aware of some information that the other is not and can control one side of the body that the other cannot. Some of the early classic demonstrations of split-brain patients involve presenting words or pictures to one or another of the two hemispheres. If a word is presented in the right visual field so that it goes to the left hemisphere, patients can verbally state what it is and write it out using their right hand. If that same word was presented to the right hemisphere, they would not be able to say what it was, but could draw a picture of it with their left hand.

Luck, Hillyard, Mangun, and Gazzaniga (1989, 1994) tested split-brain patients using a visual search task. There were two conditions in their study. In one, the test items including the target and distractors filled the entire screen. In the second condition, the items were limited to only one half of the screen. The split-brain patients located targets nearly twice as fast as the normal whole-brain individuals did, but only in the whole screen condition. The results suggest something remarkable: each hemisphere was capable of searching through the array independently of the other. In other words, the right hemisphere scanned the left side of the screen and the left hemisphere scanned the right side of the screen simultaneously, so that on average they were able to locate the target faster. This means that each hemisphere is capable of deploying its own attention mechanisms.

Similar to what we saw in the cases of binocular rivalry and ambiguous figures, the experiments on split-brain patients show us that the brain does not seem to like two or more conscious states existing at the same time. Visual consciousness is *not* like a video camera security system, where multiple images projected from different cameras can all be juxtaposed on the same screen. The preferred situation is to have a single state of consciousness and if that is not possible, then an alternation between two or more. In the case of the hemispheres the more powerful one, the left in most people, tends to dominate.

Gazzaniga and Miller (2009) posit the existence of an evaluator in the left hemisphere that unifies not just the experiences of each hemisphere but of all the different ongoing mental processes in the brain. Evidence to support its existence comes from studies with split-brain patients. In one study, they flashed the command "Stand up" to the right hemisphere of patient J.W. He then stood up as instructed. When asked why he could not reply that he had seen the statement. Instead, his left hemisphere evaluator had to create a story for why he did it in the absence of any evidence. So in this case, J.W. replied by saying something like: "I just felt like getting a coke."

These researchers propose that the right hemisphere, because it lacks an evaluator, is more impoverished than the left in split-brain subjects. This may also explain why it does not vie to control behavior and instead seems to relinquish control to the left after separation. However, Corballis (2003) suggests that the right side may have its own version of an evaluator, one that is more spatially skilled and whose job is to construct a representation of the visual world. When presented with random faces, the right hemisphere will attempt to order them, a sign that it may be evaluating and imposing pattern on visual inputs (Miller & Valsangkar-Smyth, 2005).

7 Varieties of Visual Attention

Attention is a complex, multi-faceted concept. The research on vision and attention demonstrates that there are in fact many different types. Each major type corresponds to a dichotomy in which there are two opposing forms. Some perceptual processes have been shown to be preattentive, meaning they happen very quickly and automatically before attention can "kick in." In opposition to this are processes that are slower, effortful, and require attention. Another dichotomy concerns how visual attention is allocated to the visual field. Some have likened it to a moveable spotlight, where we attend and are consciously aware of whatever falls within the aperture of the light. Others propose that the diameter of this light can be widened as in a zoom lens to take in a large area at a lower resolution or narrowed to take in a smaller area at a higher resolution.

Attention has also been described as being covert or overt. Covert attention refers to directing one's attention to a location different from fixation or where one is actually looking. In contrast, overt attention refers to paying attention to where one is actually looking. Although it may seem impossible to dissociate attention from gaze, the evidence shows that this is indeed possible. Next, we describe some of the research showing yet another differentiation, that between exogenous and endogenous attention. In the exogenous form our attention is controlled by "external" factors. For instance, our attention is drawn to movement in the periphery reflexively. Exogenous attention is more "internal" and refers to our ability to move our attention and place it where we want to.

One final difference has to do with how attention gets allocated to particular regions of the field. Most of what we have previewed so far have been examples of space-based attention in which attention gets moved from one location to another. However, there are also object-based forms of attention in which attentional resources get allocated preferentially to objects or regions within objects, even if these areas are spaced some distance apart from each other.

PREATTENTIVE AND ATTENTIVE PROCESSING

Jessica comes out of the mall after a good two hours of holiday shopping. Her hands are full of bags containing presents for her family and friends. Struggling along, she suddenly realizes that she has forgotten where she parked her car. It is a blue Toyota Camry. Looking out at the vast parking lot she sees lots of cars. Some are blue but not Camrys, others are Camrys, but not blue. Concentrating, she scans carefully through each row. After a minute or so, she finally sees her car and with a sigh of relief walks over to it.

The scenario described above is an example of what is called visual search. In the laboratory, we are able to tightly control what observers see and to examine the effect these manipulations have on search quality. In a typical visual search task, an observer is asked to locate a single target in a display that also contains distracter items. For example, a person might be asked to locate a single red letter "F." The number of distracter items on each trial is varied. On one trial, there may be as many as 32 distracters. On others there may be as few as four. Usually the target is present on half of the trials and absent in the other half.

One of the key manipulations is the similarity between the target and the distracters. For example we could have all the distracters be blue, or have them all be the red letter "S." In these cases detecting the target is very easy because it is the only red letter or the only straight letter. If we plotted how long it took to identify the target under these conditions while varying the number of distracters, we would obtain a flat function (see Figure 7.1). Participants locate the target very

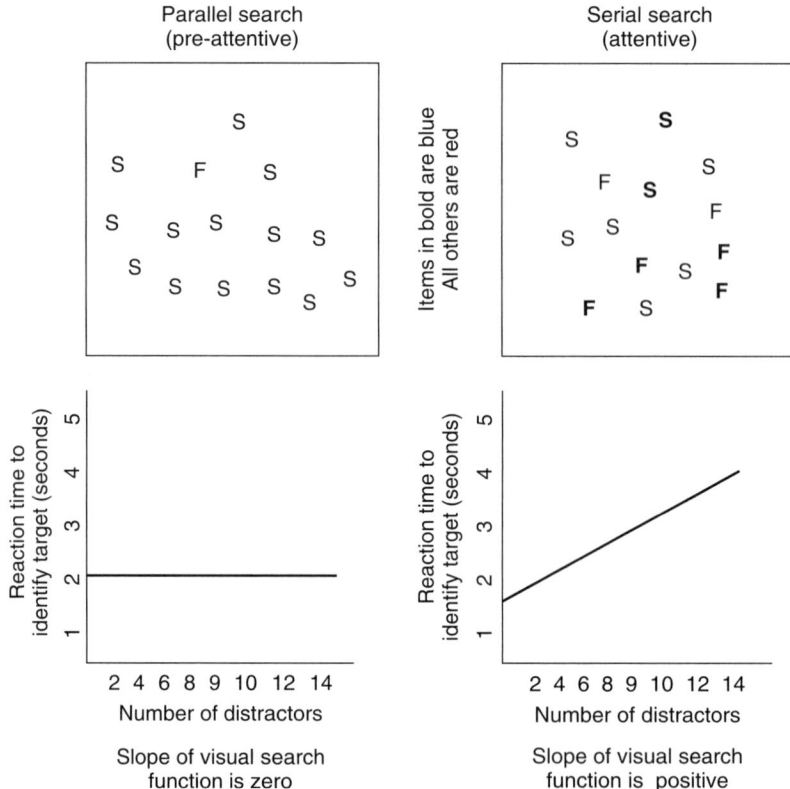

FIGURE 7.1 Examples of two visual search conditions. Looking for a red letter "F" when it is embedded in a display of other red distractor letter "S"s is easy. Looking for this same target when the distractors share both the target's shape and color is more difficult.

quickly when it is present. Furthermore, the number of distracters does not affect speed. In fact, it is so easy that the target just seems to "pop out" at them. The explanation for these results is that search under these conditions is preattentive. That is, it does not require any attention to locate the target, identification occurs automatically, quickly and effortlessly. This is also referred to as parallel search, because it seems as if you can process all the items in the display simultaneously.

Now imagine a different search scenario. You must still locate the single red letter F, only this time the distracters are more varied. There are red letters, but none of them are Fs. There are also Fs but none of them are red. So in the background we might have green Fs, and red and green Ts. In this case you cannot look only for red items or only for letter Fs. You instead must concentrate on each letter to see if it contains both of the relevant properties, the color red and the shape of the letter F. This process of looking at each letter takes a while, so that if we plot the results we see that reaction times now go up linearly with an increase in the number of distracters (see Figure 7.1). This is an example of attentive and serial search, because the items must be processed one by one in a voluntary and effortful manner, which takes more time.

Ann Treisman has formulated an outline of the role attention may play attentively and preattentively (Treisman, 1986, 1988; Treisman and Gelade, 1980). According to this view, known as feature integration theory, there are two stages to visual attention. The first preattentive stage happens early on. In this stage the visual system extracts object features such as color, size, line orientation, and direction of motion. In the second attentive stage these features are recombined to form objects that have specific shape, size, color, and movement. This is done by focusing attention at an object location. The attention acts like a "glue," cementing together the different features at that position in the visual field.

More recently, Cave and Batty (2006) have formulated another model of preattentive and attentive processes. In their framework, there are three steps. Preattentive processes first build representations of surfaces. They do this using information about color, orientation, simple 3-D structure and grouping. Selection occurs in the next step. In this stage locations and/or objects are selected based on a salience map that is constructed from information in the previous step. The salience map indicates those regions or objects in the visual field that are important and to which attention ought to be directed. In the third step, more complex perceptual and cognitive operations happen. Here, items can be compared against memory representations, categorized, and linked to associated concepts and emotions.

A recent controversy in the literature is whether or not threatening stimuli are processed preattentively or not. There is evidence that under some conditions, stimuli such as angry faces are processed more efficiently, suggesting the presence of specialized preattentive feature detectors (Horstmann, Borgstedt, & Heumann, 2006; Nothdurft, 1993; Ohman, Lunqvist, & Esteves, 2001). This makes sense from an evolutionary point of view, since these images could pose a potential threat to the organism and it would be adaptive to respond to them without slow conscious deliberation (LeDoux, 1998). This idea has been referred to as the threat-priority hypothesis.

Horstmann (2007) reviews the literature and suspects that stimulus factors and differences in experimental procedure may account for the sporadic findings. He tests examples from previous studies using a homogeneous methodology and finds a consistent advantage for detection of negative face targets among positive face distracters. However, the slope of the search functions was not flat, bringing into question whether the process is preattentive.

It seems unlikely that there would be preattentive detection of threatening stimuli like faces, spiders and snakes, simply because these are already complex stimuli that would need to be processed at later stages in order to be recognized. Preattentive processes at best may be capable of representing groups or configurations of features rather than entire objects. Any advantage for the processing of negative stimuli is probably due to strong connections between lower level feature representations and higher level conceptual ones due to practice, fear, or other factors (Cave & Batty, 2006).

What is the neural locus of preattentive and attentive vision? Kimura and Katayama (2005) used ERP in participants who performed a matching task based on color changes at attended and unattended locations. Color changes produced positivity in the occipito-temporal areas at 100–160 ms after the event. This was followed by negativity at 220–300 ms. The positivity was found for both attended and unattended locations while the negativity occurred only for the attended location, i.e., when attention was allocated to the location of the color change. They conclude that the positivity underlies preattentive processes, while the negativity underlies attentive ones.

Esterman, McGlinchey-Berroth, and Milberg (2000) examined attentional processing in three groups of patients, those with hemispatial neglect, those with hemispatial neglect and hemianopia, and a group of normal unimpaired adults as a control. Neglect patients ignore one side of their visual field even though they are consciously aware of the objects and scenes on that side. It is usually the result of damage to the hemisphere, especially the left parietal area. Hemianopia is complete blindness for everything one side of the visual field and can be caused by a variety of conditions, including damage to the optic tract. The neglect only patients showed normal preattentive search. The hemianopia patients did not. The authors conclude that neglect patients still have the ability to detect visual features, implying that this capacity may not be exclusively located in the damaged cortical areas.

SPOTLIGHT AND ZOOM LENS MODELS OF ATTENTION

Ralph is in the garage working with a power drill at night when the power goes out. Suspecting he may have blown a fuse, he stumbles through the room to find a flashlight. Once he finds the flashlight, he turns it on and sweeps it across the wall in front of him, trying to now locate the fuse box. Wherever Ralph shines the light, he can see. The first object he locates is a rake leaning against the wall. Next to that is a snow shovel. At last the flashlight reveals the fuse box. He opens the fuse box door and flips a circuit breaker switch, bringing the lights back on again.

The spotlight in this example is a good metaphor for understanding visual attention. When we look around, it is as if we shine a light on different objects. The attention or "light" in this case illuminates those objects and makes them visible. Objects that are outside the spotlight beam are difficult or impossible to make out, because there is no light (i.e., attention) shining on them. A visual attention spotlight may also act like a real spotlight in that it can shine more light over a smaller area (Figure 7.2).

There is an abundance of evidence to support the spotlight metaphor. Mostly, this comes from studies where people are cued to pay attention to one direction or another relative to a central location (Posner, 1978, 1980b). In this spatial cueing paradigm participants view a central fixation cross that is later followed by a centrally located cue. For example, the cue can be an arrow pointing left or right. After the cue a target stimulus such as a letter or word appears either to the left or right side. When the cue validly predicts targets, i.e., when the arrow points to the direction the target appears at most of the time, participants are faster and more accurate at processing the target. In contrast, when the cue is invalid, meaning it cannot reliably signal the target location, participants are slower and make more errors in processing the target. Figure 7.3 shows the trial structure for both types of cue.

These results suggest two outcomes. When observers shift their attentional spotlight to the correct location on valid cue trials, it illuminates the target when it appears and facilitates

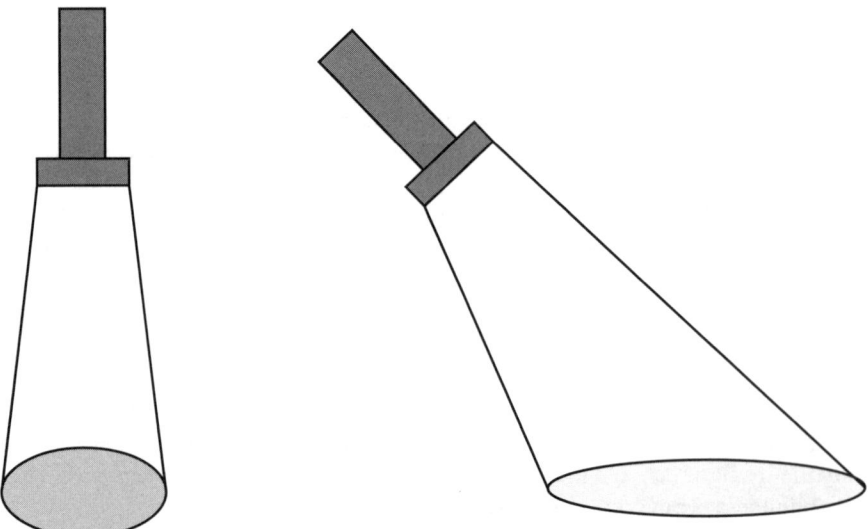

FIGURE 7.2 A flashlight's rays are more concentrated when spread over a smaller area. If we tilt the light so that it shines across a greater surface the light is more diffuse and it will be harder to make out objects. Is it the same true for visual attention?

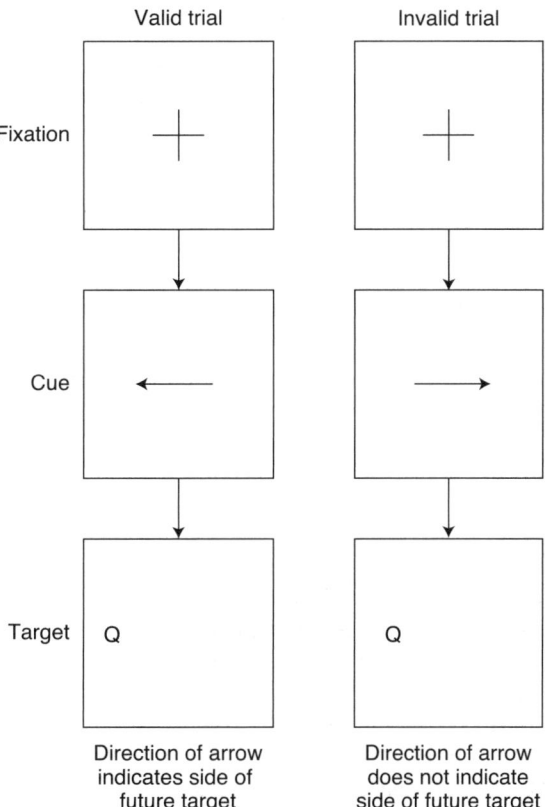

Valid trial   Invalid trial

Fixation

Cue

Target

Direction of arrow   Direction of arrow
indicates side of   does not indicate
future target   side of future target

FIGURE 7.3   In the Posner cueing paradigm, participants first see a central fixation cross. This is then followed with a cue. The cue in this case is an arrow that either points left or right. On valid trials the arrow points to the direction of the upcoming target. On invalid trials the arrow points in the opposite direction. Performance is better on valid trials.

processing of the item. When observers shift attention to the wrong location on invalid trials, they need to sweep the spotlight back to the correct location. This process takes time, and because attention is initially in the wrong location, performance under these conditions is poor.

In both outcomes described above it was initially assumed that the spotlight is shifted or moved in a continuous manner across the visual field such that if the spotlight has to travel a greater distance it will take more time. This assumption has been questioned in a number of studies (Kwak, Dagenbach, & Egeth, 1991; Sperling & Weichselgartner, 1995). Kwak et al. (1991) had observers determine whether two letters at different distances apart were the same or different. Reaction times were not related to the distance between the letters, meaning that attention was shifted in a discrete fashion between the two items. Apparently under certain conditions, visual attention can be shifted discontinuously or "jumped" between one location and another and need not be dragged across the intervening spatial interval.

In a typical flanker task, observers are asked to respond to a central target item such as a letter. Flankers surround the target. When the flankers are similar to the target, responses are fast. When they are different, responses are slowed. However, this is only usually the case when the flankers are sufficiently close to the target, within about 1 degree of visual angle. This implies that the visual spotlight cannot be narrowed any more than about 1 degree. When flankers are within this distance they are always processed because attention falls on them. When they are outside this distance, no attention is allocated to them and they can be effectively ignored. However, LaBerge, Brown, Carter, Bash, and Hatley (1991) using the flanker task showed that well-trained observers could attend to a target without any distractor influences at a distance of 0.14 degrees visual angle. This implies that practice may enable a further narrowing of the spotlight to an area less than half a degree.

Another question we can ask regarding the spotlight is its shape. The default is that it is circular. However, other shapes have been suggested, including ovals and doughnuts (Eriksen, Pan, & Botella, 1994; Juola, Bouwhuis, Cooper, & Warner, 1991). LaBerge and Brown (1989) suggest that the spotlight can adjust to the shape of a selected object. Their data imply that the visual system opens an attentional aperture that is the size and shape of the target and that this aperture remains open for a brief time following the disappearance of the selected object.

Can observers split the spotlight into two separate beams? The evidence suggests that under certain conditions this is possible. Eriksen and Yeh (1985) presented targets in a circular formation. They could appear at 12, 3, 6, or 9 o'clock. On some trials, a cue validly predicted the target location, while on others there was a chance the target could appear in the opposite location. For example if the 3 o'clock position was cued, some of the time the target could appear in the 9 o'clock position. Participants were fast to process the target in the valid cue condition, but for the invalid conditions response times were elevated. This is what would be expected if observers were unable to "split" their attentional beam and shine it on both the primary and opposing secondary locations.

However a study by LaBerge and Brown in 1989 had observers attend selectively to two separated locations. Targets were at each location while distractor letters were at intermediary locations between them. The targets and distractors were made to appear gradually to eliminate sudden onsets that might perceptually "grab" attention. They achieved this using a premask that gradually turned into the target letters. Observers were able to direct their attention to both locations, showing that the visual system can split attention when there is sufficient time and there is continuous information about the relevant locations.

Cumulatively, the experiments described above and others support the notion that visual attention is like a spotlight that can be moved or jumped from one location to another, that has a minimal spread and outer shape, and that can under some conditions be split to "shine" on two places at once. Additional research though, points to another model for visual attention. This involves a zoom lens and will be described next.

A zoom lens on a camera has the ability to vary its focus. At wide settings, the lens lets in large amounts of the visual field albeit at a low resolution. At narrow settings, the lens takes in much less, but with a higher degree of resolution. If human visual attention had this capacity it could, for instance set a wide angle to take in take in as much as possible. This would be handy when looking for a friend in a crowd when you don't know her exact location. Once you think you have spotted your friend you could then zoom into that area and process the details in order to confirm her identity.

Schulman and Wilson (1987a,b) found that responses to low spatial frequency gratings is better when observers are performing a global task such as identifying a large letter made up of smaller letters. This was also the case when the participants had to judge stimuli presented in the periphery of the visual field. In each of these cases, attention is already distributed widely and is already at a global setting. In other conditions, they found increased responding to high spatial frequency gratings when observers were making a local discrimination, this time identifying the smaller letters that make up a larger one. Responding to high spatial frequencies also benefited from judgments to stimuli presented foveally, at the center of the field.

COVERT AND OVERT VISUAL ATTENTION

The term covert attention is used to describe the focusing of attention to the extrafoveal or peripheral areas of the visual field without moving the eyes or the head (Carrasco & Frieder, 1997; Henderson & Macquistan, 1993). In contrast, the term overt attention refers to focus within the foveal or central region of the visual field (Goolkasian & Tarantino, 1999). These two areas differ in terms of cue effectiveness. Peripheral cues seem to be more effective at capturing attention (Juola, Koshino, & Warner, 1995). One explanation for this is that different attentional systems are involved. Peripheral cues appear to trigger an exogenous system that is both fast and involuntary while cues presented centrally trigger a slower endogenous system governed by more voluntary control. The magnocellular system with larger receptive fields and sensitivity to moving stimuli underlies the peripheral area while the parvocellular system with smaller receptive fields and sensitivity to shape and color underlie the central region.

Goolkasian and Tarantino (1999) cued the location of letter targets both centrally and peripherally. They found no differences in reaction time to identify the letters when they were in either of these two regions. In another experiment they introduced distrator letters, varying their distance from the target. When target location varied, i.e., when there was positional uncertainty, the distractor letters were processed along with the target regardless of distance. These results run contrary to predictions based on the spotlight theory, which would predict greater central performance because the spotlight does not have to move. These data imply that under particular conditions attention can be distributed equally well across a wide range of the visual field.

The biased competition model may be able to account for a wider variety of attentional phenomena compared to the spotlight and zoom lens models (Desimone & Duncan, 1995). In this explanation, objects attract attention to themselves, meaning that attention can be automatically distributed to the location of objects in the field and need not be tied to central locations or be moved from one location to another. In this model, objects in different parts of the visual field simultaneously activate early visual system cortical neurons. Those neurons with receptive fields at the object locations receive the most activation. Neurons whose receptive fields overlap the object location, i.e., those that are adjacent but not centered at the locations, receive slightly less activation. Those that are even farther away receive much less (Desimone, 1999). The result is multiple gradients, with attentional allocation peaking at object locations and gradually reducing with distance from them.

Kravitz and Behrmann (2008) were able to directly measure attention gradients. They varied the distance of targets relative to an object's center of mass. Targets closer to this center were detected faster even when they were both the same distance from the cue. The gradient was linear, not curvilinear, with an approximate 2 ms increase in reaction time for each degree of visual angle away from the object's center of mass. These results are in accord with an attention gradient centered at the object center that then decreases gradually with distance.

Some studies investigating gradients have found what is called the meridian effect (Eimer, 1997). If a cue and a target both appear in the same visual region, either both foveal or both extrafoveal, then identification is relatively easy. In comparison, if they both occur in different fields, one foveal, the other extrafoveal, then identification is more difficult. This is the expected result if there were two attentional systems, one for central vision, the other for peripheral vision, as described above. Dori and Henik (2006), however, found only meridian effects for linear arrangements. To account for their results, they introduce a two gradient model, whereby two different gradients develop simultaneously across the visual field. They posit the existence of an excitation gradient centered at the cue location and an inhibition gradient centered at the fixation point.

The superior colliculus is a midbrain structure responsible for guiding saccadic eye movements to different locations. Based on this we would expect activity in this area prior to the initiation of a saccade. However, this brain structure is also believed to play a role in the covert shifting of attention without eye movements. Ignashchenkova, Dicke, Haarmeir, and Their (2004) tested this hypothesis. They measured activity of neurons in the superior colliculus of rhesus monkeys while they performed overt and covert attentional shifts. They discovered that visuomotor neurons in the intermediate layer of the superior colliculus were active both during the preparation of saccades but also during covert attentional shifts. These two forms of attention apparently share a common functional module.

Another brain area implicated in control of overt saccadic eye movements is the cerebellum. Golla, Their, and Haarmeier (2005) tested normal controls and cerebellar patients, those with damage to the cerebellum, on overt and covert attentional tasks. The cerebellar patients showed saccadic deficits on the overt task. They demonstrated larger position errors and a greater number of corrective eye movements compared to the controls. In contrast, their ability to shift attention covertly without eye movements was unimpaired. The cerebellum thus appears to guide eye movements but to not play any major role in covert shifts of visual attention.

EXOGENOUS AND ENDOGENOUS ATTENTION

There are two major influences on where visual attention is directed. First, there are external stimuli that capture our attention. For example, we automatically and reflexively orient our attention to a moving object in peripheral vision by moving the eyes or head. This has been called the visual "grasp" reflex and is mediated in humans and other vertebrates by subcortical midbrain circuits (Easton, 1973). There is an obvious visual advantage to this behavior in terms of detecting prey, predators, or other survival relevant stimuli (Ingle, 1973). This type of attention can be labeled as exogenous or bottom-up because it is primarily driven by stimulus characteristics.

The second major influence over attention is endogenous or internal. In this case, attention is controlled by conceptual or top-down factors. For example, when watching a baseball game, one may decide to pay attention to different parts of the visual field. One could focus first on the batter, then on the pitcher, and then on the outfielders. Endogenous attention is voluntarily controlled.

One way to study these two types of attention is the cue paradigm described earlier (Posner, 1980a; Posner, Snyder, & Davidson, 1980). When the cue is symbolic as is the case with the arrows, it is considered to be a test of endogenous attention. That is because the direction of the arrow must interpreted cognitively. However, exogenous cues can also be used. For instance, the left or right peripheral field can be brightened momentarily prior to target appearance. If the brightening happens on the same side as the target, processing is enhanced, if on the opposite side, it is delayed and more error-prone. This type of cue seems to automatically attract attention toward itself, regardless of voluntary control.

Jonides (1981) points out a number of differences between the two cue types. Exogenous attention appears to be less influenced by cognitive load than endogenous attention. In attentional load studies subjects are given a secondary task that is made progressively more difficult. If the primary task suffers increasingly as a result, then it must also utilize those same attentional resources. This implies that exogenous attention is rapid and preattentive, meaning it relies very little or not at all on attentional resources.

A second difference is that it is easier to ignore endogenous cues in comparison to exogenous ones. The peripheral stimulus thus appears to grab attention regardless of voluntary control. In other words it is automatic, stimulus-driven, and cannot be altered by a conscious act of will. Third, exogenous cues generally produce stronger effects than endogenous ones. They are more primary. Finally, exogenous cues are less susceptible to cognitive factors, the predictive validity of the cue and other expectations.

Yet another difference between these two forms of attention concerns their time course. Endogenous attention builds up more slowly. It appears to be spread out over a broad area at first and then narrows to a smaller region (Shepherd & Muller, 1989). The broad effect occurs at a stimulus onset asynchrony (SOA) of 150 ms, while the narrowing effect occurs later on at around 500 ms. SOA is the time between the onset of the cue and the target. Exogenous attention is more rapid, peaking at an SOA of 50 ms (Cheal & Lyon, 1991).

Several studies have looked at the neural mechanisms underlying these two forms of attention. Corbetta et al. (2000) used event-related fMRI (ER-fMRI) to separate out the different brain areas involved. They found that cues activated the inferior and superior parietal lobe. Valid targets activated the superior parietal lobe and the superior frontal cortex. Invalid targets activated the frontal eye field, superior parietal lobe, and the temporal-parietal junction. They hypothesize that voluntary attention and maintenance of attention at cued locations are mediated by the intraparietal sulcus. On the other hand, reorienting attention toward stimuli at unexpected locations seems to be handled by the temporal-parietal junction (Tootell & Hadjikhani, 2000). Finally, it has been speculated that infrequent or task-irrelevant events activate the ventral frontal cortex (VFC) along with the inferior and middle frontal gyri.

Based on this and other data, Corbetta and Schulman (2002) argue that there are two attentional brain networks. One is devoted to endogenous orienting and the generation of attentional sets. It includes the intraparietal sulcus and the frontal eye field. The second is an exogenous orienting system. It includes the temporal-parietal junction and the VFC, both in the right hemisphere. Its putative role is to interrupt cognitive activity when an important stimulus is detected. More recent work supports the notion of two autonomous neural networks. Berger, Henik and Rafal (2005) examined exogenous and endogenous orienting cues in four different tasks. In almost all of the tasks, with the exception a difficult identification procedure, they found independent effects for the two cue types, suggesting that these really are separate mechanisms.

OBJECT- AND SPACE-BASED ATTENTION

The question of where attention gets allocated has been the source of extensive research and debate over the past several decades. Two theories of attention have dominated the scene. Space-based attention models have attention going to spatial locations. A number of studies support this account. In the classic flanker task described earlier, facilitation and interference effects both attenuate with distance (Eriksen & Hoffman, 1972). In divided attention tasks, the cost of splitting attention between two areas increases with distance (Hoffman & Nelson, 1981). The spatial cueing paradigm also supports the space-based view, since the beneficial effect of valid cues drops with an increase in the distance between cue and target.

On the other side of the debate we have object-based models of attention. According to this view, attention gets allocated to perceptual objects defined by uniform connectedness or Gestalt grouping rules (Duncan, 1984; Palmer & Rock, 1994). Uniform connectedness simply means that a common boundary line encloses objects and groups them together.

According to Lauwereyns (1998) three different types of evidence support object-based attention. First, the ability to report two or more properties is improved when the properties are located on the same object (Baylis & Driver, 1993; Duncan, 1984; Kramer & Watson, 1995; Vecera & Farah, 1994). Second, it is difficult to ignore distractors when they belong to the same object as the target or relevant items (Baylis & Driver, 1992; Driver & Baylis, 1989; Kramer & Jacobson, 1991). Finally, detection of targets is improved at the areas occupied by an object (Egly, Driver, & Rafal, 1994; Umilta, Castiello, Fontana, & Vestri, 1995; Yantis, 1992).

Duncan (1984) used a box and a line that were superimposed. He asked his participants to report the line's tilt, the box's height, and which side of the box contained a gap. It turned out that two of these judgments were easier when they involved the same object rather than two objects. This result has since been replicated with the two objects spatially separated (Vecera & Farah, 1994).

One issue when studying object-based attention is whether or not it is under mandatory or strategic control. If it were mandatory, whenever attention is allocated to an object, it completely fills that object. In this case, other items inside that object will be difficult to ignore. If it were strategic, then observers would have some degree of control over the process and would be able to limit the spread of attention to the target region of the object. Under this scenario, it would be possible to ignore distractors in the object.

The literature addressing this question has produced varying results. Davis and Holmes (2005) controlled for stimulus factors used in other experiments. In a divided attention task they actually found same-object costs, where features that are part of a single object are processed more slowly than those that belong to separated objects. Goldsmith and Yeari (2003) using exogenous and endogenous cues found attentional spreading within objects when this mode of processing was encouraged but this was attenuated when focused attentional processing was encouraged. Ho and Atchley (2009) found object-based attentional spreading under conditions of low attentional load, but for high load attention was limited to object locations close to the cue.

Yeari and Goldsmith (2010) used a central arrow cue that formed part of an object, where the subsequent target item could either be part of that object or a separate object. When the cue was invalid and the target could appear at either object they obtained a same object effect indicating a mandatory spreading of attention. But when the cue was valid and targets were more likely to appear at the different object location, this effect disappeared, indicating that participants were able to suppress attentional spreading within the cue object and allocate it instead to the different object. They conclude that mandatory object-based attentional spreading is a default mode, but can be overridden by strategic control. He, Fan, Zhou, and Chen (2004) derive similar conclusions. Their data suggest that object-based attention is reflexive while space-based attention is more under voluntary control.

The results of all these studies support the notion that both types of visual attention are possible, with one or another being utilized under particular conditions. Thus, space-based and object-based attention need not be viewed as mutually exclusive options. Vecera and Farah (1994) argue that the stimulus representation used in the task can influence which is selected. If the task requires shape discrimination then object-based attention ought to be used since these properties can be best computed within an object-centered representation. If the task requires other properties then space-based attention can be utilized.

Another case where task makes a difference is in symmetry detection. Bertamini, Friedenberg, and Kubovy (1997) had subjects judge whether two contours were reflected (mirror image versions of each other) or translated (identical but separated in space). There was a single object advantage for detecting reflected contours, which are typically part of the same object. However, there was a two-object advantage for translated contours, which typically form parts of two separated objects. In this latter case, the contours fit into each other by a lock-and-key transformation, much the same way two puzzle pieces fit together. These results have since been replicated for multiple orientations and for rotational contours (Bertamini, Friedenberg, & Argyle, 2002; Friedenberg & Bertamini, 2000).

We can now turn to the neural mechanisms underlying these two kinds of visual attention. Sinnett, Snyder, and Kingstone (2009) tested patients with unilateral damage to the dorsolateral prefrontal cortex, patients with damage to parietal cortex, and healthy controls. Those with frontal lesions had difficulty performing object-based attention tasks in the contralateral hemi-field. They conclude that frontal cortex is necessary for allocating attention to object-based representations while posterior regions are necessary for attending to objects at particular locations in the visual scene.

Arrington, Carr, Mayer, and Rao (2000) used ER-fMRI to measure brain activity in two tasks, one where attention was oriented to a region bounded by an object and to a region without any such border. In the object-based task they found widespread activation strongly lateralized to the left hemisphere. Areas included parietal and temporal cortex that modulate attention, parts of the visual ventral stream pathway including occipital, temporal, and parahippocampal cortex, and areas implicated in voluntary control such as the prefrontal cortex. In addition they examined the difference in brain activity for valid and invalid cue trials. There was much greater activity during invalid trials, strongly lateralized to the right hemisphere. These areas included the posterior temporal and inferior parietal lobes. These additional regions seem to mediate the reorienting of attention from an invalid cue location to the target.

8 Your Attention Please

Many times when walking about our attention may be drawn to something. Let's use Clarence to illustrate. Clarence is taking a stroll through the park on a sunny spring day. Looking straight ahead down the path in front of him, he finds his attention quickly diverted to the right. Turning his head in that direction he realizes that a Frisbee has floated down and landed on that side of the path next to him. He crouches down to pick it up and then flings it back to the couple who were playing with it. This is an example of attentional orienting in which some stimulus or event grabs our attention and more or less "forces" us to orient either our eyes or head and pay attention to it. In this case, we can think of certain types of stimuli that are prioritized by the visual system. If they are detected, our gaze is automatically directed toward them through an orienting action, whether we want to pay attention to them or not. We provide another example of attentional orienting later in this chapter.

Short of actually moving our eyes or head, we can also ask what other types of things grab our attention. There are a number of these, and they include not just motion but any singleton, or item, that varies from those around it. For instance we are more likely to pay attention to something red if it occurs in a field of other things that are all green. In this case we can say that the item is very salient, and that it "pops" out from its background and causes attention to be directed toward it. Researchers have developed saliency maps as a concise way of depicting the salience of different objects in space.

Before discussing either salience or orienting we need to backpedal a bit and describe two classic paradigms in psychology. These are the Stroop task and the flanker task. These two paradigms show that even though we try to pay attention to A and ignore B, that B can still intrude into our awareness and influence what we see and how we respond. In the Stroop task, we are asked to either name the color of a word and ignore the name or name the name and ignore the color. As we will see, the former of these two situations is more difficult. In the flanker task, we are asked to pay attention to a central target and to ignore distractors that lie to either side. In many cases, we are unable to ignore these flankers and based on their similarity to the target, they can influence how we respond.

THE STROOP TASK

Perhaps one of the most-studied topics in psychology is the Stroop effect (Stroop, 1935). MacLeod (1991) in a comprehensive review reports more than 700 Stroop-related articles. Many more studies have been conducted since then. In this task participants are asked to either name a word or the color of a word that appears before them. For example, the word "RED" may appear on a screen. The word can either be in the same color that it spells out, red in this case, or in a different one, say green. When asked to name the word, participants are faster in the compatible or congruent condition when the two are the same color (RED in the color red) than in the incompatible or incongruent condition (RED in the color green). When asked to name the color, responses are also faster in the compatible than the incompatible condition. However, there is an asymmetry in these results. Responses are much slower for color naming when the color and word are different, than they are for word naming for this same condition.

Words that are color-related have also been found to cause interference. For instance, the word "GRASS" which implies a green color, interfered more with color naming when the color of this word was non-green, i.e., when it appeared as red, in comparison to when it is green

(Dalrymple-Alford, 1972). This makes sense according to a semantic network interpretation of memory by which associated concepts are adjacent and prime one another through spreading activation. Alperson (1967) trained subjects on word pair associations. When these word associates were used as the irrelevant feature for color naming, they also produced interference. This demonstrates that even newly learned associations can produce Stroop interference. A number of studies have shown that Stroop facilitation, although present in most studies, is generally weaker than interference (MacLeod, 1991).

The classical interpretation of this effect is that it is harder to ignore or suppress responding to the word when one is asked to name the color than it is to suppress the color when asked to name the word. One reason for this is automaticity. We are so well practiced at processing meaningful words that they automatically enter our attentional awareness and interfere with the other contents of working memory, in this case the word's color. This intrusion is apparently fast and beyond our voluntary control. In contrast, we don't spend much time naming colors. This process is therefore not learned and automatic. Because of this the color does not intrude into awareness and interfere with our naming of the word. In this latter case we are apparently able to use voluntary control processes to suppress or inhibit the color information.

Another theoretical interpretation of this effect is the speed-of-processing view. Word naming interferes because this process operates more quickly and is completed before the color naming process. In one of these "horse race" models the processes compete with each other to determine a response, which comes at the end of their computations. Treisman (1969) and Dyer (1973) phrase this process in more attentional terms. They claim that an attentional selection mechanism must chose the results of either the word analyzer or the color analyzer because of a bottleneck that will only allow one possible response through at a time. This view has since been dubbed "response competition" (Posner & Snyder, 1975). By these accounts facilitation in congruent conditions occurs because whichever result reaches the response mechanism first will trigger an output. The "winner" thus always gets to determine the response, so on average the reaction times in this condition will be faster.

Speed-of-processing accounts are examples of late-selection models of attention, because the selection is taking place at the response level after the analyzers have already done their job. However, perceptual encoding theories argue that selection can take place earlier. Hock and Egeth (1970) presented data supporting the notion that color-related words are recognized earlier and thus more likely to distract from encoding ink color. We talk more about early and late selection models of attention in the selective and divided section of the book.

Early models of the Stroop effect were sequential in which processing at one stage had to be complete before the next stage could start. They consisted of an encoding stage, an analysis stage, a response stage, and in some cases an additional disambiguation stage (Morton & Chambers, 1973). Later models were more parallel in nature, allowing either stimulus dimension process to run to completion (Logan, 1980). Researchers were less in favor of a limited-capacity response stage with a bottleneck and more in favor of viewing attention as a resource. In this view, resources get allocated to different tasks. Those with the greatest amount of resources are able to complete their computations sooner (Kahneman, 1973). In parallel models, evidence for a response is accrued. Once enough evidence is obtained, a response is automatically triggered. There is thus no need for a separate response stage.

Cohen, Dunbar, and McClelland (1990) developed a three-layer artificial neural network model of the Stroop effect that was nicely able to capture much of the findings in the literature. In this model, two pathways, one for color naming, the other for word naming, share a response mechanism. Task-specific units, one for color naming and another for word reading, have connections to hidden units. If they are active the resting level activity of the hidden units for one of the two possible inputs is increased. This in turn biases the amount of activation the output units receive from these two streams. The one with the most bias is more likely to reach a threshold of activation sooner and trigger a response.

THE FLANKER TASK

In the classic flanker task, observers must respond to a central target while ignoring flankers, which are distractors typically located to either side of the target. Eriksen and Eriksen (1974) had subjects push one key if they saw one of two letters (S and C) in a central location. They were to push another key if one of two other possible letters (H and K) appeared. Two other letters, to the left and right flanked the central letter. These flanker letters could be either the same as the central target (SSS), from the same response category (CSC) or from the opposite response category (HSH). Response times to classify the target were slowed by the flankers, but only when they were within about 1 degree of visual angle. The slowed responses were greatest for the opposite category condition. Table 8.1 shows the different conditions and results for the classic Eriksen experiment.

The flanker effect has been studied under a number of conditions, both physical and related to the type of stimulus or conceptual and related to variables such as semantic category and attentional set. A partial list of variables that have been studied and found to impact on the effect are size (Miller, 1991), color (Harms & Bundesen, 1983), distance between target and distractors (Eriksen & Eriksen, 1974), motion (Driver & Baylis, 1989), and categorical overlap (Paquet & Lortie, 1990). We refer the reader to these articles to learn more about the direction of each effect, i.e., whether they facilitate or interfere with target responding.

Fenske and Eastwood (2003) employed schematic facial stimuli in the flanker test. They presented positive or negative affect faces as targets and surrounded them by positive, negative, or neutral affect flankers. Previous research has shown that negative emotion faces capture attention more than positive ones do. If this were the case, then the negative target face conditions should show less of a flanker effect. In other words there should be less facilitation when the distractors are the same and less interference when they are different. That is because the central target will be drawing more attention to itself and presumably less attention will be available to the distractors. In contrast, if the positive affect faces are less effective at capturing attention, attention will be more broadly distributed and the distractors should have more of an impact. This is in fact exactly what they found.

Even though participants in the flanker tasks know where the target is and are told to ignore the distractors, they still influence responding. What does this mean for attention? These findings

---

TABLE 8.1

The Conditions in the Eriksen & Eriksen (1974) Experiment. Observers are told to make one response, such as a left button push, when the central letters are an "S" or a "C." They are asked to make a second response, such as right button push, when the central letters are either an "H" or a "K"

Response Categories: (S and C) and (H and K).

Condition	Letter Combinations				Results
Same Letter	SSS	CCC	HHH	KKK	Fastest
Same Response Category	CSC	SCS	KHK	HKH	Intermediate
Opposite Response Category	HSH	HCH	SHS	SKS	Slowest
	KSK	KCK	CHC	CKC	

have been interpreted in terms of the spotlight and zoom lens models of attention in which the diameter of the attentional window cannot be made small enough to exclude the flankers when they are near. Hence, they intrude unintentionally into the window area and compete for attention. For compatible conditions they facilitate responding because they are mapped onto the same response as the target. For the incompatible conditions they interfere with responding because they are associated with a different response (Cohen & Shoup, 1997). However, it is not entirely clear whether these effects are occurring at the response level, the stimulus level, or both (Kornblum, Hasbroucq, & Osman, 1990).

Diedrichsen, Ivry, Cohen, and Danziger (2000) varied the location of a single distractor, placing it either to the left or right of the target. Flanker effects were greater when the distractor was on the same side of the response. They posit that this is due to an induced shift of attention toward that side. This hypothesis was further supported by the fact that observers were more accurate at identifying letters presented for a brief duration on the response side. Hubner and Lehle (2007) had participants perform a dual flanker task. In some trials, the participants had to process not only the target, but also the flanker in a secondary task. It was found that they could not ignore these flankers, even in trials where they were irrelevant to either the primary or secondary tasks.

Is visual attention even required to obtain the flanker task? The answer to this question might surprise you. Cohen, Ivry, Rafal, and Kohn (1995) found flanker interference for the contralesional hemifield of spatial neglect patients. The flankers exerted their influence even though the patients could not allocate attention to that region of space and were apparently unaware of them. In another set of experiments Ro, Kanwisher, Rafal, and Robert (2002) used the Posner cueing paradigm to manipulate exogenous orienting of attention either toward or away from a single flanker. The investigators did this by outlining the distractor location with a box to cause an involuntary attentional shift. They found flanker effects in both directions, either toward or away from the cue. This was also true when the attention was endogenously oriented, i.e., when they used central arrows that pointed to either direction. The flanker effect thus seems possible without any allocation of visual attention. How can we interpret these results? One possibility is that the stimuli directly activate response channels. That is, they can impact on the representations responsible for producing one of the two responses. This is a process that supposedly does not require visual attention in order to operate.

What parts of the brain are engaged during the flanker task? Purmann, Badde, Luna-Rodriguez, and Wendt (2011) investigated this question using an event-related potential design. They compared early visual responding, characterized by a P1 indicator from posterior occipital regions, and compared this to later attentional responding, characterized by an N2 indicator from anterior fronto-central regions. The N2 is known to reflect conflict monitoring while the P1 does not. They expected that the magnitude of the anterior response would decrease with repeated presentations as participants adapted to the task. Their prediction was supported. This suggests that flanker adaptation is not a lower level visual process, but instead involves frontal regions involved more in executive control and monitoring. Willemssen, Hoormann, Hohnsbein, and Falkenstein (2004) in an ERP study also found central and parietal activation.

SALIENCE

Imagine looking out at a natural landscape scene. Areas that might "stick out" in such a scene are the colors of flowers against a green background or perhaps the movement of a bird as it flies across the sky. Areas such as these are candidates that may be of more usefulness to the organism. They may indicate a food source or the location of predators.

The phrase attentional capture is used to describe the situation where an object of attention is more or less automatically determined by certain stimulus properties. Studies have shown that salient feature changes and abrupt onsets have been found to attract attention (Yantis & Hillstrom, 1994). Theeuwes (1994, 1995) found that attention is captured by the most salient singleton. A singleton is an object in a display that differs from all others on some feature dimension. This was true in a visual search task, even when the singleton was not relevant to the target. To illustrate, if one was looking for a red item among blue items, a blue item with a sharp contrast would capture attention before the red target item, even though it was unrelated to the target in any way. These results suggest that search mechanisms are set up to detect contrast of any type, but there are exceptions to this discussed below.

A saliency map is a representation of the visual field with areas coded to signal their relative importance for attentional processing (Findlay & Walker, 1999; Henderson, Weeks, & Hollingworth, 1999; Itti & Koch, 2000; Koch & Ullman, 1985; Parkhurst, Law, & Niebur, 2002). Figure 8.1 shows what a salience map for a visual search display might look like. High priority regions in the map can be activated by bottom-up or top-down influences (Cave, 1999). Bottom-up factors are driven by visual inputs only and would include areas that differ sufficiently from their surrounding region on some attribute such as color, orientation, shape, or motion. Top-down factors are driven by instructions or other cognitive factors. If you suspect that a lion might attack you from the bushes, then the region representing the bushes in the map would be more salient.

Traditional models of saliency share some similarities with the classical visual search model (Treisman & Gelade, 1980). Saliency in this view is determined at first by separate feature maps (Itti & Koch, 2000; Koch & Ullman, 1985). So for instance a color feature map would code solely for color across the visual field. Color saliency would be computed as those regions in the color feature map where color changes occur. Other feature maps such as the one for orientation would record saliency for locations where orientation changes happen and so on. In a second step, the output of each of the separate feature maps would be combined into a featureless location map that would then be used represent saliency over the entire visual field. Those locations with the most feature changes would receive the highest saliency values and have the highest priority for attention allocation.

Studies have shown that people fixate at areas of luminance contrast in an image (Krieger, Rentschler, Hauske, Schill, & Zetzsche, 2000; Reinagel & Zador, 1999). This would suggest that luminance contrast in the salience map would be a strong bias for the direction of eye movements for overt attention (Parkhurst et al., 2002). Einhauser and Konig (2003) tested this idea. They presented natural images to participants and measured where they fixated. They did find that

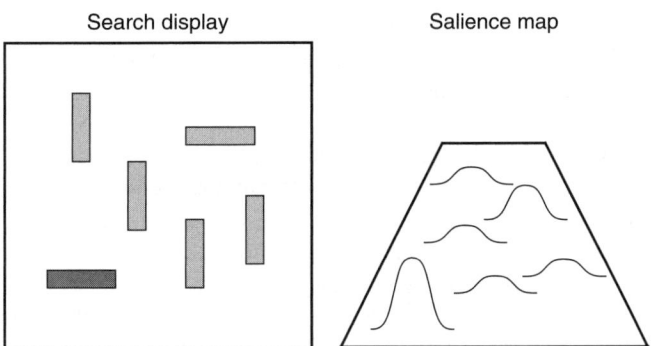

FIGURE 8.1 In a visual search task in which the target is a green horizontal line, the target location at the lower left would have the greatest salience. Of secondary salience would be a blue horizontal line at the upper right of the display. All the remaining distractors would have little or no salience at their individual locations. These are indicated by the height of the distributions for each item.

contrasts were elevated at fixation points but this was true only for low spatial frequencies and during a particular time frame after image presentation. They next elevated luminance contrast at different areas in the images and found that this did not attract fixations. Conversely, regions of lowered contrast did not repel fixation and in some cases attracted fixation. The authors conclude that luminance contrast does not appear to be used to guide overt attention but that it may be correlated with higher order properties of natural scenes that do attract attention.

Underwood, Foulsham, van Loon, Humphreys, and Bloyce (2006) presented pictures of natural office scenes to participants. In each scene there were two objects. One of the objects, such as a piece of fruit, had a low contour density and homogeneous coloring. A second object, such as a coffee mug, was more visually complex and had a higher saliency. In one experiment, the participants were instructed to inspect the scene knowing that there would be a memory test following. In this study, fixations were distributed to the complex object, as would be predicted by the salience map. For the second experiment, the participants were instructed to locate a low saliency target. Now the results showed that the fixations were seldom located on the high saliency object. In other words, observers under these instructions were able to ignore the high salience regions in the image. This study very nicely shows that cognitive set or top-down factors by themselves are powerful enough to "over-ride" stimulus salience.

Several investigators have constructed biologically plausible computational models of salience driven attention. We summarize a few of them here. The Ban, Lee, and Yang (2004) model is specific to face perception and has both top-down and bottom-up influences. They have used it to successfully locate faces in complex natural scenes. De Brecht and Saki (2006) have implemented a neural network model that can determine saliency in dynamic images. It is capable of explaining how sudden-onset stimuli can attract attention. Li (2002) formulated a stimulus driven model that operates entirely off of VI cell activity in primary visual cortex. This model is more economical than older models that require calculating salience across multiple separate feature maps and then summating across them. The biological underpinnings of this model are described in more detail below (Zhaoping & Snowden, 2006).

Where is the saliency map? Li (2002) proposes that the visual cortex generates a saliency map directly from visual inputs with regions higher in salience determined by the most responsive V1 cells regardless of their feature selectivity. So a green horizontal bar could be signaled by a cell tuned to green or another cell tuned to a horizontal orientation, whichever is the most active. However note that in other views of salience maps different cells, such as those in the parietal lobe that are not tuned specifically to any feature, may code for saliency (Itti & Koch, 2001). The view that V1 cells in primary visual cortex serve as the saliency map has economy to recommend it, as no further processing or connections to other areas are needed. It is also supported by anatomical findings. V1 sends outputs to the superior colliculus, whose job is to generate saccades (Shipp, 2004). The colliculus could thus be viewed as "reading out" the saliency map and using it to move the eyes to regions of significance.

Zhaoping and Snowden (2006) created a model of the saliency map that involves both the input strength of a V1 cell and its context. Whereas the input strength is determined primarily by contrast determined locally within its receptive field, context is determined by the difference between the local region and the surrounding area. A horizontal bar will thus stand out only if it deviates sufficiently in orientation from its neighbors. It would be salient if it was surrounded by vertical bars, but not horizontal ones. This requires connectivity with nearby cells coding for the same feature attribute (Nothdurft, 2000). The activity of a cell driven by a particular orientation is suppressed dramatically when the surrounding cells code for that same orientation, an effect called iso-orientation suppression (Knierim & van Essen, 1992). This type of suppression has also been observed for color and is believed to be the neural process underlying pop-out in visual search.

Other than area V1, what other brain regions are involved in saliency? Kusunoki, Gottlieb, and Goldberg (2000) argue that neurons in the LIP area represent salient stimuli. These neurons respond more to recently flashed stimuli brought into their receptive field by saccades than they do to task-irrelevant unchanging stimuli also brought in by saccades. In addition, these neurons respond to constant stimuli that are the anticipated targets for an eye movement but not to identical saccades without such a target.

Geng and Mangun (2009) measured activity in two brain areas, the frontal eye fields (FEF) and the anterior intraparietal sulcus (aIPS), while participants performed an attention task with relevant and nonrelevant targets. They found that aIPS but not FEF activity was affected by the perceptual salience of the targets, while the FEF but not the aIPS was affected by the direction of spatial attention. They conclude that the aIPS is governed more by bottom-up stimulus salience while the FEF helps to control the top-down direction of intended spatial attention. Van Koningsbruggen, Gabay, Sapir, Henik, and Rafal (2010) used TMS to disrupt activity in the intraparietal cortex (AIPCx) during an attentional task. TMS application only to the right AIPCx interfered. Their results support the view that the right AIPCx is responsible for updating a salience map after eye movements.

ORIENTING

You are walking across a busy city street when suddenly out of the corner of your eye you glimpse something moving. You move your eyes to see a taxi speeding through a yellow light. You step back just in time to avoid being hit and after your heart slows down you breathe a sigh of relief that you noticed in time. In this section we will examine the different kinds of stimuli that produce attention orienting responses such as this and the neural mechanisms that underlie the effect.

Research shows that motion onset (Abrams & Christ, 2003), the onset of an object (Cole, Kuhn, & Liversedge, 2007), or a looming object (Franconeri & Simons, 2003) serve to orient covert attention. Recall that covert attention involves the attraction of attention to the peripheral visual field without moving the eyes or head. In contrast higher level factors such as expecting where an object will appear (Ehinger, Hidalgo-Sotelo, Torralba, & Oliva, 2009) and familiarity with a scene (Underwood, Foulsham, & Humphrey, 2009) influence overt attention, which is for central locations that involve eye movements. However, some behavioral tendencies also affect covert attention. These include the frequency of making certain types of eye movements (Tatler & Vincent, 2009) or the bias to look toward the center of a computer screen (Tatler, 2007).

One important stimulus that influences where we attend are faces. A number of studies have shown that we orient our attention to angry facial expressions (Mogg & Bradley, 2002) and to fearful faces (Fox, 2002). Other emotion-laden stimuli that can elicit orienting effects are pictures of weapons or mutilations (Koster, Crombez, Verschuere, & De Houwer, 2004), snakes and spiders (Beaver, Mogg & Bradley, 2005), and emotional words (Hunt, Keogh, & French, 2006). These types of stimuli signal a potential threat to an observer and so may "grab" attention, either through evolutionarily selected mechanisms (LeDoux, 1996) or environmental conditioning (Armony & Dolan, 2002, Beaver et al., 2005).

Bradley, Mogg, and Millar (2000) presented threatening, sad, happy, and neutral faces to participants varying in their level of anxiety. Each observer was shown a pair of faces to either side of a central fixation cross. A small probe then appeared in the position of one of the two faces. Observers pressed a button either to the left or right responding to the probe's location. Reaction times (RT) and direction of eye movements were both measured. They found attentional vigilance for threat faces (as measured by lowered probe detection RTs and eye movement direction to such faces), but only for individuals with moderate and high levels of anxiety. The

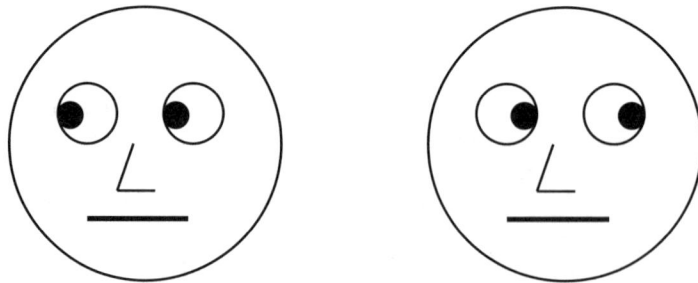

FIGURE 8.2   When looking at these faces, in which direction do your eyes move?

entire sample of observers was more vigilant for threat as compared to sad faces. They also found that anxious and depressed participants showed an avoidance pattern for happy faces. It is not clear whether this is a result of or a contributing factor toward their negative affect.

An important social cue for knowing where to attend in the environment is gaze direction (see Figure 8.2). If we see that our friend is looking to the left, we may infer that there is something interesting going on over there and move our eyes in the same direction. Research shows that this is indeed the case. We rapidly and automatically orient our attention to the direction of another person's gaze (Friesen & Kingstone, 1998). This ability is found early on in development. Three-month old infants will show attention shifts in response to an adult's gaze direction (Hood, Willen, & Driver, 1998) although it is possible that this ability does not arrive until somewhat later, at the age of one and half years (Moore & Corkum, 1998). The ability to share an attentional focus is known as joint attention and is necessary to interpret other people's thoughts, what is termed a theory of mind.

The basic testing procedure in eye gaze experiments is to have a face appear in a central location. The eyes of the face can look either to the left or right or straight ahead. A target is then presented to either direction. Facilitation in the form of lowered RTs or increased accuracy is found for targets appearing in the same direction of the eye gaze and interference as measured by increased RTs or decreased accuracy is obtained for trials in which the gaze is in the opposite direction. This is true even when observers are told that gaze direction is uninformative or that the target will appear on the side opposite to gaze direction (Driver et al., 1999; Friesen & Kingstone, 1998). Such results imply that the effect is automatic and not under voluntary control, i.e., that it is an instance of covert rather than overt attention.

Posner and Petersen (1990) and later Matchock and Mordkoff (2009) differentiate between three different attention networks. These networks, their function, brain locus, and associated transmitter systems are outlined in Table 8.2. The alert system is designed to generally keep attention sustained over a given time period so that if something important appears, it will be noticed more easily. If such a stimulus appears, the orienting system would then activate, drawing visual attention toward the location of the object or event. Once this occurs an executive control system would then be deployed that could allocate attention in order to make a decision or action. These three systems put orienting mechanisms in context and show that they are part of an overall network of attention systems that interact with one another.

An important question to ask then is to what extent these three attention systems interact with one another. The results are controversial. There is some experimental evidence to suggest that the executive control system interacts with the other two components (Fuentes, 2004). However there is more debate on the relationship between the alerting and the orienting systems. Various

TABLE 8.2

There are Three Main Attentional Networks, Each Associated with a Unique Function, Brain Area, and Transmitter System (after Matchock & Morkdoff, 2009)

Attention Network	Alerting	Orienting	Executive Control
Function	Increase and sustain vigilance	Select specific information from what's available	Planning and decision making
Brain Loci	Reticular formation and right frontal and parietal lobes	Parietal lobe, frontal eye fields, and superior colliculus	Lateral prefrontal cortex and anterior cingulate cortex
Neurotransmitter System	Norepinephrine in locus coeruleus	Acetlycholine from basal forebrain area	Dopamine, dopaminergic system tegmental

researchers have failed to find a correlation between the two using the ANT or attention network test (Fan, McCandliss, Sommer, Raz, & Posner, 2002). However, Fuentes and Campoy (2008) obtained shorter orienting RTs when an alerting tone was used compared to a no tone control. Their data support the conclusion that the alerting system improves rather than accelerates orienting effects.

Studies using ERPs have examined which brain areas become active at what time during attention orienting tasks. When orienting there is an early P1 component with an onset at 70–90 ms followed by an N1 component with an onset at 100–120 ms, both of these occurring at lateral occipital locations (Anllo-Vento, Schoenfeld, & Hillyard, 2004). An early direction attention negativity (EDAN) in the ERP readout is found at posterior electrodes at 200–400 ms after a cue is presented. This is believed to correspond to the observer interpreting the meaning of the cue and then starting an attentional shift to the cued location (Hopf & Mangun, 2000). Fu, Caggiano, Greenwood, and Parasuraman (2005) found that on valid cue trials, where the cue was an accurate predictor of target location, there was a larger and later contralateral P1 component and a smaller and later P1 component. In contrast, there was only a larger amplitude of the P1 during attentional focusing. They conclude that there are dissociable mechanisms for orienting as opposed to focused visuospatial attention.

Kincade, Abrams, Astafiev, Shulman, and Corbetta (2005) measured attention using ER-fMRI. They found that voluntary shifts in attention produced more preparatory activity in the FEF and intraparietal sulcus, areas that seem to play a role in endogenous control of attention. There was activation in the occipital and parietal regions as well as the FEF for stimulus-driven attention shifts marked by a color difference that corresponded to exogenous control of attention. They conclude that there is partial overlap between the neural circuits coding for these two forms of orienting. De Haan, Morgan, and Rorden (2008) obtained similar results. They found that the brain areas activated by overt and covert attention shifts are very similar but that overt shifts produced overall higher levels of activation.

9 Now You See It, Now You Don't

In this chapter we review studies on priming and masking. Priming involves presenting a first stimulus that then affects perception of a subsequent stimulus. Primes can be conceptual, in which case they are meaningfully related to a target that follows. They can also be perceptual, where they share some physical or sensory property with the target. Primes can also be cognitive or affective. Examples of affective primes are faces with specific emotional expressions such as anger, happiness, and sadness. Research shows that paying more attention to a prime or to things related to it can influence processing of the stimuli that follow. However, primes can also be completely subliminal and affect processing even when the participant is completely unaware of them.

In masking, a second stimulus is presented that affects perception of one that came before it. For example, one could present a word, but then immediately follow it with a screen filled with randomly oriented lines. The mask in this case ensures that the stimulus is only processed for as long as it was presented and that it does not persist in visual iconic memory after it was removed. Masking effects have traditionally been explained to be the result of a combination of the mask with the target. Target processing is then impeded because these two stimuli are merged into one and treated as a single item. In the object substitution explanation, however, masks are treated by the visual system as the presence of a second object or as an updated version of the initial target. This is postulated as disrupting a reentrant process in which the representation of the target is compared against new incoming information.

Experiments have shown that focusing on a mask can increase its effectiveness. Also, targets that are important or meaningful, such as your name or a smiling face, are more resistant to masking than neutral stimuli, probably because they capture attention. Some studies have shown that for face stimuli, very brief masked durations are all that is necessary for identification. If this is true, then recognition can take place without any reentrant processing, which takes considerably more time.

PRIMING

Priming in the most basic sense refers to having experienced one thing first that affects your experience of something later. For example, having looked at a picture of a boat you may now be able to recognize a second image of a boat more quickly. In experimental terminology the first stimulus is called the prime and the second is called the target. Primes come first and can be presented for a very short time in which case participants are assumed to not have any conscious awareness of them. Alternatively they can be presented for longer times and are processed consciously. In more complicated studies, a prime may be masked. In this context a mask stimulus is presented at the same time as or slightly after the prime and usually degrades the prime, reducing its effect.

In the literature, two broad categories of priming are studied. In semantic or conceptual priming words are typically used as primes and their influence on comprehending the meaning of subsequent words is tested. In one classic study, participants were asked to judge whether a stimulus was a word or not, what is known as a lexical decision task. People were much faster to

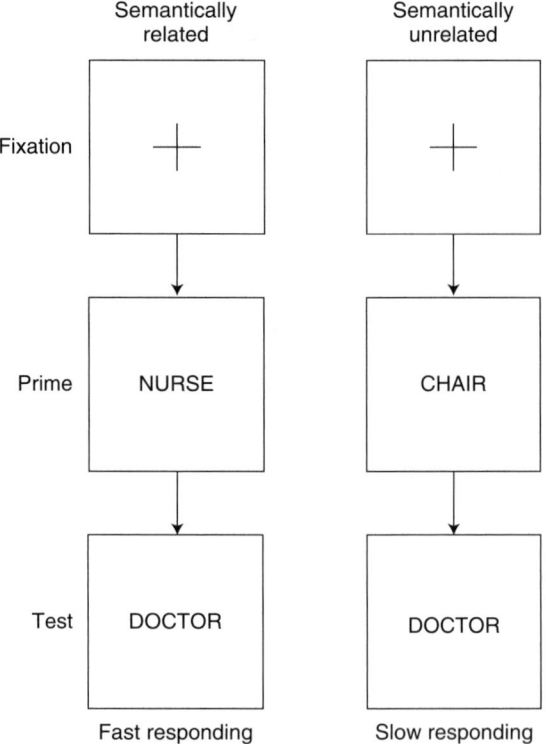

Semantically   Semantically
related   unrelated

Fixation

Prime   NURSE   CHAIR

Test   DOCTOR   DOCTOR

Fast responding   Slow responding

FIGURE 9.1   In a classic priming study, responding to a test word that is semantically related to a prime is faster than to an unrelated word (after Meyer & Schvaneveldt, 1971).

judge that the letter string DOCTOR is a word if it follows the word NURSE than if it follows the word CHAIR (Meyer & Schvaneveldt, 1971). The structure of a trial for their experiment is shown in Figure 9.1. These studies have proven very useful for understanding the mental lexicon and the organization of semantic knowledge in long-term memory.

In perceptual priming the physical aspect of a stimulus such as a picture or pattern is manipulated and its influence on the perception or response to subsequent patterns is investigated. For example, one could present a left-pointing arrow as a prime. If this was followed with a left-pointing arrow as a target that required a left hand button push, then responses would be speeded. If the prime was a right-pointing arrow preceding a left-pointing target, then responses to this same key press would be slowed. This line of research has been fruitful to understanding attention, consciousness, and processing stages in early vision. It is this body of literature that we review primarily here.

Brain imaging studies show that perceptual priming is associated with an increased representational sharpening in early sensory regions. More specifically, the number of neurons representing the stimulus is reduced, leading to a more specific activation of neurons standing for the object in higher order processing areas (Moldakarimov, Bazhenov, & Sejnowski, 2010). Conceptual priming is associated with reduced blood flow in the left prefrontal cortex (Demb et al., 1995). It is this region that is responsible for decoding word meaning (Gabrielli, Poldrack, & Desmond, 1998). Other brain areas are also probably involved (Dehaene, Kerszberg, & Changeux, 1998).

Martens, Ansorge, and Kiefer (2011) examined some of the differences between semantic and perceptual priming. They had participants perform an induction task where they paid attention to semantic or perceptual level object features. The idea was that this would get them to think about objects either conceptually in terms of their meaning or perceptually in terms of their physical appearance. Behavioral measures and brain activity both showed semantic priming after the semantic induction task but not after the perceptual induction task. Conversely, visuomotor priming was shown after the perceptual induction task but not after the semantic induction task. In effect, the tasks served to activate one of the prime types but not the other: one can think of them as "priming the primes." These data imply that conscious processing strategies can modulate unconscious processes.

Two important influences on priming are bottom-up stimulus strength and top-down attentional focus. One can assume that if a prime is made stronger perceptually by being made larger or more salient then its effect on subsequent processing will be greater. Similarly if an observer pays more attention to a prime by directing or maintaining attention to it, then the prime should also be made stronger. Van den Bussche, Hughes, Van Humbeeck, and Reynvoet (2010) tested these ideas empirically. They had observers attend primes or not and presented primes either subliminally or not. When primes were attended or presented subliminally, a priming effect was present. In other words, either one of these measures alone was enough to elicit an effect. When both of these conditions were present simultaneously the priming effect was boosted.

Metacognitive abilities refer to the ability to "think about thinking." For instance, if someone was very tired while studying for an exam they might realize they were not comprehending or remembering the information. This might prompt them to take a break, get some coffee, or postpone studying to the following morning. However, would any of these decisions be made if the individual were not consciously aware of their fatigue or of their inability to learn the material? Van den Bussche, Segers, and Reynvoet (2008) hypothesized that conscious awareness is necessary in such situations. In a priming experiment they manipulated the proportion of Arabic/number word targets. The targets were easily perceived and so the participants were completely aware of them. In a second experiment they manipulated the proportion of Arabic/number word primes. The primes were presented subliminally and participants were not consciously aware of them. Only in the target condition were the participants able to use the manipulation to enhance task performance. The results imply that metacognitive processing of this sort must be conscious.

AFFECTIVE PRIMING

Emotional priming has been studied for some time. In these paradigms an emotional stimulus such as an angry face is presented and its effect on a subsequent stimulus is measured. One question we can ask of these studies is whether one needs to be consciously aware of the prime stimulus or not for the effect to occur. Several studies have shown that priming under some conditions can be stronger when participants are completely unaware of the priming stimulus (MacLeod & Hagan, 1992; Murphy, Monahan, & Zajonc, 1995).

Murphy and Zajonc (1993) in one condition presented observers with affective faces that had either a happy or angry expression. In another condition they presented observers with nonaffective faces with neutral expressions or with polygons. Presentation was either suboptimal (nonconscious) being presented at a very short ~10 ms or optimal (conscious) being presented at 1,000 ms. The affective faces led to a consonant change in the evaluation of Chinese idiographs, with happy faces inducing more positive evaluations and angry faces inducing more negative evaluations. This was true even when the faces had been presented at the short exposure duration, far too short for any conscious awareness. It was not the case for other nonaffective types of priming. Primes for size, symmetry, or for masculinity/femininity worked only at the optimal conscious level.

Suboptimal nonconscious priming has also been found in a variant of the Stroop effect. MacLeod and Hagan (1992) and MacLeod and Rutherford (1992) found greater interference for subliminal threat words in anxious observers using a Stroop paradigm. Interference also correlated with state anxiety in these studies. Additional examples of suboptimal/subliminal priming include judging whether pictures depict sex or plants, pronunciation of adjectives, and a design employing the mere exposure effect (Bargh, Chaiken, Raymond, & Hymes, 1996; Bornstein, 1989; Bornstein & d'Agostino, 1992; Janssen, Everaerd, Spiering, & Janssen, 2000). In each of these cases the prime was affective in nature and induced its effect without conscious awareness on the part of the participants.

Rotteveel, de Groot, Geutskens, and Hans Phaf (2001) replicated the Murphy and Zajonc (1993) study using a different measure of affective priming. They employed a facial electromyography (EMG) to record the electrical activity of specific facial muscles. The musculus zygomaticus major used in smiling and the musculus corrugator supercilii used in frowning have in earlier studies served successfully as an indication of induced emotional state (Lang, 1995). The results were as predicted, with priming inducing significant valence-related changes in these muscles. This effect was greater in the subliminal than in the optimal condition.

The authors in the above study conclude that conscious and nonconscious processing of affective stimuli can be dissociated. In LeDoux's (1996) dual model there is a fast direct pathway to the amygdala that mediates fast responses to danger and a slow, more indirect pathway that involves cortical processing and cognition. Suboptimal processing of facial expression may follow the direct path that could be less accessible to conscious awareness.

MASKED PRIMING

In the masked priming technique a prime is presented prior to a mask that in turn precedes a target. Participants are asked to choose as quickly as possible between one of two responses based on the target and their reaction time is measured (a speeded two-option-choice reaction time task). Typically, participants are not consciously aware of the prime (Eimer & Schlaghecken, 2002). The prime and the target can be associated with the same response, for example they can both be right-pointing arrows that require a right-side button push. These are called compatible trials. Alternatively, the prime and target can be associated with two different responses. An example in this case would be a prime with a left-pointing arrow and a target with a right-pointing arrow. These are incompatible responses. On neutral trials the prime has no associated response.

Reaction times for compatible trials are lowered relative to the neutral condition and raised for incompatible trials relative to neutral. These two findings are collectively referred to as the positive compatibility effect (PCE). However, the PCE only happens when the target follows the masked prime at an interstimulus interval (ISI) between 0 and 60 ms. When the ISI is longer, on the order of 100–150 ms, there is a negative compatibility effect (NCE). This is characterized by slowed responses on compatible trials and faster responses on incompatible trials (Eimer & Schlaghecken, 2002; Eimer, Schubo, & Schlaghecken, 2002; Seiss & Praamstra, 2004).

Schlaghecken and Eimer (2006) argue that masked primes trigger an initial response, activating their assigned response outputs while inhibiting competing response alternatives. This produces the PCE result. Presentation of the mask terminates this initial response and negates any effect of the prime. They believe that an active self-inhibition process occurs next that serves as a sort of "emergency brake" to suppress the outdated representation. The resulting disinhibition produces the opposite pattern of result seen in the NCE. This self-inhibition process is motoric in nature and happens as part of the behavioral response process, not as part of stimulus processing.

Verleger, Jaskowski, Aydemir, van der Lubbe, and Groen (2004) dispute the self-inhibition process. They argue that the mask causes the NCE when it has certain features characteristic of the opposite response. For instance, in some studies the mask contains two superimposed arrows pointing in both directions. If the prime was the left arrow and a left and right arrow were both partially visible in the mask then the right arrow could activate the opposing right response. Subsequent data from studies using neutral primes shows that the NCE disappears, providing some support for this hypothesis (Lleras & Enns, 2004; Verleger et al., 2004). However, Schlaghecken and Eimer (2006) conducted several experiments with neutral primes consisting of horizontal and vertical lines, or a random checkerboard mask that should not bias any arrow-shaped responses. Despite this, they still obtained the NCE. These data again support the self-inhibition explanation.

Unconvinced, Lleras and Enns (2006) present two arguments for why an NCE can be obtained with "neutral" masks that does not involve motoric self-inhibition. According to the onset-triggered suppression hypothesis, the onset of the mask itself is enough to suppress a primed response representation, what they call an "oh no" reaction. They are careful to distinguish this from the self-inhibition mechanism and posit it as part of stimulus processing, not motor processing. Secondarily, they propose the repeated location advantage hypothesis, whereby priming is more powerful when target and prime are in the same or nearby locations. To test these hypotheses they predict that positive priming (PCE) will be obtained when masks do not contain response relevant features, when they do not look like targets in their temporal characteristics and when they appear in different locations. In contrast, negative priming (NCE) should be obtained when masks contain task-relevant features, when they appear with an abrupt onset, and when they occur in the same location.

The results of their study support both hypotheses, essentially that the more similar the prime and the mask were to each other in their geometric, spatial, and temporal properties, the more likely they were to obtain positive priming. The less similar they were to each other, the more likely they were to obtain negative priming. These results are in accord with the object substitution explanation of masking, discussed below. The visual system is more likely to treat the mask as a second occurrence of the same object when they are alike and more likely to treat the mask as a first occurrence of a different object when they are different. It makes sense that attention might be switched or reallocated when a new object appears as this could signal potentially useful information to the organism. New objects may need to be treated differently from old ones, so it is also useful to prepare a different, perhaps opposite response to them.

MASKING

In backward masking experiments a target stimulus is presented and then followed by a mask (Breitmeyer & Ogmen, 2000; Enns & Di Lollo, 2000). In forward masking the mask precedes the target. Metacontrast masking occurs when the contours of the target and mask overlap or are in close spatial proximity. If this contour relationship is present and the mask precedes the target it is known as paracontrast masking. In typical backward masking experiments, both the target and mask are presented for a very short duration, usually less than 50 ms. In these studies, the target stimulus is typically chosen such that it would be fairly easy to identify if it were presented in isolation, with no mask present. Yet, when a mask is introduced only 100 ms after target offset, the ability to process it markedly reduced, with many observers unable to see the target at all. Backward masking has been studied in its own right but is also commonly used in many perceptual experiments to limit how long a particular stimulus is processed.

The variable most often manipulated in backward masking experiments is stimulus onset asynchrony (SOA). This is the time between the target onset and the mask onset. Performance plotted as a function of SOA is called a masking function. There are two primary types of masking

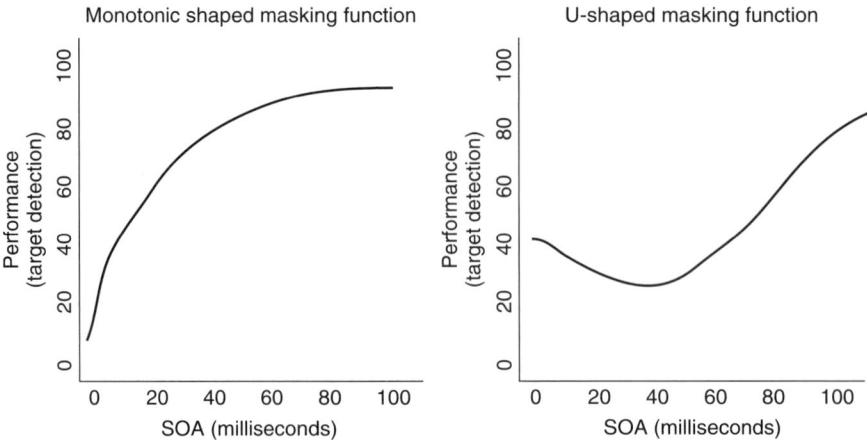

FIGURE 9.2   On the left is a monotonic masking function showing a gradual increase in performance with an increase in stimulus onset asynchrony (SOA). On the right is a U-shaped masking function with higher performance at lower and higher SOAs and lower performance in-between.

function found in the literature (Francis & Cho, 2006). The first is a monotonic increase in performance with increased SOA. The second is a U-shaped function with performance better at very short SOAs, a dip at intermediate values and then a subsequent rise. Figure 9.2 shows examples of both.

There have been a variety of proposed explanations for these two patterns of result. Francis and Cho (2006) list six different contributing factors. The type of mask for instance, could have an impact. Noise masks that contain a random arrangement of dots or other features, pattern masks made up of ordered stimuli-like letters or other features, and light masks that consist of a flashed white or colored screen all tend to result in monotonic-shaped functions. In comparison, masks where the shape of the mask does not overlap spatially with the target shape, tend to produce the U-shaped function. Notice the similarity between this U-shaped function and the two-peak response function in the attentional blink phenomena.

There appear to be two types of masking effect, each producing different results (Eriksen, 1966; Haber, 1969). In integration masking the target and mask temporally combine such that the target cannot be processed easily. Monotonic SOA masking functions are a consequence of this because integration weakens with increased time separation. In interruption masking, the mask is believed to interfere with the processing of target information. This produces the U-shaped curve. Francis and Herzog (2004), through a variety of computer model simulations, have shown that when a mask is weak, each model produces the U-shaped function but when the mask is stronger, each model produced the monotonic-shaped function. A strong mask could be one that is for instance brighter or more centrally located.

OBJECT SUBSTITUTION

Enns, Lleras, and Di Lollo (2006) argue for a reentrant view of visual masking. According to the reentrant view the visual system resolves ambiguity by passing information back and forth between lower and higher visual areas. Lower areas include the retina, lateral geniculate nucleus, and area V1. Higher areas include extrastriate cortical regions and the temporal cortex. The lower areas contain unembellished stimulus information while the higher areas contain learned information that can help identify what has been seen. Historically, these two regions have been referred to as "bottom-up" vs. "top-down," "stimulus driven" vs. "conceptually driven" or as "sensation" vs. "perception" (Hochberg, 1968; Neisser, 1967). Feedforward processes drive information forward through the ascending pathways while feedback processes send information back through descending pathways. The initial feedforward stage is taken as a given. What is uncertain is the extent of the feedback process: how many cyclical iterations occur, for what types of information and under what conditions (Lamme & Roelfsema, 2000; Zeki, 1993).

In the Enns et al. account conscious perception of a target during backward masking is the result of reentrant activity between lower and upper levels. Initially the target stimulus is encoded in the lower levels and then passed upward to allow for recognition and identification. However, a stimulus object may be difficult to recognize because it is incomplete or similar to other objects. To resolve this ambiguity the lower level representation can be compared against upper level representations. These comparisons take place during the reentrant process. If reentrant information does not match the initial input, as when the mask information arrives, a new representation emerges and continued iterative processing is necessary. So in this account the mask is not entirely considered as just interfering with the target, it instead is taken by the visual system as an updated version of the target or as an entirely new object that must be dealt with. They refer to this process as masking by object substitution (see Figure 9.3).

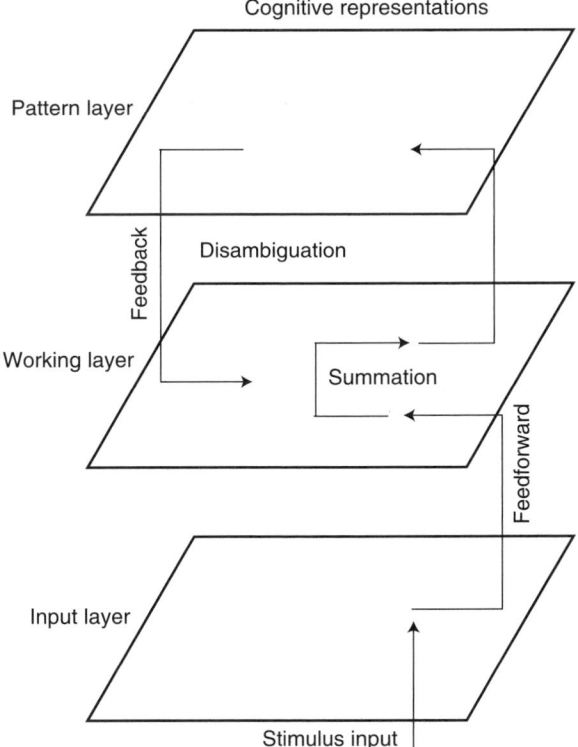

FIGURE 9.3 A computational model for object substitution (after Di Lollo, Enns, & Rensink, 2000). Stimuli are represented in the input layer. These basic level features are summated with information in the workspace and fed up to the pattern layer. Information there can be used to disambiguate representations at lower levels.

A lingering sparse mask that does not physically touch the target causes object substitution masking (Di Lollo, Enns, & Rensink, 2000). For instance, the mask can be four dots at each corner of the space occupied by the object. If this four-dot mask is removed at the same time as the target, no masking occurs. If the mask persists past target offset, masking effects are seen. Object substitution masking procedurally is distinguished from other types of backward masking in two key ways (Hirose & Osaka, 2010). First, it is strongly modulated by visual attention. If the target is the only item visible, if it segregates strongly from distractors, or is singled out by a cue, then substitution masking is either diminished or eliminated (Enns, 2004; Luiga & Bachmann, 2007). In backward masking there is some attentional modulation but always with residual masking due to lower level stimulus interference from local contour interactions or temporal integration of the target and mask (Atchley & Hoffman, 2004). Second, object substitution occurs without target and mask contour overlap. In the case of the four-dot mask, none of the dots occupies the same space as the target and the dots are very diffuse spatially (Moore & Lleras, 2005).

Jiang and Chun (2001) found what has been deemed asymmetric substitution masking. They found stronger masking effects when the mask was presented in the periphery, farther away from the fixation point than comparable masks shown more centrally. One explanation for this is attentional momentum: peripheral mask onset may capture attention and drag it away from the target location. They tested for this by pre-cuing the target location or having the target pop-out. These manipulations did decrease the extent of substitution masking but did not eliminate the asymmetry effect, so other factors must also be at work.

Masking and Attention

One question we can ask about masking is whether or not it requires attention. The traditional view on this has been that it does not and that masking effects are rapid and preattentive (Breitmeyer, 1984). More recent evidence throws this view into question. Ramachandran and Cobb (1995) presented observers with a central disc flanked by two other discs, one to the left and the other to the right. Two vertical columns, one pair above the central disc and one pair below, followed as the mask. They discovered greater masking when the observers were asked to attend to the mask than when they attended to the discs and conclude that voluntary attention can affect the extent of any masking effect.

If voluntary top-down attention can influence masking then it is possible that involuntary bottom-up attention can as well. Involuntary attention in this sense refers to stimuli that grab attention and that one cannot at least initially ignore. Mack and Rock (1998) found that inattentional blindness (looking right at something but no seeing it) did not occur for highly meaningful and emotional stimuli including a person's name and a smiley face. Based on these results they decided to see if these same stimuli would also be resistant to masking.

Shelley-Tremblay and Mack (1999) tested this issue in a separate study. In one experiment happy faces were found to be considerably more resistant to masking than inverted or scrambled face controls. In a second experiment they found that a person's own name was more mask resistant than a scrambled variant equated in number of letters, luminance, and spatial frequency. In a final experiment they showed that when these same attention-capturing stimuli were used as masks, that they were more effective than controls. These results demonstrate that meaningful stimuli such as these capture attention even when they are presented at very short durations. Their attention-grabbing properties reduce the effectiveness of a mask when they are employed as targets. Conversely, they are better at redirecting attention away from the targets and so serve as more effective masks.

Luiga and Bachmann (2007) directly tested whether endogenous (voluntary) or exogenous (involuntary) attention is more important for masking. In one of their experiments they directed attention to the target using a four-dot mask that appeared around the target location. In this condition attention was automatically and involuntary drawn to the target and masking was attenuated. Masking effects were present, however, when there was no pre-cue or when the pre-cue was a centrally located arrow indicating target direction. The results suggest that exogenous attention plays a more important role in masking than does endogenous attention.

There is abundant research showing that emotional stimuli such as fearful and angry faces, emotional words, and pictures of weapons and mutilation can attract covert visual attention (Fox, 2002; Hunt, Keogh, & French, 2006; Koster, Crombez, Verschuere, & De Houwer, 2004; MacLeod & Matthews, 1988; Mogg & Bradley, 2002). In these studies two faces, one with and the other without threat-related content are displayed to either side. A dot probe then cues a response to one of the two sides. Participants are faster to respond to the cued direction if the face that previously appeared on that side was threat related (congruent trials) than if it was not (incongruent trials).

In a follow-up to these studies, Carlson and Reinke (2008) added a masking technique. In their trials they followed the initial presentation of fearful and neutral faces with additional face masks to limit their processing time and resolve a number of methodological issues. They obtained the same result, namely speeded responding to congruent and slowed responding to incongruent trial types. They conclude that there is an automatic directing or shifting of attention to the location of the fearful face even when it is masked. This effect was not due to a general increase in arousal and instead implied a narrowing of the spotlight of attention to the location of the possible threat. Note also that in this study the face masks used, being either a smiling face or an emotionally neutral face, were insufficient to block the effect. In other words, a fearful face was powerful enough to resist masking by another face with emotional but not threat-related content.

MASKING AND THE BRAIN

What neural mechanisms are at work during masking? According to the "two-channel" theory, neural activity in one channel inhibits neural activity in another (Macknik & Livingstone, 1998). Breitmeyer and Ganz (1976) propose that each stimulus initiates activity in a transient channel with a short latency representing low spatial frequencies of fast-changing stimuli, and a sustained channel whose latency is longer, representing higher spatial frequencies such as details of more static figural stimulus characteristics. Activity in the sustained channel is activated first by the target. The mask then activates the sustained channel, which in turn suppresses mask activity in the sustained channel. These effects only hold for a particular range of SOA values, when the mask is sufficiently strong, i.e., when the mask contains sufficient contour, and when the mask contours are in sufficiently close spatial proximity to the target contours.

Rolls (2006) provides a summary of research by himself and his colleagues investigating the neurophysiological events associated with masking. Rolls and Tovee (1994) and Rolls, Tovee, Purcell, Stewart, and Azzopardi (1994) measured activity in neurons located in the macaque inferior temporal cortex. It is this region in the monkey that is associated with perception of complex features and holistic aspects of form. Neurons in this area in monkeys and in the fusiform face area in humans respond selectively to entire faces. The researchers in these studies presented faces as test figures for 16 ms. A backward mask presented for 300 ms was made up of overlapping letters of the alphabet. SOAs in these experiments ranged from 20 to 1,000 ms. The primary dependent measure here was the duration of neural firing. With no mask these neurons remained active for 200–330 ms. At an SOA of 20 ms, neuronal firing was limited to 30 ms, while for an SOA of 40 ms, it was limited to 50 ms. In essence the effect of the mask was to curtail how long these cells fired.

Results with monkeys were next compared to another study with human participants (Rolls et al., 1994). The stimuli and timing were the same. Five faces familiar to the observers were used. In a forced choice condition the response was to specify whether a face was normal or rearranged and to identify the face by name. For an SOA of 20 ms none of the observers were consciously aware that faces had been presented and could not perform any correct identification. When SOA was 40 ms, however, face identification was nearly perfect and the subjects were much more consciously aware of face identity.

If we juxtapose the monkey and human data Rolls (2006) concludes that 30 ms is just enough time for inferior temporal neurons to enable identification and conscious registration of a face. This time, however, is far shorter than the duration of time required for any sort of reentrant activity between higher and lower processing levels in the visual system, which seem to require the 200–300 ms of post-stimulus activity found in the no-mask condition. He concludes therefore that feedback activity is not necessary for conscious perception, in direct opposition to other views on this subject (Crick & Koch, 1990).

An information-theoretic analysis shows that there is considerable information about the stimulus even at these short response times. Rolls, Tovee, and Panzeri (1999) calculate that there are 0.1 bits available from each neuron at an SOA of 20 ms and 0.14 bits of information at an SOA of 40 ms. Expressed differently, 33 percent of information available without a mask is present under backward masking when neural firing duration is allowed to be 30 ms long. If the target face is present for only 16 ms, without a mask, it still contains 65–75 percent of the information available from a 500 ms (unmasked) stimulus. Apparently, the visual system is capable of extracting stimulus information very quickly using a fast feedforward process only. There is evidence to support recurrent processing with anterior inferior temporal cortex that can be used to sharpen stimulus ambiguity, but this does not appear to be evident in early nonspecific firing (Hochstein & Ahissar, 2002).

10 Looking without Seeing

Perhaps some of the most fascinating findings in vision research are those showing that it is possible to be looking right at something and not even see it. Not being able to see it in this context means not having it enter conscious awareness. In the attentional blink, looking at one target in a rapid display makes it difficult to identify a subsequent target that follows it by a certain lag time. Repetition blindness also involves a failure to identify a second item in a string of briefly presented items but in this case the items must bear some similarity to one another. In each of these cases attention is "occupied" with the first item, and so misses the second.

In change blindness we fail to notice even obvious changes between two scenes that are presented in alternation. This may be due to the fact that visual attention is limited and cannot be stretched to cover the entire visual field. The work on change blindness casts doubt on the idea that we hold detailed representations of a visual scene in mind after seeing them, although alternate interpretations are possible. Other work shows that we may be able to recognize that changes have happened but not be able to identify what they are, a so-called "mindsight."

The effects described thus far all involve presentation of several scenes, one after the other. Blindness in these cases might be expected because there is an abrupt change between scenes. But looking without awareness is also possible when there is only a single scene present. In these studies, observers are shown a video and asked to pay attention to one area or perform some visual task related to content in the scene. A target item is then presented and observers are asked whether or not they noticed it. The surprising result is that the target is missed in most cases, even when it is presented in the exact area where observers are fixating. Inattentional blindness demonstrates that we aren't always paying attention to where we are looking. This conclusion should sound familiar, because it is a demonstration of covert attention.

ATTENTIONAL BLINK

The attentional blink (AB) effect requires the very rapid presentation of several items, in a technique known as a rapid serial visual presentation (RSVP). In a typical trial, an observer views an RSVP stream of about 30 letters. They are asked to identify one target, such as a white letter "T" that appears in the stream of other black letters. On half the trials there is a second item called the probe, such as a black letter "H" that appears after the first target. The observer must attempt to identify both the target and the probe (Shapiro, 1994).

The main manipulation in these experiments is the relative position of the probe. It can be the next letter in the sequence, or it can follow at some distance to it, say eight items after the target. The responses of interest are observer's ability to detect the probe on trials where they have also successfully identified the target. Figure 10.1 shows what the trial structure of an attentional blink study is like.

In Figure 10.2 we see a plot of the results that might be obtained in a typical AB study. The shape of the function demonstrates three effects. At very short delays when T2 follows right "on the heels" of T1, detection is somewhat good. However, performance drops during the second or third positions. From that point onward we see a gradual increase in performance that peaks at seven or eight locations following. The first peak may be due to an attention "window" that has opened up in order to process the first target. If this window is currently open, the second target may also enter and be processed. The secondary dip in the function is probably the result of a temporary depletion of attention resources, a refractory period during which visual attention

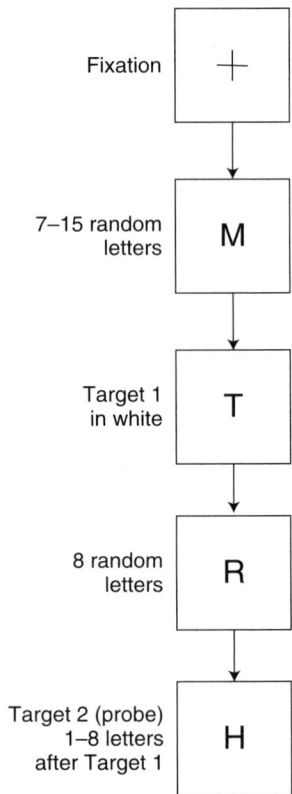

Fixation

7–15 random
letters

Target 1
in white

8 random
letters

Target 2 (probe)
1–8 letters
after Target 1

FIGURE 10.1   The trial structure for an attentional blink experiment. The task is to identify both targets. The crucial manipulation is the delay in the presentation of Target 2 relative to Target 1. It can come anywhere between one letter to eight letters behind Target 1. In the experiment blank screens follow each letter. These are not shown in this figure.

builds up again. This gradual increase is manifested in the rise in performance that peaks seven or eight positions later.

One question we now ask is why we are so poor at identifying the probe, especially since it is appearing in the exact same location as the first target. According to the working memory hypothesis, an item, in order to be consciously reported, must be consolidated into working memory. This process requires attention. If attention is devoted to processing the target that comes first, then there is less available for the probe that follows. This leaves the probe open to interference from the distractors that are also competing for entry into memory. The result is that the probe is less likely to enter conscious awareness and be reported (Chun & Potter, 1995; Jolicoeur, Dell'Acqua, & Crebolder, 2000; Shapiro, Raymond, & Arnell, 1994).

Several researchers have studied the role of similarity in the AB. When the target and the distractors are similar perceptually or categorically, the AB effect is enhanced (Chun & Potter, 1995; Shapiro et al., 1994). The postulated reason is that both types of items being alike are now treated the same and compete for limited attentional resources. Target–target similarity also has an impact. When both types of target are similar, the RB effect is more severe, but only when the similarity is task-relevant. Sy and Giesbrecht (2009) demonstrated this using face stimuli. When the two targets were both different faces of the same gender, the blink was more pronounced in

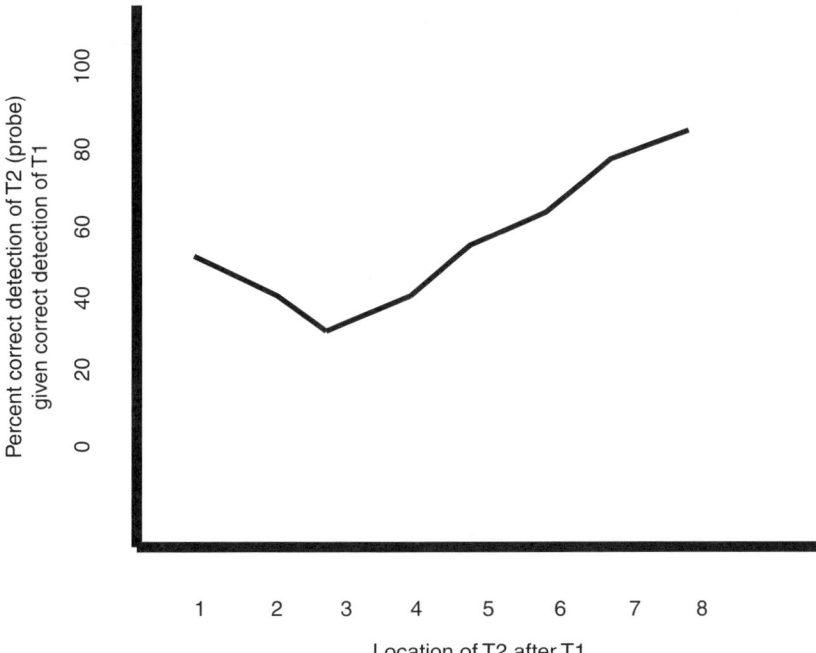

FIGURE 10.2   A plot showing the results of a typical attentional blink experiment.

comparison to two different faces of different genders. Again, the explanation is that similar items demand the same kind of processing or resources (Awh et al., 2004).

Observers in many AB experiments report not seeing the probe. However, just because it is not consciously perceived does not mean that it fails to influence perception. Visser, Merikle, and Di Lollo (2005) presented RSVP streams with two targets amidst distractors. The first target was a string of identical digits. The second target was either an English word or a non-word. Each of these word conditions were presented equally often. Each stream terminated with a three-letter word-stem. When the probe was a word, the word-stem consisted of its first three letters. Participants were more likely to complete the stem under the word probe conditions. This demonstrates that even unconscious probes can still prime subsequent related items for up to one second after they appear.

Sergent and Dehaene (2004) tested whether conscious perception of the probe item is graded or all-or-none. They had observers rate their subjective awareness for probes either inside or outside the blink interval. They found that subjective consciousness of the probe items in the blink were either as good as those identified outside of it or they were either not identified at all. There was no continuous or gradual increase in awareness for increased lag times. They interpret these results using a two-stage model couched in neural terms (Chun & Potter, 1995; Dehaene et al., 1998). In the first stage stimulus information propagates into the visual system in a feed-forward manner (Lamme, 2003). In this stage there is no conscious awareness of a stimulus. During the second stage, top-down and bottom-up inputs overlap and reinforce each other, producing widespread neural activation between distant brain areas. This pattern of activity corresponds to conscious awareness of a stimulus.

On some trials, the probe is only in stage one and goes unrecognized. This is the neural equivalent of the attentional blink. However, on other trials the probe reaches stage two and is consciously perceived. It is unclear what determines these two possibilities. It could be small differences in the initial wave of activation, noise, or baseline activity preceding the stimulus (Sergent & Dehaene, 2004). A neural network simulation of this model successfully reproduced the bimodal rating scale data, so the model has neural plausibility (Dehaene, Sergent, & Changeux, 2003). These authors in a later ERP study obtained additional evidence in support of their model (Sergent, Baillet, & Dehaene, 2005).

Hommel et al. (2006) have formulated an alternate neural model of the AB. In their account, there are four main brain areas that together constitute an attentional network. These are the lateral portion of the frontal lobes that mediate goal attainment, the inferotemporal lobes that perform target identification, the posterior-parietal regions responsible for target selection, and the visual occipital regions where stimulus processing first begins. AB in this model is the result of top-down bias created from parietal–frontal interactions and competition between stimulus codes in the temporal cortex.

REPETITION BLINDNESS

Teresa waits in her car outside the entrance to an elementary school. She watches the exit door looking for her daughter Elizabeth. A stream of children comes running out as the school bell rings. Elizabeth has blonde hair and is wearing a red dress. After several minutes, all the children have left but Teresa did not see Elizabeth. Just then two girls approach the car. It is Elizabeth with her friend Mary. Both are blonde and are wearing red dresses today. Because of their similar appearance and because Elizabeth came out directly behind Mary, Teresa failed to notice her daughter. This is an example of repetition blindness (RB), a failure to notice the repetition of an item when it is presented in a series of briefly presented items.

A typical RSVP display in the lab consists of a stream of individual stimuli, each of which is presented one at a time for a given duration. Observers are asked to locate a critical item. If for instance the critical item is the letter T, most observers will be able to successfully locate the first instance (C1) of the letter. If however a second critical item identical in appearance to the first follows it closely (C2), it is often missed. In order for RB to occur the rate of presentation must be about 100–180 ms/stimulus and the lag time between repetitions about three or four items.

RB has been found for words in lists and in sentences (Kanwisher, 1987), letters in words and in spatial arrangements (Kanwisher, 1991), as well as words that are pronounced the same way but differ in meaning and/or spelling, such as bare/bear, i.e., homophones (Bavelier & Potter, 1992). RB for nonwords has been found in some studies but not for others and seems to depend on list length and participant strategy (Morris & Still, 2008). RB has also been obtained with colors (Kanwisher, 1991), pictures of familiar objects (Kanwisher, Yin, & Wojciulik, 1999), and pseudoobject pictures (Arnell & Jolicoeur, 1997).

Several theories for RB have been proposed. Kanwisher (1987) believes that the presentation of the first target item activates a single stimulus representation or type in episodic long-term memory. Because this memory trace has just been activated, it cannot be updated by the appearance of the second item. In this account, the two occurrences essentially compete with each other with the first one usually winning. Chun and Potter (1995) and Potter (1999) propose a two-stage version of this theory. They argue that words are first recognized as types, the general category or concept to which they belong. This first stage occurs automatically and unconsciously and does not require attention. In the second stage token individuation happens. Here, instances or examples of the type called tokens are specified as having occurred in a particular time and place. This stage is conscious and does require attention. If there are insufficient attentional resources the first token only may get attached to the type. The result is an awareness of having seen one of the two words.

Although type-token accounts of RB like those mentioned above have been popular, they are controversial and conflicting evidence exists. Harris and Morris (2004) found RB for word–nonword pairs (noon noof), words that are similar in structure (glome glame) and same repetitions (plass plass). They conclude that RB happens at the sublexical level and that meaning does not play a role. Whittlesea and Masson (2005) failed to obtain RB in several experiments where tokenization would predict the effect.

Alternate RB theories focus on later post-perceptual stages of processing. In these views, the problem happens at the report or decision-making stage. For instance, RB could be due to retrieval failure, an inability to correctly access the items in memory after they have already been created (Armstrong & Mewhort, 1995), or to problems reconstructing the right memory (Whittlesea, Dorken, & Podrouzek, 1995). There may also be biases against reporting items that appear more than once (Fagot & Pashler, 1995). However, it should be noted once again that there is conflicting evidence for these theories. Johnston, Hochaus, and Ruthruff (2002) reduced memory loads by eliminating the need to report target identity, separating repeating and nonrepeating targets into separate blocks and using immediate "online" responses. In every case they obtained strong RB effects. They conclude that RB happens at the perceptual level.

Hayward, Man, Zhou, and Harris (2010) presented line drawings and shaded images of objects in an RSVP display. They varied the orientation of these objects about different orientation axes in several experiments. In most cases, these changes in viewpoint failed to reduce RB, implying the effect is orientation invariant. If this effect were dependent on the perceptual appearance of the items, that is, if it happened at an earlier perceptual stage of processing based on similar visual appearance, then RB should have gone away. The fact that it remained suggests the effect is taking place at a deeper conceptual level, where the object is coded in a more abstract way that is not dependent on its exact physical appearance. Orientation invariance for RB has been obtained in other studies as well (Coltheart, Mondy, & Coltheart, 2005).

How can we reconcile these conflicting accounts of RB? Some theories posit that it happens early on and is perceptual in nature. Others argue that it happens later on and is more conceptual in nature. Some data support the hypothesis that it is based on appearance while other results put the emphasis on meaning. RB can apparently occur as a perceptual, memory, or decision-making process. In all likelihood, it may be that all of these accounts have some validity. There might be different versions of RB caused by problems at each of these different processing stages. The research on this topic mimics earlier research on attention where some studies supported early selection (Broadbent, 1958), then later selection (Deutsch & Deutsch, 1963), and then both (Johnston & Heinz, 1978).

CHANGE BLINDNESS

Imagine looking out the window at a busy city street. If you took in a single glance you might see storefronts, cars on the street, and people on the sidewalk. Now close your eyes quickly and then open them again. Does the scene look different? Well, it should. If the cars and the pedestrians were moving they would now be in different locations. The question we are going to ask in this section is how accurate we are at noticing such changes. One might expect that we are pretty good at it, since we perceive the visual scene as being coherent despite changes due to movements of our eyes, head, and body. The research, however, proves this assumption wrong. It turns out we are notoriously poor at detecting even major changes that occur to scenes, an effect referred to as change blindness (CB).

In a typical CB study researchers present a drawing or photograph of a scene. This is then replaced with a blank screen for a short interval, followed by another picture of the scene where something has been altered (Figure 10.3). These alterations can include the appearance or

FIGURE 10.3   Can you tell the difference between these two photos?

disappearance of an object, or a change in the color of an object or background. The two frames alternate with the intervening blank screen between them for a given amount of time. The observer is then asked to describe what changes have occurred. Most observers fail to recognize even large changes to these scenes (Simons & Levin, 1997).

Is attention necessary for change detection? The evidence suggests that it might be. Changes to objects in the "center of interest" in a scene are detected more easily than those in the periphery that are of "marginal interest" (Rensink, O'Regan, & Clark, 1997). This makes sense if attention is focused more or more often on central objects. The assumption here is that attentional resources are limited. They may be able to focus on one or more objects in a scene, but not on the entire scene. If the change occurs where attention is allocated, it has a greater chance of being detected. If it happens somewhere outside of the attentional region it will in all likelihood be missed.

Rensink et al. (1997) argue that in order to detect change we need to attend to the location of that change. Because scenes are so large, they cannot all be fixated or attended to at once. Instead, a person must scan the image, attending to different regions in turn. An observer must then retain this information from one view of the scene to the next. The encoded information can then be compared against the next available view of the scene to see if it is the same or different (Simons, 1996). For a single object, this process may be easy, but for scenes with multiple objects it is not possible to encode all the objects and features.

CB studies thus seem to refute the idea that the visual system integrates specific images across saccadic eye movements to create a coherent world percept. Based on the CB results it would appear that most of the information from one fixation to another appears to be lost. In other words, our perception of stability does not seem to be the result of a detailed representation held in iconic or short-term memory. However, we may be jumping to conclusions too soon. It could be that we retain a detailed representation but are not able to compare it to the current percept. Alternatively, we may have a detailed representation but lack conscious access to it.

There are other possibilities (Simons, 2000). It may be that the second image overwrites the first, erasing it. Under the first impressions explanation, we retain a representation for the first image but fail to do this for the second. Alternately, it may be that a representation is formed but not stored. One other possibility is that both images are formed by not compared to one another. Finally, it could be possible that we blend or combine the features of the two images together.

We are beginning to disentangle these accounts. Recent work implies some sort of visual representation is retained. Hollingworth and Henderson (2002) found that observers could recognize an object they had previously attended even though they did not identify a change to that object. Participants have also been found to recognize prechange and postchange objects at better-than-chance performance even though they again did not detect the change itself (Mitroff, Simons, & Levin, 2004). Rensink (2004) proposes that we can sense changes without seeing them. He calls this ability "mindsight." If this capacity exists, it means individuals may be able to detect change without focused attention to the changed region. Mindsight implies the existence of a subconscious or implicit change detection process that may operate differently than an overt or conscious one.

What parts of the brain are used in CB? Beck, Rees, Frith, and Lavie (2001) used ER-fMRI to address this question. They discovered different patterns of neural activity for trials on which changes were detected vs. those on which a change was missed (CB). When a change was noticed, there was increased activation in the parietal lobe, the right dorsolateral prefrontal cortex, and category-specific regions of extrastriate visual cortex. For instance, when face stimuli were used, there was more activity in the fusiform gyrus (the neural area that processes face information). During CB there was substantially less activation in dorsal regions. They conclude that the dorsal stream pathway (responsible for processing visual object location) and parietal area activity (implicated in attention) are responsible for awareness of change.

Given that there has been over a decade of research on CB, where do we stand now? Simons and Ambinder (2005) provide a brief summary of the CB literature and conclude that there are several core findings. These are summarized in Table 10.1. They also raise a set of questions that remain to be addressed. For instance, we still don't know what draws attention to certain scene elements over others. Also, the observer's expectations certainly play a key role in what gets attended to. For instance, if one likes sport cars, then attention may first be directed to a sport car

TABLE 10.1

Four Core Findings in the Change Blindness Literature (after Simons & Ambinder, 2005)

Core Finding 1	Change blindness occurs whenever attention is diverted from the change signal.
Core Finding 2	Changes that are easier to detect include visually distinctive objects and objects whose meaning is important to the scene.
Core Finding 3	Attention seems to be minimally necessary to detect changes, as changes to objects that are not attended aren't noticed.
Core Finding 4	Attention by itself may not be all that is needed to perceive change, as oftentimes observers fail to notice important changes even when they are paying attention to them.

in the image of a scene. The role that individual preferences play in CB and how these might interact with stimulus factors has yet to be fully examined.

INATTENTIONAL BLINDNESS

You're walking down the street looking for your friend Tom who is going to meet you in front of the movie theater. Unbeknownst to you, your cousin Jeff is also standing in front of the theater, right next to Tom. You see Tom and walk up to him to say hi, completely failing to notice Jeff, even though he is in close proximity. This phenomenon is called inattentional blindness (IB) and simply put is the failure to see something right where you are looking because you were distracted or paying attention to something else (Mack, 2003).

The classic demonstration of IB in the lab comes from a study by Simons and Chabris in 1999. They showed a video clip of a group of people passing a basketball back and forth. Observers were asked to count the number of passes. About half way through a person dressed in a gorilla suit walks into the center of the group, beats his chest, and then walks off. A significant percentage, 73 percent, of the viewers failed to recognize the gorilla!

A number of researchers have studied the relationship between eye movements and IB. Koivisto, Hyona, and Revonsuo (2004) found strong IB effects even when the unattended item was fixated and appeared in an expected location. If we infer that spatial attention is located at the point of fixation, then clearly it is not necessary for conscious awareness. Memmert (2006) also measured eye movements and discovered that observers who did not notice an unexpected object spent as much time, about one second, looking at it as did those who did actually notice it. This work shows that attentional focus and fixation are not necessarily linked and can apparently be decoupled from one another.

In one interesting take on how to study IB, Kuhn and Findlay (2010) created a magic trick in which they could misdirect where observers were looking. For some of the participants, conscious perception for an event was not where they fixated. However, when observers did detect the event they quickly moved their eyes toward it. The researchers speculate that overt conscious attention and covert subconscious attention interact. Unconscious vision can apparently inform conscious visual processes where to look, up to two or three saccadic eye movements ahead of the current fixation position.

Most et al. (2001) studied the role similarity plays in IB. In one of their experiments, participants were asked to track black or white letters moving across a computer screen. The primary task was to count the number of times these letters "bounced" off the edge of the screen. On some of the trials a cross varying in similarity to the attended letters appeared. After these trials, the observers were asked if they had seen the unexpected cross and to describe it. When the cross was the same luminance as the attended letters, 94 percent of the observers noticed it. When the cross was the same luminance as the irrelevant letters, the ones they were supposed to ignore, it was hardly ever noticed.

These results show that top-down perception or attentional set makes a difference. If we are asked to pay attention to stimuli with certain characteristics, then processing of objects with those characteristics is better even if they are unexpected and not central to the primary task. Put another way, it is harder to ignore objects if they share features with objects you are supposed to pay attention to. In our example above, if Tom is wearing a green shirt and you are looking for green shirts, then you would be less likely to miss Jeff if he too was wearing a green shirt.

An important issue to investigate in IB research is the extent to which the unexpected object is processed by the visual system. If the object is missed completely, then it should have little influence over any subsequent task. Research shows that this is not the case. Moore and Egeth (1997) found that grouping processes occurring outside of awareness affected perception of the Muller–Lyer illusion. Grouping is considered a rapid, lower level of visual processing and is thought to occur before any meaningful interpretation of a stimulus. So these results imply that unattended objects are at least processed to the level at which features or parts of an object are assembled into wholes.

Other work, however, shows that meaningfulness does seem to be processed outside of aware-ness. In these studies, changes to meaningful stimuli like inverting a happy face or a changing one letter of a participant's name produce a substantial increase in the IB effect by capturing attention (Mack & Rock, 1998). These results imply that we do process stimuli to the level of meaning even when they are not directly attended. Evidence from brain imaging experiments supports this view. Super, Spekreijse, and Lamme (2001) found similar patterns of neural activity for a grouping task when the stimuli were attended and seen and when they were unattended and not seen. Although the type of brain action was similar, there was a greater amount of activity in the seen condition.

Bressan and Pizzighello (2008) further explored depth of processing for the unexpected item. In their study accuracy was lower in a primary task only when the irrelevant item failed to reach awareness. This result is counterintuitive since one might expect greater interference for increased attentional allocation to a secondary task. In their account an unexpected stimulus triggers a state of alert in the observer. This state would ordinarily cause an attentional shift to the item. However, this shift fails to occur because most attentional resources are already committed to the primary task. If sufficient resources are left over and are allocated to the unexpected object it may be enough to disrupt performance but not so much that the object can be recognized and then ignored. This is an interesting interpretation because it suggests that attention is necessary to ignore items as well as to pay focus on them. With more attention, irrelevant items may be easier to ignore and therefore less disruptive.

11 The Damaged Brain: Agnosias

Oliver Sacks describes several case histories of patients with strange disorders in his book *The Man Who Mistook His Wife for a Hat* (Sacks, 1985). To start there is the case a music teacher, who we will refer to as P. Patient P. is unable to recognize some common objects. He describes a rose as "a convoluted red form with a linear green attachment." On one occasion, P. took hold of his wife's head as he apparently tried to lift it and put it on his own head. Sacks reports: "He had . . . mistaken his wife for a hat!" Patients such as P. have a pattern recognition disorder that is referred to as visual agnosia. A visual agnosia in general terms is a failure to identify objects or certain object properties due to brain damage. In this chapter we will review each of the major agnosias. We start with those that might be considered "low level" as they are an inability to normally process certain visual attributes like color or motion. Then we will examine agnosias that might be considered "high level" because they are deficits related to parts of objects or of larger objects such as faces. Finally, we will end by reviewing a very strange disorder in which a person has a visual deficit but is not aware of it, what might be considered a "meta-level" agnosia. We will characterize each of these types based on their unique cognitive and neuroscience signatures, and where applicable address their relation to attention and conscious visual experience.

CEREBRAL ACHROMATOPSIA

Cerebral achromatopsia is a kind of color-blindness that is caused by damage to the cerebral cortex. It is frequently confused with congenital achromatopsia, a genetic color blindness in which one or more of the genes that code for color pigments is missing. In the cerebral version, there is extensive bilateral damage to the inferior occipital and temporal regions. Owing to the specificity of the region and the bilateral component, it is a very rare condition. The disorder is usually comorbid with prosopagnosia, as the same brain regions appear to underlie each (Bouvier & Engel, 2006).

Patients with cerebral achromatopsia are unable to perceive the world in color. Some say they see things only in shades of gray. However, testing reveals that they can still detect borders defined by color differences. For instance, they can see a green square against a red background, even when the two areas are equated in luminance. There appears to be some residual color vision capability in at least some of these individuals as almost one-third of those tested can pass the Ishihara plate test. Cole, Heywood, Kentridge, Fairholm, and Cowey (2003) found attentional capture in an achromatic observer based on a color-defined motion signal. When the chromatic contours of the signal were obscured by luminance contrast, attentional capture was eliminated. They argue that the motion effect is due to chromatic contrast handled by intact color-opponent mechanisms. Cowey and Heywood (1997) also found intact color abilities in a cerebral achromatic patient. This person could perceive shape from color and determine motion direction in striped color stimuli. These patients may have "blindsight for color" in that they have certain color processes that are intact but which do not have access to phenomenal awareness.

Oliver Sacks in his 1996 book *An Anthropologist on Mars* describes in detail what it is like to be a cerebral achromat. In the chapter titled "The Case of the Colorblind Painter" he presents a case study of a patient named "Jonathan I." After damage to his occipital lobes Jonathan I. now describes people as "animated gray statues." He finds the color of flesh abhorrent and likens it to the color of rats. As a result he becomes a social recluse and cannot bear to see even his own face in the mirror. Jonathan I.'s visual imagery is intact, but this is of little solace because even when he closed his eyes, his visual images are colorless and perceived in this same horrific gray. The appearance of food is disgusting to him, so he closes his eyes when eating but can still perceive a mental image of the food in that repulsive gray. In contrast to this, another 74-year old female achromatic patient reported having color visual imagery intact (Bartolomeo, 1997). These differences are probably due to difference in lesion location.

Cowey, Heywood, and Irving-Bell (2001) lesioned macaque brains in order to more specifically determine what cortical regions subsume the disorder. They compared three groups of subjects. The first were macaques with removal of temporal areas TEO/TE while sparing areas of the perirhinal temporal cortex and the superior temporal sulcus. The second were macaques with lateral parietal lesions only. The third were human patients with cerebral achromatopsia. The monkeys were tested postoperatively using a two-choice color discrimination task and a nine-choice oddity task. In this later case they had to choose a color target item from among equated gray distractor items. Those with the more extensive lesions had problems learning and remembering both of these tasks compared with the lateral parietal group. However, they still performed better than the human group.

Area V4 is considered to be one of the primary cortical areas for color processing. In the study just described area V4 was not lesioned. In studies where it is, the deficits are less severe than those witnessed here (Heywood, Gadotti, & Cowey, 1992). Animals with V4 lesions only show mild deficits on the color oddity task. The authors conclude that there is no one "color area" that is totally responsible for color perception. It appears that wide areas of the ventral temporal lobe are responsible for color perception and that all of this area must be destroyed to eliminate all forms of color discrimination.

AKINETOPSIA

Some patients following bilateral posterior brain damage suffer from a deficit in perceiving visual motion. This condition is known as akinetopsia, or more simply, as motion-blindness, abbreviated as MB (Zeki, 1991). A less severe form of MB has been diagnosed that follows unilateral damage (Schenk & Zihl, 1997; Vaina, Cowey, Eskey, LeMay, & Kemper, 2001). The disorder has been produced in macaque monkeys by ablation of unilateral or bilateral area MT/V5 (Pasternak & Merigan, 1994; Rudolph & Pasternak, 1999). Researchers have also been able to induce temporary MB in healthy human participants using TMS over extrastriate regions (Hotson, Braun, Herberg, & Boman, 1994; Pascual-Leone & Walsh, 2001). Although damage to area MT is the usual cause of akinetopsia, motion perception deficits have also been found in patients suffering from other forms of brain damage, including cerebrellar lesions, midbrain lesions, vestibular dysfunction, and amblyopia (Nawrot, 2003). There are also a multitude of different diseases that can produce motion deficits, among them Alzheimer's disease, schizophrenia, William's syndrome, and nefazodone toxicity (Nawrot, 2003).

We have already mentioned that area MT is responsible for motion perception so you may be able to predict what happens when this area is damaged. One patient, L.M., suffered bilateral damage to area MT and some other surrounding brain regions. When tested, researchers discovered that she had difficulty perceiving moving objects. L.M. was unable to pour liquid into a glass because she could not detect the rise of the fluid in the container. She had problems understanding what people were saying due to an inability to see facial expression, mouth movement or hand gestures. She became very confused if there were more than a few people in a room because the people seemed to jump abruptly from one location to another. Koch (2004) remarks that her world was much like that seen with a stroboscope or disco light where objects are frozen in place because their movement in-between flashes can't be detected.

Schenk, Mai, Ditterich, and Zihi (2000) measured L.M.'s reaching ability. If she were capable of reaching toward moving objects, then this would indicate that her vision-for-action system (dorsal stream) motion capabilities were intact, since it is already apparent from testing that her vision-for-perception (ventral stream) motion capabilities are impaired. A series of experiments revealed that L.M. was able to successfully reach for objects that were moving at 0.5 m/s or less, while normal matched controls could do so at higher speeds of 1.0 m/s. She was also able to adjust the speed of her moving hand to the speed of the target. However, in order to perform accurate reaching she needed longer looking times and had to see her moving hand. These results therefore show deficits in both systems. Neuro-imaging revealed that L.M. had damage to the human areas equivalent to MT/V5 in the macaque. This area receives information from earlier striate cortex and after processing feeds output to both perception and action systems.

Area MT is known to contain direction-selective neurons in a columnar organization (Albright, Desimone, & Gross, 1984). Since MB patients have widespread damage throughout this area it follows that they would have a pan-directional deficit, i.e., to have difficulties perceiving motion in any direction, and this is indeed the case. If this area could be damaged or stimulated locally the result might be directionally sensitive MB, in which a subject would have problems seeing motion in only one direction. Blanke, Landis, Safran, and Seeck (2002) set out to test this hypothesis. They applied electrical stimulation directly to the cortical surface (area MT/V5) in a patient undergoing brain surgery for epilepsy. They were able to induce temporary unidirectional MB, whereby the individual could not perceive motion in one direction, but whose vision for other directions was normal.

APPERCEPTIVE AGNOSIA

Most of the basic visual functioning in patients suffering from apperceptive agnosia is intact. They can see details, discriminate between lights of different brightness, and perceive color. However, they have a difficult time identifying, matching, or copying simple visual forms. In a typical task patients may be asked to indicate which of four drawings of common objects is the same as a single comparison drawing. Patient S. was unable to do this. In one trial he matched a circle to a triangle and a paperclip to a key. S. was also unable to copy letters of the alphabet. While attempting to copy a capital letter "X," he drew two distinct but not overlapping oblique lines. Figure 11.1 provides an example of how apperceptive agnosics might respond in a matching task.

Two primary theories have been proposed to explain the mechanisms underlying apperceptive agnosia (Vecera & Gilds, 1998). In the first account, it is because of viewing the world through a "peppery mask" caused by multiple scotomas (Campion, 1987). In the second it is because of a breakdown in perceptual grouping (Farah, 1990). According to the peppery mask account patients have multiple infarcts (localized cell death due to anoxia) that cause the visual system to be "peppered" with scotomas varying in size and location (Campion, 1987). In the grouping deficit account, apperceptive patients have suffered damage to a perceptual grouping mechanism that collects features together using the Gestalt rules to produce a coherent object percept. This view also predicts damage to figure-ground organization processes.

In order to determine which of these explanations is correct, Vecera and Gilds (1998) attempted to simulate apperceptive agnosia in neurologically intact participants. All of the subjects performed a Posner-type cueing task. For the first peppery mask experiment, a random dot pattern was superimposed upon the display. For the second grouping experiment targets were grouped or not grouped by placing them inside rectangles based on non-accidental properties. The results in

FIGURE 11.1   An example of a matching task completed by an appereptive agnostic. The task is to match the object presented on the left with one of the four objects on the right. In each case the patient has marked off an incorrect response.

the first experiment in normal subjects did not follow that of an apperceptive patient while in the second experiment it did. The data thus supported the grouping deficit hypothesis but not the peppery mask hypothesis.

Another debate concerning apperceptive agnosia is whether it is based on damage to either the parvocellular or magnocellular pathways. The parvocelluar pathways are based on ganglion cells with smaller receptive fields and carry information about details, local features, and color. The magnocelluar pathways are based on ganglion cells with large receptive fields and carry information about global form and motion. Apperceptive agnosia has been posited as a defect of the magnocellular pathway resulting in an inability to segregate figure and ground by sampling information across extended areas of space (Davidoff & Warrington, 1993; Milner et al., 1991).

Hildebrandt, Schutze, Ebke, and Spang (2004) tested these alternatives in a patient named A.M. Testing revealed A.M. to have impaired motion perception and a reduced ERP response to a course achromatic checkerboard, suggestive of magnocellular pathway damage. However, he showed normal ERP response to colored and fine-grained achromatic checkerboards, indicative of intact parvocellular pathways. These results are consistent with the damaged magnocellular account of apperceptive agnosia but with an intact parvocellular system that preserves detection of color and local features.

What is the conscious experience of an apperceptive agnosic like? Based on case studies we can speculate that they may see features "free-floating," without being attached to objects. This perceptual experience may be akin to the illusory conjunctions we discussed earlier, in which aspects of one object such as its color may attach to aspects of another object such as its shape. For example, when looking at a house, an apperceptive agnosic may see the windows and doors as separate objects, or may be combine a door with a feature of a second object, such as a car. As a result, these individuals may rely on global object characteristics, such as their location or general size, in order to make sense of the world (Shelton, Bowers, Duara, & Heilman, 1994).

ASSOCIATIVE AGNOSIA

J.M.P. is a highly educated man in his sixties. After cardiac arrest he suffered cerebral anoxia along with some frontal lobe impairment. He has complete alexia, an inability to perceive written words and apraxia, an inability to make purposeful movements. His object recognition abilities are severely reduced and he can recognize only a handful of photographs of all categories of stimuli including animate and inanimate objects, faces and buildings. However, he scores well on judgment tasks that involve comparing two visual objects and deciding whether they are the same or different. This last result means that his basic perceptual faculties are intact and that his impairment must stem from a failure to use visual representations derived from perceptual processes. J.M.P. is diagnosed as having associative agnosia (Charnallet, Carbonnel, David, & Moreaud, 2008).

There are three diagnostic criteria that define associative agnosia. To start, the affected individuals have problems with visual object recognition. However, they can recognize objects using other sensory modalities. For instance, they can identify a bird if played a recording of birdsong or a dinner plate if allowed to touch one without seeing it. Finally, they can perceive objects holistically, at least in the operational sense of being able to copy or match drawings. It is here where we see they differ from apperceptive agnosics who are incapable of either copying or matching. One associative patient, L.H., reproduced line drawings of a teabag, a diamond ring, and a pen accurately, but could not identify any of the items by name (Levine & Calvanio, 1989). These patients are thus able to perceive objects holistically but not provide a name for what they see.

Farah (1990) provides several theoretical explanations for this disorder. Early accounts posited a disconnection between language areas that contain linguistic representations from memory and visual representations from perceptual processing. In this view the two areas are intact; it is the connection between them that is damaged. This means that they can see objects fine and have intact cognitive knowledge of such objects but cannot match one to the other. In a slightly different version of this story, Humphreys and Riddoch (1987) argue that the deficit is due to a disruption of a system containing stored visual object representations. Hinton (1981) has implemented a neural network model that simulates some of these pattern recognition deficits.

Where exactly are the lesion sites in associative agnostics? Feinberg et al. (1994) examined computed axial tomography (CAT) scans of three patients with deficits for objects and words but not faces. They showed unilateral occipito-temporal damage. However, another four subjects with similar symptoms showed damage to other brain areas including parahippocampal, fusiform, and lingual gyri. There was also white matter damage of the inferior longitudinal fasciculus present in all subjects. In some patients there were also lesions to the splenium of the corpus callosum.

The conscious experience of having associative agnosia must be disconcerting but not quite so disabling as the apperceptive form. Patients have relatively normal perceptual abilities and can navigate and interact with others in a mostly normal way. In some aspects, this disorder is more of a memory than a perceptual deficit, as there are problems for some patients regarding semantic knowledge. For instance, they may have difficulty choosing between objects that are meaningfully related or in being able to classify objects into different categories based on shared meaning (Iorio, Falanga, Fragassi, & Grossi, 1992).

PROSOPAGNOSIA

Patient F.G. is right-handed and 71 years of age. He shows a gradual deterioration in his capacity to recognize faces, whether they are famous or familiar. He was approached on the street one day and engaged in a conversation by a woman he did not know. It turned out this woman was someone with whom he had lived for several years and with whom he had a child! He has learned to rely on the sound of people's voices in order to identify them. His perceptual and cognitive abilities are intact. His IQ when tested was above normal and he scored well on batteries assessing language, praxic, executive functioning, and visuoperceptual skills (Joubert et al., 2003). He does, however, have some memory deficits related specifically to the retention of newly acquired visual and verbal information. A neurological examination showed atrophy of his right fusiform gyrus and parahippocampal cortex. Although F.G. has a developmental or deteriorative form of prosopagnosia, his brain is damaged in the same place and his symptoms are similar to prosopagnosic patients who have acquired brain damage by accident.

Prosopagnosia is characterized as the inability to recognize faces, despite the ability to recognize other kinds of visual stimuli and generally intact cognitive functioning. Prosopagnosia can be thought of as a type of associative agnosia because the ability to perceive faces is intact while the capacity to identify them is lost. Prosopagnosics are sometimes unable to recognize close friends, family members, and, in some cases, even the reflection of their own face in the mirror (Burton, Young, Bruce, Johnston, & Ellis, 1991; Parkin, 1996). The disorder is one of discrimination as well, as patients will also have problems in telling faces apart from each other. It should be noted that there are congenital and developmental forms of prosopagnosia that may not be associated with overt structural brain deficits (Behrmann, Avidan, Marotta, & Kimchi, 2005; Kress & Daum, 2003). In this section we focus on the acquired version.

Faces are perceived configurally. This means that we process the relationships between features as much or equally to the extent that we process individual features in isolation. For example, we might identify our father simply by looking at his nose. The nose by itself could be enough to determine if it is our father, based on its length, curvature, and other physical aspects. Usually this is not enough, however, in which case we need to process relational information such as the distance of the nose to the eyes and to the lips, and the shape of the spaces in-between those features.

Evidence to support configural or holistic face perception comes from what is called the face-inversion effect whereby people are good at recognizing upright faces but quite poor at recognizing them when they are upside-down (Valentine, 1988). Another way to demonstrate this effect is to alter facial features by changing their direction. When the face is now flipped, we don't notice anything wrong. This is because we have now altered the relationships with regard to a spatial frame of reference. For an inverted face the nose is no longer above the mouth, but now below it. Because these relationships have changed and our visual system relies upon them it is now much more difficult to process them.

Research shows that prosopagnosics rely on individual features rather than configural relations when perceiving faces (Joubert et al., 2003). In one case study a single prosopagnosic patient, named P.S., was found to use a less than optimal processing strategy. She failed to use the eyes or the spacing between them to identify faces as normal control subjects do. Instead, she relied on the lower part of the face including the mouth and external contours (Caldara et al., 2005). This reliance on individual features is the same strategy adopted by normal observers when attempting to recognize unfamiliar faces. Schmalzl, Palermo, Harris, and Coltheart (2009) also find a congenital prosopagnosic who focuses on local features when perceiving faces. The data suggest that these patients have suffered damage to a specialized recognition mechanism that relies on configural processing. Since they can recognize other objects without much difficulty, this implies that there are at least two forms of object recognition, one for faces, the other for non-facial stimuli (Duchaine, Yovel, Butterworth, & Nakayama, 2006; Riddoch, Johnston, Bracewell, Boutsen, & Humphreys, 2008; Yovel & Duchaine, 2006).

Prosopagnosia has been linked to bilateral damage in the occipito-temporal region. Farah (1990) surveyed 71 cases and found that 65 percent had bilateral lesions, 29 percent had a right-side lesion, and 6 percent had a left-side lesion. In another study of 11 patients lesions were found in the fusiform and lingual gyri affecting the calcarine fissure with striate cortex and the hippocampus. These results are in agreement with those measuring face recognition in normal subjects that shows activation in the fusiform and inferior occipital cortices (Damasio, Damasio, & Van Hoesen, 1982). Some researchers have additionally looked at brain function following recovery from damage. Dricot, Sorger, Schiltz, Goebel, and Rossion (2008) discovered that the ventral portion of the lateral occipital complex (vLOC) was being activated during face perception in a recovering prosopagnosic. This area is not implicated in face processing for normal individuals.

Single cell recording data from animal studies has revealed the existence of cells that respond selectively to faces. The area in question is the inferotemporal (IT) cortex, part of the ventral pathway that is responsible for object recognition. Bruce, Desimone, and Gross (1981) found that some IT neurons fired most rapidly when the animal was presented with the stimulus of a complete face, either that of a monkey or a human being. The neurons fired less rapidly when the monkeys were presented with images of incomplete faces, such as those with certain features like the eyes removed. Wachsmuth, Oram, and Perret (1994) also measured neural firing in area IT in monkeys. They found cells that increased their firing rate when the animal was shown a picture of either a face by itself or a picture of a face and a body together. Responses dropped significantly when the stimulus consisted of a picture of a body only without a face.

In human participants, "face cells" of the sort described above have been located in the fusiform face area (FFA). Imaging studies show that pictures of faces activate this area, located in the fusiform gyrus of the human IT (Clark et al., 1996; Puce, Alison, Gore, & McCarthy, 1995). This region appears to be dedicated to the processing of face information (Kanwisher, McDermott, & Chum, 1997). Figure 11.2 shows the location of the fusiform gyrus on the temporal lobe of a human brain.

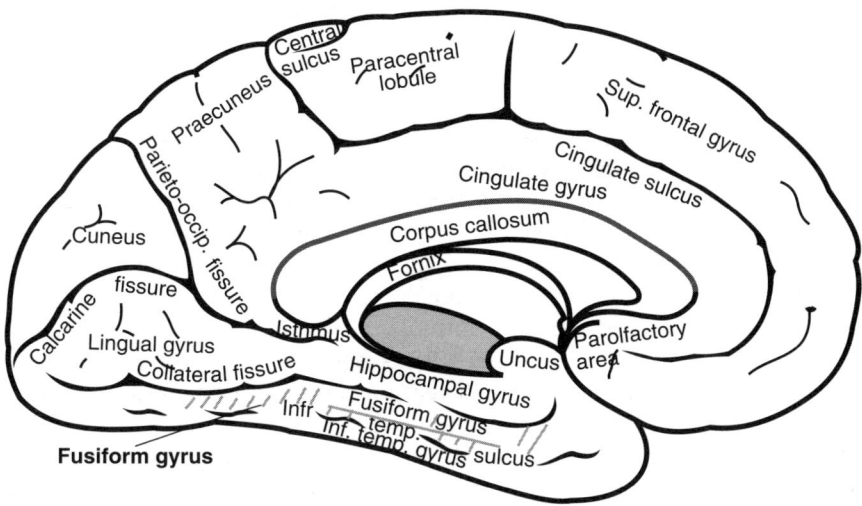

FIGURE 11.2   The fusiform face area (FFA) located on the fusiform gyrus plays a key role in identifying faces. Damage to this area results in prosopagnosia.

CAPGRAS SYNDROME

Ms. C is a white, right-handed female, 45 years old. She has been hospitalized over the past decade for psychotic episodes, depression, and paranoid delusions. Previously diagnosed with schizophrenia, she was treated with Xanax and Mellaril although she had a history of not taking medications. When admitted to a Virginia hospital she reported someone had taken the place of her father and this imposter wanted to kill her. While on a recent camping trip with her father, she took a walk. When returning from the walk, she entered her room and reported that she found a man in the room pretending to be her father. At this point she became very angry and needed to be held back by park rangers. As bizarre as this may seem, it is a real case history. Ms. C is suffering from Capgras Syndrome, CS (Sautter, Briscoe, & Farkas, 1991).

CS is characterized by the delusional belief that an imposter who looks very similar to someone we know has replaced and is impersonating them (Edelstyn & Oyebode, 1999). Usually there is more than one imposter and the number of imposters tends to increase over time (Cenec-Thaly, Frelot, Guinard, Trio, & Lacour, 1962; Edelstyn, Oyebode, Booker, & Humphreys, 1998; Oyebode & Sargeant, 1996). When questioned about this the patients say they understand there are two versions of each person, but claim that the original person they know is no longer present. Small differences in appearance such hairstyle, or in behavior such as posture, are perceived by the patient and used to discriminate between the known person and his/her supposed doppelganger (Frazer & Roberts, 1994; Todd, Dewhurst, & Wallis, 1981). This delusional belief holds also for the self, pets/animals, and inanimate objects (Anderson & Williams, 1994; Cutting, 1991; Paillere-Martinot et al., 1994; Signer, 1994; Silva, Leong, Weinstock, & Penny, 1995).

CS tends to be comorbid, occurring along with other disorders. Estimates are that symptoms are present in 4 percent of psychotic patients (Frazer & Roberts, 1994; Kirov, Jones, & Lewis, 1994) and 30 percent of Alzheimer's disease individuals (Ballard et al., 1995; Forstl, Almeida, & Iacoponi, 1991). Recent work shows that 25–40 percent of cases are also linked to dementia, stroke, and epilepsy (Edelstyn & Oyebode, 1999). In the majority of cases though, it is associated with paranoid schizophrenia (Odom-White, de Leon, Stanilla, Cloud, & Simpson, 1995; Silva & Leong, 1995) and to a lesser extent schizoaffective disorder (Edelstyn et. al., 1998; Forstl, Almeida, & Iacoponi, 1991) and affective disorder (Kimura, 1986; Nilsson & Perris, 1971). CS can be either transient or persistent and the delusion has been known to recur in some patients over time (Oyebode & Sargeant, 1996). The disorder occurs among all types of ethnicities (Forstl, Almeida, Owen, Burns, & Howard, 1991; Mak, Wong, & Lo, 1985) and ages (Burns, 1985; Sverd, 1995). Some reports claim a higher incidence among women (Anderson & Williams, 1994; Sims & White, 1973).

Right hemisphere lesions are commonly found in CS patients, as are bilateral lesions (Silva, Leong, & Wine, 1993). The damage is found mostly in the frontal (Signer, 1994), parietal, and temporal (Diesfeldt & Troost 1995; Joseph, 1986) lobes. Brain imaging techniques show bilateral frontal and temporal cortex atrophy in schizophrenic subjects (Joseph, O'Leary, & Wheeler, 1990). Additional work shows global brain atrophy and right hemisphere damage for cases involving dementia (Forstl, Almeida, & Iacoponi, 1991). There is unusual glucose metabolism in paralimbic and temporal areas in those with Alzheimer's (Mentis et al., 1995).

Given the variety of different brain areas affected and the number of comorbid disorders, it has been notoriously difficult to produce a coherent cognitive or psychological description of CS. One explanation posits that there is a disconnect between stored memories of people and new information about them after some amount of time has elapsed, i.e., after friends or relatives return from a long vacation (Staton, Brumback, & Wilson, 1982). The failure to update these episodic memories produces a discrepancy between the current perceptual input of the person's face, and the older, remembered image of that face. In another view, Cutting (1991, 1994) argues that the right hemisphere is responsible for recognizing the identity or uniqueness of a visual object such as a face. Damage to this area in CS patients prevents them from accessing memories. The individuals then confabulate, they produce a narrative to explain what they see.

   The most current explanation is that CS individuals have damaged the dorsal "where" visual system while their ventral "what" pathway is still intact. The dorsal pathway runs from the visual cortex to the limbic system by way of the inferior parietal lobule. The function of this lobule is to register the emotional significance of a face. This disconnection results in the expression of inappropriate emotional responses to faces. In this sense, CS is the opposite of prosopagnosia, where the dorsal system is damaged but the ventral system is intact (Ellis, Young, Quayle, & de Pauw, 1997; Young, 1994). Hirstein and Ramachandran (1997) provide some experimental data that support this model.

ANOSOGNOSIA

Anosognosia is perhaps the most interesting of all the agnosias. The agnosias we have discussed so far are all perceptual in nature. They involve an inability to process some perceptual aspect of the external world. Anosognosia in contrast is more internal. It is an inability to be aware that one even has a deficit. It occurs most often after right hemisphere damage that produces paralysis or impairment of limbs on the left side of the body. In some instances, these patients will form delusional beliefs about the affected limbs (Feinberg, 2001; Feinberg & Keenan, 2005; Ramachandran, 1995). They will believe that their limbs can move, have moved, or they will move the opposite side limb when asked to move the paralytic one (Feinberg, Roane, & Ali, 2000; Kaplan-Solms & Solms, 2000). There is a less severe form of this disorder, called anosodiaphoria, in which patients will acknowledge that they have a deficit but express little concern about it (Feinberg, 2001; Feinberg & Keenan, 2005). Anosognosic patients will often develop delusional beliefs about their impairment, claiming that a limb is only temporarily disabled (Kaplan-Solms & Solms, 2000; Ramachandran & Blakeslee, 1998).

   Schacter (1990, 1992) argues that anosognosia is the result of damage to a system that generates awareness. Other accounts posit that it is the result of disruption to a sensory feedback process (Heilman, Barrett, & Adair, 1998). In many patients it is as if incoming sensory information is either shut off or fails to reach a mechanism that enables its understanding and use. The afferent pathways that convey information about the paralyzed side in patients with hemiplegia (one-sided paralysis) are intact. The problem seems to be in how that information is received and used to generate awareness.

   Venneri and Shanks (2004) report a case study on patient E.N., an 85-year-old woman who suffered large-scale damage to her right hemisphere. Much of her normal cognitive abilities were intact. When tested, her scores on memory, object recognition, reasoning, and language were all within the normal range. Brain imaging revealed loss of blood supply to the right parietotemporal cortex, extending to associative cortex in the right frontal area. Her deficit cannot be attributed to perceptual or cognitive dysfunction. These investigators speculate that the damaged areas may be responsible for the ability to monitor reality and to evaluate the validity of mental contents.

   Fotopoulou, Pernigo, Maeda, Rudd, and Kopelman (2010) compared a group of hemiplegic anosognosiacs to a control group of those with right hemisphere lesions on an implicit and explicit awareness test. All participants were shown short sentences with deficit-related themes. In the explicit task they were asked to rate how relevant the sentences were to themselves. In the implicit task they had to inhibit completing each sentence. The asoagnosiacs were significantly slower in the implicit task compared to the controls. These investigators then compared the lesions of these groups. The asoagnosiacs had damage to the insula, inferior motor areas, basal ganglia structures, limbic structures, and deep white matter. They propose that an awareness of the disorder requires a re-representation of sensory and motor input to the insular cortex. Apparently, the failure to do this results in nonconscious perception of the deficit.

Another similar account by some of the same investigators has been recently proposed. Jenkinson and Fotopoulou (2010) formulated a computational model of anosognosia for hemiplegia (AHP), claiming that it is a failure of monitoring both intentional and actual movement. The false belief that anosognosics have moved a paralyzed limb may arise from a breakdown in a mechanism that registers discrepancies between intended and actual movement. This system then seems to deceive conscious awareness of what happened.

One amazing report provides hope for treatment of this disorder. Fotopoulou, Rudd, Holmes, and Kopelman (2009) cured an AHP patient by having her watch a video replay of herself. She recovered instantly and permanently after the viewing! They believe it was the third-person perspective seen at a later time that was responsible. The patient apparently needed an objective view apart from the personal perspective of her own body and one that was "off-line," i.e., happening at a time after the intended movement. These results are similar to earlier findings on the treatment of phantom limb pain. The cognitive scientist V. S. Ramachandran discovered that phantom limb pain vanished in patients who were able to view a mirror image of their intact limb moving, apparently because it simulated the visual appearance of the missing limb in action.

12 The Damaged Brain: Other Disorders

In this chapter we review several major visual disorders that are a consequence of brain damage but that are not agnosias. A scotoma is a blind region of the visual field that in many instances is not even noticed by patients. Scotomas appear to be filled-in just as the blind spots are. In blindsight an individual suffers widespread damage to primary visual areas and is thus considered completely blind in the normal sense. However, these patients retain some remarkable capabilities. They are able to point to the location of objects and have some primitive form perception, yet they have no conscious awareness of what they are doing. These patients still have some visual pathways intact, particularly those that bypass area V1 and feed into the dorsal stream pathway. These secondary pathways support object location and movement but appear to have only limited conscious access.

In visual neglect damage to one hemisphere produces an inability to perceive anything in the contralateral visual field. Remarkably, some of these patients are not even aware of their deficit. Visual extinction in other patients happens when an object in one portion of the field becomes invisible, but only when another competing object is placed in a corresponding location in the opposite field. The last disorder we survey here is Balint's syndrome, a severe spatial disorder characterized by a difficulty in locating objects. These patients have difficulty tracking moving objects, copying an object at a location relative to another, and at navigating themselves through space.

SCOTOMAS

A scotoma, broadly defined, is a region in the visual field within which nothing can be perceived (Ramachandran, 1993). Scotomas can be the result of brain damage, but the blind spot is actually an instance of a "natural" scotoma. Just as we "fill-in" the blind spot, many patients with brain damage also fill-in their scotomas. Remarkably, as we are unaware of our own blind spot, so are some of those with damage-induced scotomas. For example, if such a patient looked at a wallpaper pattern, they would not see a blank or dark region on the wall corresponding to the scotoma. They would instead see the color, texture, and pattern of the wallpaper covering or extending through the scotoma.

In this section we will extend our discussion of the filling-in process that we began in Chapter 3. However, as we will see, the two processes are not identical. Ramachandran (1992) examined two patients, each of whom had damage to the right occipital cortex. This produced a scotoma that was six degrees of visual angle in extent to the left of fixation. They then presented two halves of a vertical line, one above, the other below the scotoma (Figure 12.1). After a delay of about four or five seconds, they reported seeing the lines completed. Even more interestingly, they next offset the two lines so that they were misaligned by approximately two degrees visual angle. In this instance the patients reported seeing the two vertical lines move toward each other horizontally so that they were lined up and then became completed (see Figure 12.1)! There was also a delay of several seconds before this happened. These delays do not occur when the procedure is performed in the blind spot, suggesting that the filling-in process for scotomas may be different for than that for the blind spot.

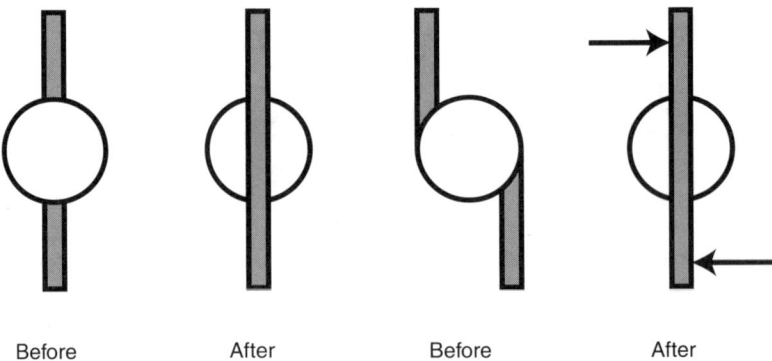

Before   After   Before   After

FIGURE 12.1   The open circle indicates the region of the scotoma. If two halves of a dark, vertical line are placed above and below the scotoma as we see in the left-most figure, the resulting percept is that the line continues through to connect both halves. To the right we see the lines have now been separated with the top line shifted left and the bottom line shifted right. The resulting percept is that the top line moves right and the bottom line moves left, so that they each resume their former alignment (after Ramachandran, 1993).

As opposed to cortical damage, it is also possible to create scotomas artificially using TMS. In this procedure, placing a coil over the scalp that emits a magnetic pulse can stimulate the cerebral cortex. In humans the result is suppression of cortical function (Epstein, Verson, & Zangaladze, 1996). Kamitani and Shimojo (1999) presented a large circular grid pattern to subjects followed by a short TMS magnetic pulse. Depending upon the cortical locus, this produced a missing gray patch in the grating. So, if the center of the coil was on the right hemisphere, the patch would appear in the left visual field. The authors were able to induce scotomas very precisely in different portions of the visual field by moving the coil. In this study, there was only a partial filling-in, where the stripes along the boundary of the scotoma extended into, but not all the way across, the patch region. This may be due in part to the suppressive effect of the coil.

There was another notable effect in this study. The researchers presented a brief gray field both before and after the grid. This produced a perceived gray patch as the scotoma. Next, they varied the color of these fields. When preceded and followed by a red field, the observers perceived the scotoma as red. When preceded by red and followed by green it was perceived as green and when preceded by green and followed by red, it was perceived as red. Clearly, the filling-in process is tapping into the subsequently presented field and using this content to "paint" in the region, much as a painter would dip a brush into ink. The effect may be referred to as backward temporal filling. It remains to be seen what other properties are backward filled. For example, one might predict that the texture, brightness and other qualities of the following field also get filled in.

BLINDSIGHT

Patient D.B. underwent surgery at the National Hospital in London to entirely remove his right occipital cortex to treat a tumor. This procedure results in blindness for the contralateral visual field and is called hemianopia. In this case, D.B. reported being unable to see anything on his left side. After this surgery D.B. was tested in the laboratory by the presentation of various stimuli in his "blind" left side. Remarkably, he could tell if a grating there was oriented in a particular direction, could detect where a stimulus was and could localize objects by reaching out with his arm to grasp them. He was able to do all this despite not being consciously aware of anything! That is, he was not consciously aware of any of the stimuli presented to that field (Weiskranz, Warrington, Sanders, & Marshall, 1974). D.B.'s condition later became known as blindsight.

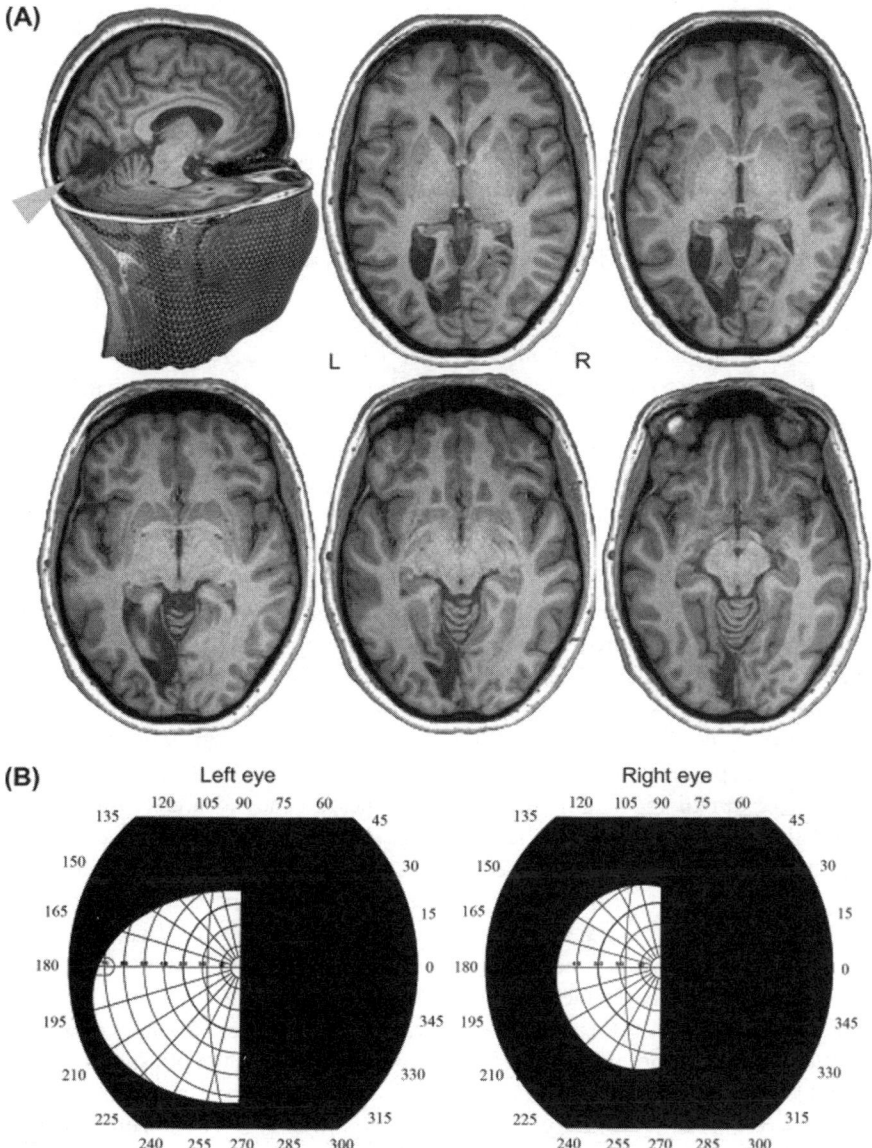

FIGURE 12.2 Panel A shows saggital and axial slices of an MRI can of patient S. J. Although she has left hemisphere damage to her occipital lobe she is able to immediately reach out into the "blind" right visual field depcited in panel B and ajust her grasp ot the width of objects without being consciously aware of them.

Blindsight refers to the capacity to perform visually at above chance level in a blind portion of the visual field even though there is no conscious awareness of having done so. It results from cortical damage to area V1, either on one hemisphere or both, producing either hemifield or full-field blindness (see Figure 12.2). The type of tasks that can be performed in blindsight include limited form perception, target localization, discrimination of motion and wavelength, and even semantic priming (Magnussen & Mathiesen, 1989; Marcel, 1998; Morland et al., 1999).

Blindsight patients can also be conditioned to fear responses when a stimulus in the blind field is paired with an aversive stimulus, showing that emotional responses to visual stimuli can occur in the absence of primary visual cortex (Anders et al., 2004; Hamm et al., 2003).

There is some variation in symptoms between blindsight patients that has led to a two-fold categorization. Type I patients have to be induced to guess to demonstrate their abilities, while type II patients report vague sensations. Neither type however, claims being able to see anything in the normal sense (Cowey, 2010). (For comprehensive reviews of the literature see Cowey, 2010; Stoerig & Cowey, 1997.) The issue of whether blindsight is even a legitimate phenomenon has been debated over the past few decades. One recent suggestion is that it is just degraded normal vision (Scharli, Brugger, Regard, Mohr, & Landis, 2003; Weiskrantz, 2009).

Despite brain damage blindsight patients are believed to have secondary visual pathways intact. These can operate even in the absence of inputs from V1 (Danckert & Goodale, 2000; Danckert & Rossetti, 2005). The retinal path that leads to the superior colliculus is typically undamaged. This pathway connects to visual areas via the thalamic pulvinar region (Cowey, 2010; Stoerig & Cowey, 1997). In the monkey there are projections from the LGN to areas MT and V5 (Sincinch, Park, Wohlgemuth, & Horton, 2004). These have also been found in at least one blindsight patient (Rees, 2008).

An alternative explanation to the intact pathways argument is that there are islands of cortical tissue that are undamaged and still functioning in V1. Fendrich, Wessinger, and Gazzaniga (1992) tested a human participant who had hemifield blindness due to a stroke. MRI revealed a small region of functional cortical tissue that was within the blind region but for which he demonstrated blindsight abilities. The obvious conclusion here is that this tissue and perhaps other areas like it that were not detected are responsible.

Weiskrantz (1995) describes the results of a study he conducted with John Barbur where they measured the motion perception of patient G.Y. They moved a spot of light in various trajectories across his blind hemifield and found that he could detect the spot accurately throughout a large region of the blind field. It is possible that a widespread collection of small intact islands could account for these results. However, a subsequent high resolution MRI scan showed only a single small patch near the back of the striate region (Barbur, Watson, Frackowiak, & Zeki, 1993). A separate PET imaging study of G.Y. showed no activity whatsoever in V1. Based on these results, the island explanation is probably incorrect. Other work employing different methods also casts doubt on this explanation (Kentridge, Heywood, & Weiskrantz, 1997).

Another explanation that may account for blindsight is extraocular and intraocular scatter. This is light that scatters from the stimuli in the blind hemifield to the portion of the retina that processes light from the visually intact hemifield (Faubert, Diaconu, Ptito, & Ptito, 1999; King, Azzopardi, Cowey, Oxbury, & Oxbury, 1996). Some experiments have controlled for this but the results are not conclusive. The possibility remains that blindsight may be due to scatter for some patients but not others (Danckert & Culham, 2010).

Blindsight has interesting implications for a theory of consciousness (Kroustallis, 2005). How is it that these patients can perform visual tasks yet not be aware of them? Milner and Goodale (1995) argue that blindsight capacities are carried out by the dorsal "where" stream that is specialized for action but not recognition. This system is used to carry out tasks such as reaching that do not require conscious awareness. For example, one blindsight patient when tested could not discriminate between different orientations, yet was able to rotate a letter into the proper orientation to insert it into a slot (Milner, 1998). This proposal has merit because retinal inputs can feed visual information to extrastriate regions, including dorsal stream areas, via the superior colliculus pathway rather than through V1.

There may be a kind of awareness associated with dorsal stream activity. This would explain why it is that some blindsight individuals report that they had a "feeling" that a light was in a particular location without being able to actually see it. Another patient when asked how he did it, replied that he had an impression that something was "there" and that the location information was subjectively quite powerful (Weiskrantz, 1980). This all makes sense if the "where" pathway was being used. These patients, because they have some level of subjective awareness would be classified as falling under the type II designation mentioned above.

Blindsight cannot be characterized as an attentional deficit. That is because there are effects of cueing in the blind field. A cue presented in the blind field that specifies the upcoming location of a target that is also in the blind field improves performance for the target when it appears at that location. Conversely, when the cue biases a different location, target performance is hindered. This happens even when the subject is incapable of recognizing either the cue or target (Kentridge, Heywood, & Weiskrantz, 1999). So even though there is no subjective form perception in these individuals, there is still some selective attentional capacity to voluntarily move attention around inside the blind field.

NEGLECT

A 65-year-old woman, for our purposes abbreviated L.G., appears at the hospital complaining she is weak on her left side. She also ignores anything that appears to her left. When food is placed in front of her she eats only from the right side of the tray and even chews food only in the right side of her mouth. When doctors or family members walk into the room she turns when they approach, but only toward the right. LG. is also unable to move her left arm when asked. Over the next several weeks her fatigue diminishes and she is able to go home. An MRI of her brain shows that she has suffered a stroke and that there is a lesion at the posterior portion of her right parietal lobe.

The case study described above is an example of what is called unilateral visual neglect. Patients suffering from this are unaware of the space located opposite the site of their lesion. It is as if they are incapable of noticing or allocating attention to one whole side of the visual field. The ignored side in most cases is the left and results from right side parietal lobe damage although it can also occur for the right side with left side parietal lobe damage as well. Although contra-lesional side deficits have been studied almost exclusively, there is evidence of ipsilesional problems. Snow and Mattingley (2006) found that right hemisphere damage led to an impairment in selectively inhibiting task-irrelevant information within the ipsilesional field.

It should be noted that neglect can be either for space in the visual field, called extrapersonal neglect, or neglect for parts of the patient's own body, what is known as personal neglect (Chatterjee, 2002). Another distinction is between motor neglect, a failure to act in or toward the left side of space, and perceptual neglect, a failure to perceive objects and events on the contralesional side (Bisiach, Geminiani, Berti, & Rusconi, 1990). In this section we are primarily concerned with the extrapersonal and perceptual forms of neglect.

Extrapersonal neglect is measured in a variety of ways. In a line cancellation task, the patient is presented with a set of lines and asked to cross off the ones they can see. For left-side unilateral neglect, they will cross off the ones only on the right side (Albert, 1973; Mark & Heilman, 1997). When asked to copy a figure of an object such as a house, they will draw only the right side of the object (Marshall & Halligan, 1993; Seki & Ishii, 1996). Figure 12.3 shows examples of both. Measures using line bisection and reading are also used as assessment tools.

Attentional theories posit neglect as a disorder of spatial attention. In this view, patients have lost the ability to select a region or object in space from among other possible regions or objects in order to perceive and/or act upon them. It should be noted that in most neglect patients, preattentive processes are intact. They can perform figure–ground segregation and are susceptible to illusions thought to require preattentive vision (Mattingley, Davis, & Driver, 1997; Vallar, Daini, & Antonucci, 2000). According to Posner and his colleagues, right superior parietal damage

Line cancellation task

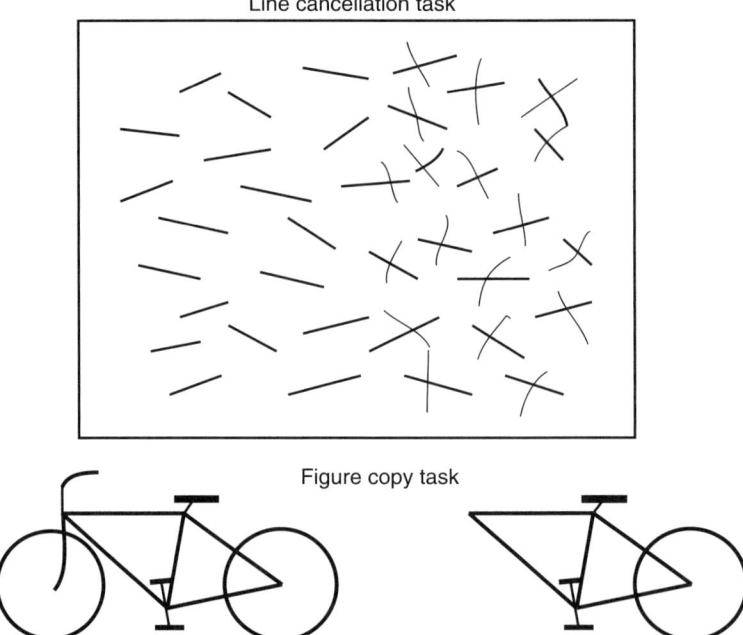

Figure copy task

FIGURE 12.3   Two tests commonly used to assess hemifield neglect. In the line cancellation test, the patient is instructed to cross out all the lines he or she can see. In the figure copy task the patient is told to draw the object they see. In both cases, those with left hemifield neglect will only cross out the lines on the right hand side or draw the right side of the figure.

destroys the neural basis to disengage attention from the right side of objects before they would then shift to pay attention to the left (Posner & Dehaene, 1994). Deficits in engagement and disengagement of attention are related to posterior cortical and subcortical lesions (Sieroff, Decaix, Chokron, & Bartolomeo, 2007).

A number of researchers have investigated hemispheric differences and their relation to neglect. Kinsbourne (1987) conjectures that each hemisphere directs visual attention to the contralateral visual field but that the right side is weaker at this than the left. Each hemisphere also inhibits the other in this regard. When the right hemisphere is damaged, it loses the ability to inhibit the left and its right side bias becomes even more pronounced. In another view, the right hemisphere has been suggested to direct attention to both sides of the visual field whereas the left hemisphere only directs attention to the right visual field (Heilman & Van Den Abell, 1980; Mesulam, 1981). When the right is damaged the remaining left hemisphere results in right side attention only. Brain imaging studies in normal individuals without brain damage substantiate this claim, as there is greater left hemisphere activation when shifting attention to the right but greater right hemisphere activation when shifting to either direction (Gitelman et al., 1999; Kim et al., 1999).

Visual neglect is associated with more than just cortical lesions. It has been found with dorsolateral prefrontal damage as well as damage to the cingulate gyrus (Husaim & Kennard, 1996; Watson, Heilman, Cauthen, & King, 1973). Damage to the posterior-superior and the inferior-frontal fascili have also been implicated (Leibovitch et al., 1998). A number of subcortical structures play a role in spatial attention. Lesions in these areas result in neglect as well. They include the thalamus, basal ganglia and midbrain (Hier, Davis, Richardson, & Mohr, 1977; Watson,

Valenstein, & Heilman, 1981). As a result of these studies, several researchers have formulated distributed network models of spatial attention where different brain areas subsume different functions (Heilman, 1979; Mesulam, 1990; Watson et al., 1981).

In terms of conscious experience, patients with neglect fail to notice their deficit. They are not aware that they cannot perceive space or objects contralaterally even though this is validated in testing. For these individuals, the brain appears to provide a subjective sense of spatial and object completion. Walker and Mattingley (1997) found that patients with neglect claimed to have conscious veridical perception in the affected portion of their visual field and in some cases could complete partial figures such as half of a square or circle. They refer to this phenomenon as "pathological visual completion." However, they believe that this is characterized more by unawareness of visual loss rather than an active filling-in process.

EXTINCTION

Patient M.B. undergoes a test by his neuropsychologist after suffering right parietal damage. First, a spoon is held up in his right visual field. He can report that he sees it without any problem. A fork is then held up in his left visual field. Once more, he has no problem identifying it. Now at the same time a spoon is presented on the right while a fork is presented on the left. At this point M.B. identifies the spoon but fails to see the fork. In fact, he reports that he sees nothing at all on the left side! This deficit is called extinction and is characterized as an inability to report a brief contralesional visual event when it occurs concurrently with an event on the ipsilesional side. This happens despite normal reporting for the same contralesional stimulus when it occurs in isolation (Mattingley et al., 2000).

Many patients suffering from neglect manifest extinction and some investigators characterize extinction as a symptom of neglect or even as a milder version of it. Extinction is more prevalent after right hemisphere damage (Vallar, Rusconi, Bignamini, Geminiani, & Perani, 1994). It can linger after recovery from severe neglect (Karnath, 1988). However, some evidence shows that it may be a distinct disorder with different mechanisms, as some neglect patients don't have extinction symptoms (Bisiach, 1991; Liu, Bolton, Price, & Weintraub, 1992). The results of other studies suggest that extinction may be due to weak or delayed sensory inputs to the damaged hemisphere rather than to functional impairment of the hemisphere itself (Farah, Monheit, & Wallace, 1991; Marzi et al., 1996; Vallar et al., 1994).

Mattingley et al. (2000) report a case study where the patient can detect targets when both are presented on the same side of the retinal midline. That is, she can identify objects when they are both on the left or both on the right, but not when one is on the left and the other is on the right. However, she could do this only when she was able to allocate her attention exclusively to one side. When the targets appeared unpredictably to either side of fixation, this ability disappeared. The authors conclude that extinction results from competition between oculomotor programs that generate eye movements toward potential targets.

Smania et al. (1998) presented light flashes at varying eccentricities to either visual field in right hemisphere neglect individuals. Reaction time and detection rate were worse in the contra-lateral field as might be expected. Performance for the impaired visual field deteriorated with increased eccentricity. Surprisingly, however, response speed and detection accuracy increased with peripheral presentation for the ipsilateral field. They attribute this difference to an exaggerated attention gradient toward the ipsilateral field. In a separate study they manipulated the predictability of the light flashes by blocking trials. Response speed was now enhanced for both hemifields, suggesting that the patients could voluntarily focus attention to either side. However, the difference in responding between the same side and opposite side visual fields remained implying this effect is due to abnormal automatic attentional processes.

Rafal, Danziger, Grossi, Machado, and Ward (2002) presented digits and numerical words bilaterally to neglect patients. They found that extinction was greater when the digit and the spelling of the word were the same. For instance, if the word "TWO" were presented to the left visual field and the digit "2" was presented to the right visual field and both shared the same response. They found the same effect when homophones were presented bilaterally, i.e., when two words that sound alike but have different meaning such as "ONE" and "WON." The homophones resulted in greater extinction than comparable trials where the two items were different, "TWO" and "SIX." This similarity effect thus holds not just for physical resemblance but also for semantic resemblance, demonstrating that extinction happens at the level at which a stimulus is selected for action. In other words, it happens at a semantic or response-based level of attentional selection.

Vuilleumier and Rafal (2000) varied the location, either bilateral or unilateral, the number, one or two, and the shape, stars and triangles, to four patients with right parietal damage. The participants showed extinction for reporting location of bilateral displays but not for counting them. They also showed extinction for contralesional targets when asked to count or differentiate between stars and irrelevant shapes. Extinction for star shapes was worse contralesionally on the left when a second star was present on the right side rather than irrelevant triangles. The data show that visual extinction is strongly influenced by task demands and relevance of the stimuli, rather than physical stimulus characteristics. This supports the notion that extinction is an attentional disorder and not a sensory one.

To what extent are neglect patients conscious of extinguished stimuli? Do they have any awareness at all for the concurrently presented contralateral object? Are they conscious of some stimulus attributes but not others? A study by Gordon Baylis and his colleagues sheds some light on this issue (Baylis, Gore, Rodriguez, & Shisler, 2001). They found that contralateral performance was fairly good when neglect patients were asked to localize or count stimuli. Error rates were also low when the task was to identify but not locate them. In comparison identity and localization together produced the worst performance. This suggests that extinction is a difficulty in binding identity to location. Either task by itself is not difficult, but both tasks together are.

According to feature integration theory, the role of focused attention is to bind stimulus attributes together. If this attention "glue" is missing features can "float," disassociating from one another. Right parietal damage thus seems to impair this binding process. The result is a failure to perceive a coherent object with all its attributes together. Another way to think about this problem is as a failure to integrate information from the dorsal "where" pathway with the ventral "what" pathway (Baylis, Driver, & Rafal, 1993). This explanation makes sense because in some patients, there is damage not only to the parietal lobe itself, but also to the pathways that connect it to the temporal lobe.

BALINT'S SYNDROME

Patient R.M. is a middle-aged man who has suffered two strokes, damaging both his left and right parietal lobes (Rafal, 2002). He was capable of reading individual words and could identify shapes, color, objects, and faces. His spatial orientation ability was poor, however, as he could not navigate on his own and got confused about his location anywhere except in his own home. His depth perception was impaired and he suffered from optic ataxia, an inability to guide his hand to an object using visual information. He could not track the movement of even a very slowly moving object with smooth pursuit saccades. MRI revealed almost identical lesions to both left and right side parietal-occipital regions. Primary visual areas and the temporal lobe were both completely intact.

R.M. is suffering from Balint's syndrome, a disorder characterized by an inability to interact visually with objects even though they can identify them (Husain & Stein, 1988). Objects seem to appear and disappear and object features can appear scrambled. Patients with this syndrome are effectively "lost in space" as they cannot make any sense of their visual environment. There are several key features of Balint's syndrome. The first is simultagnosia, a constriction of visual attention such that the person can focus on only one object at a time. The second is spatial disorientation, a failure to know where they are in the world in relation to objects and other features in the environment. Patients are easily lost and cannot remember how to get from one point to another even if they have been shown just moments before. Balint's patients may also display optic apraxia, an inability to fixate and follow an object with one's eyes as well as an impairment in target pointing under visual guidance, what is called optic ataxia.

When drawn one figure at a time on a page, patients can name them. However, when a second object is drawn around or on top of another they cannot. This simultagnosia can be diagnosed using the overlapping figures test, in which several objects are drawn superimposed upon each other. There are pronounced difficulties reading as some individuals report being too distracted by competing words. When writing they cannot place letters in line with each other. The letters can be seen to move, overlap with each other, or disappear (Coslett & Saffran, 1991; Luria, 1959). Any task involving the comparison of two objects is additionally impaired. These patients can't tell which of two objects is longer or larger than another. Jackson, Swainson, Mort, Husain, and Jackson (2009) argue that Balint's patients lack the attentional resources to select from among the many competing objects in the visual field. With this selective ability gone, there is a fierce competition among the objects, which all vie for attention producing the confusion.

Balint's syndrome can help us understand better the debate between space-based and object-based attention. In one study Cooper and Humphreys (2000) presented figures of equal and unequal length to a patient. When the features were within a single object they were fairly accurate. However, when the features belonged to two separate objects, performance plummeted. This implies that within-object (object-based attention) but not between-object (space-based) attentional switching is possible for this person.

As in neglect patients, those suffering from Balint's seem to have most of their preattentive automatic attention processes intact. Humphreys (1998) found that performance was enhanced when two items were perceptually grouped based on various Gestalt grouping principles such as brightness, collinearity, connectedness, and surroundedness. Baylis, Driver, Baylis, and Rafal (1994) found that a Balint's patient could identify letters of meaningful words better than when they were presented in a meaningless string, demonstrating the so called "word superiority effect." These results and others show that grouping of features and semantic processing capabilities are intact.

What is the neurological basis of this syndrome? As mentioned earlier, Balint's patients have bilateral damage to the occipital and parietal regions in contrast to neglect patients who have damage only on one hemisphere, typically the right) The angular gyrus is also usually destroyed as well. In many cases, there are lesions to the supramarginal gyrus and the back portion of the superior temporal gyrus on the right side but not on the left (Friedman-Hill, Robertson, & Treisman, 1995; Verfaellie, Rapcsak, & Heilman, 1990). **FIGURE 12.3**   Two tests commonly used to assess hemifield neglect. In the line cancellation test, the patient is instructed to cross out all the lines he or she can see. In the figure copy task the patient is told to draw the object they see. In both cases, those with lefthemifield neglect will only cross out the lines on the right hand side or draw the right side of the figure.

13 Conclusion

In this final chapter, we will examine an issue related to all of the findings we have surveyed so far. That is the topic of evolution and how it relates to attention and consciousness. If we are conscious, then according to evolutionary theory we must be so for some reason that has contributed to our survival. We will examine some of these evolutionary theories. We then describe a very general theory of consciousness, one that fits our understanding of neural function in the visual system as well as other forms of awareness. Following this, we introduce three types of models of visual attention/consciousness: neural, cognitive, and computational, then outline the differences between them and how they can be integrated. Finally, we conclude with several suggestions for how to advance our scientific understanding of consciousness.

CONSCIOUSNESS AND EVOLUTION

THE EVOLUTION OF CONSCIOUSNESS

By evolutionary theory, a trait needs to have some adaptive function in order to be selected for. This raises an interesting question. Is consciousness, more specifically visual consciousness, adaptive? It is easier to answer this question for cognitive abilities. We have little difficulty seeing the survival advantages conveyed by language, memory, or perception. Obviously, visual capacities such as pattern recognition and depth, motion, and color perception also are adaptive. But all of these can take place automatically as information processing in an automaton. They don't need to be conscious properties.

Blackmore (2012) lists four ways of thinking about the evolution of consciousness. The first is conscious inessentialism. According to this view consciousness is different from adaptive traits, does not help us in any way, and has no discernible effects. The question we must ask ourselves in adopting this view is why evolution under these conditions would produce consciousness at all. If it does not, then we can think of it as an epiphenomenon, as something that is produced by brains in much the same way smoke or steam is released from a locomotive. In this analogy, it is not essential for the locomotive to function but is a consequence or byproduct of its normal function.

In the second view, we admit that consciousness does have an adaptive function. It is still separable from cognitive processes but is there for a reason. In this case we need to ask what this function might be. Why would being conscious have helped our hominid ancestors to survive? We can extend this argument when talking about animals. If animals are conscious, the adaptive function it serves in them is probably the same as it is for us. One of the more promising hypotheses on this question is that consciousness allows important information to be decided and acted upon. We discuss this in the next section.

Another argument we can make is that consciousness is "attached" to mental functions and can't be separated from them. In other words, we are conscious when we think, feel, perceive, etc. but this awareness does not give us any adaptive value over and above those capacities by themselves. Conscious is "along for the ride," so to speak. We can argue that seeing depth is adaptive because it allows one to move through the environment better. Being aware of depth doesn't give us any additional benefit. The question here is why would consciousness come about in creatures like us that evolved these particular abilities.

The remaining possibility is that consciousness is illusory. It may or may not exist but the real issue here is why we care about it so much. Why are we obsessed with this notion of consciousness? Is it because we are conscious? Is this a topic we should just give up on? Some would say yes (Norretranders, 1999).

THE FUNCTION OF CONSCIOUSNESS

What advantage does being conscious bestow on us? As we have learned, much of what the visual system does, such as program eye movements, is automatized and unconscious. Why can't all of vision, even all of cognition and our other brain functions be automatized? Why aren't we mindless automatons? There seems to be no reason in principle why consciousness seems necessary.

Crick and Koch (1995) argue that visual awareness is necessary because it summarizes the most critical aspects of the outside world and then sends this information to the executive part of the brain where it can be used to inform decisions. These decisions in turn determine our behavior and actions, what we should do next in any given moment. An analogy might help here. If we treat the brain as an ocean liner then consciousness is like the captain doing the steering. The automatic or unconscious aspects of vision would then correspond to the crew tending the engine, cleaning rooms, and performing myriad other tasks. It is the captain that makes the important decisions such as where the boat goes. However, if awareness isn't directed properly, poor actions can have dire consequences; witness the *Titanic*.

So in order to act in a complex and dynamic visual world, it helps to be conscious. This state allows us to choose among competing actions and to suppress irrelevant ones. Koch (2004) points out that planning and decision-making are not themselves necessarily conscious states, but that the interface between planning and visual processing is. Just as there are some visual processes that are unconscious, there may be decision-making processes that are too. Another important point to mention is that new unconscious processes, i.e., visual zombies, can be created through learning. For instance, a soccer player who practices kicking a ball over and over will eventually be able to do it without thinking. In this case, a new unconscious but fast sensory-motor process has been created.

Cognitive psychologists often contrast procedural knowledge with declarative knowledge. Procedural knowledge consists of skill, knowing how to perform in a situation and is demonstrated through doing. An example of this would be being able to ride a bicycle. Declarative knowledge consists of facts and is demonstrated by talking, for example knowing that George Washington was the first US president. These two types of knowledge correspond roughly to the vision-for-action system and the vision-for-perception system, which can also be conceptualized as instantiated in the dorsal and ventral streams of the visual system. Actions, once learned, are fast. One needs to focus attention while learning but not thereafter. Thoughts, on the other hand, operate more slowly. So in this thesis consciousness seems to be necessary for reasoned thought processes but not for well-practiced actions.

Gray (2004) is among those who argue that consciousness is adaptive. He states that it is a "late" error detector. He uses the term late because many of the rapid responses we have to the world, such as reflexes or visual zombies are automatized and happen without any awareness. Consciousness is a slower process that is disconnected from the immediate demands of the here and now. It takes as input the result of a comparison between the world as it is and a predicted possible future outcome and uses it to plan or evaluate what to do next. According to Gray the hippocampus is the likely neural site for such a comparator. One way to think of this is that the senses "present" the world while consciousness "re-presents" it (Crook, 1980).

Humphrey (2002) provides a perception-based view of consciousness. He argues that it evolved as an "inner eye" designed to see certain internal events as opposed to external ones (see Figure 13.1). This inner view tells the subject only what she needs to know and in a format that

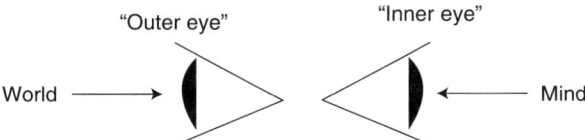

FIGURE 13.1 According to Humphrey (2006), consciousness is an "inner eye" that allows us to read our mental states. This capacity allows us to think about each other and the world in a more effective way.

is understandable. This format is the subjective state that we experience as consciousness. It came into being to let us do natural psychology, that is, to perceive and think about our mind in a way that helps us survive and get along with others. Other theorists have their own take on such inner eye views. Dawkins (1976) says that the brain's function is to simulate the world and that consciousness is the result of simulating a model of our self.

Humphrey (2006) believes that there is no separate function for consciousness apart from cognitive abilities and focuses instead on explaining how it evolved. According to him primitive creatures such as amoebas started off having localized reflexes that responded selectively to specific stimuli. Gradually during evolution these simple responses underwent self-monitoring. That is, part of an organism's nervous system evolved to process and control these reactions. The result is a privatization and internalization of experience.

THE DYNAMIC CORE HYPOTHESIS

Edelman and Tononi (2000) have developed a very general neural model of consciousness called the dynamic core. The dynamic core is a constantly changing, distributed pattern of neural activity that corresponds to conscious experience. In their own words, they state that:

1. A group of neurons can contribute directly to conscious experience only if it is part of a distributed functional cluster that, through reentrant interactions in the thalamocortical system achieves high integration in hundreds of milliseconds.
2. To sustain conscious experience, it is essential that this functional cluster be highly differentiated, as indicated by high values of complexity. (Edelman & Tononi, 2000, p. 144)

In order to make sense of these two statements we need to define some of their terms. First, a functional cluster is a group of elements within a system that interact more strongly with each other than with the rest of the system. A corollary of this is that not all neurons in the brain need to be active in order to produce a conscious experience. As we have shown throughout this book, it is not even necessary that all neurons in the visual system be active in order to be visually conscious.

Reentry refers to cyclical or repeated neural activity within a given network in the brain. This repeated activity serves to coordinate processing between brain areas that may be separated from one another. In their view recurrent activity in the thalamocortical system is believed to be the network responsible for conscious experience (see Figure 13.2). As previously noted, the thalamus is the sensory gateway to the cortex. Information from the different senses project to specific thalamic nuclei. From there, they project to the specific cortical regions for processing different sensory modalities. These pathways are two-way as messages from the cortex also feed back to the thalamus. The visual system compromises one of these recurrent pathways.

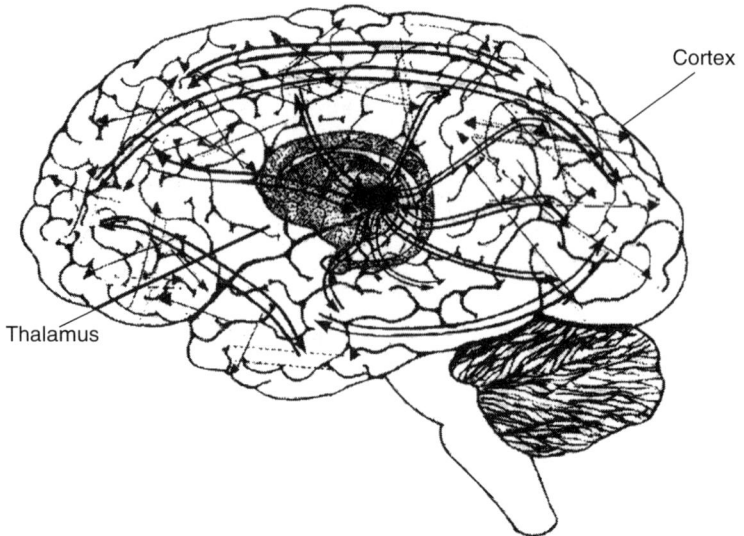

Cortex

Thalamus

FIGURE 13.2 Edelman and Tononi (2000) argue that reentrant activity between the thalamus and the cortex and between different areas of cortex is what underlies subjective conscious experience (after Edelman and Tononi, 2000).

The term integration is used here to mean the collective organization of many different patterns of brain activity. The binding problem in vision best illustrates this. The areas for processing color, form, and movement are each integrated, perhaps through neural synchrony to unite the different features corresponding to a single object. Time-wise, a single conscious experience needs to take place quite quickly. This is especially true for vision where interacting with a complex changing environment requires the continual creation of new visual objects. The authors estimate that the formation of conscious experience should take about 150 ms.

One criterion for a functional cluster is that it be highly differentiated. By this, they mean that there are billions of possible conscious states that one can enter into in any given moment and that can produce different behaviors. Each of the different thoughts that one can have constitutes one set of these possibilities. Although the number of thoughts that we can hold in awareness may be limited to a small number, the number of possible states that we can select between is enormous.

There are several reasons why a conscious experience should have a high degree of differentiation. First, brain states that correspond to unconscious states, such as the slow wave stages of sleep, epileptic seizures, or states of coma, are characterized by ordered neural activity. These states don't appear to support mental awareness and are too simple, since large neural populations are all firing together. On the other hand, if neurons were wired up to each other at random, there would be too little coordination and the resulting patterns of activation would be too complex. Only in the middle ground between these extremes do we see the right amount of differentiation and complexity. These are supported by a network that is wired up with high degrees of connectivity within certain specialized areas, and some amount of differentiation, with connectivity between them. This is the connectivity pattern we see in brains. For example, the visual system has wiring within the color, shape, and form modules but there is also wiring between each of these areas.

GENERAL PROPERTIES OF CONSCIOUSNESS

Edelman and Tononi (2000) next flesh out the general properties of consciousness and show that their dynamic core hypothesis can account for them. We will describe each of these and show how the visual system also applies to them.

1. *Consciousness as an integrated process*. The dynamic core is defined by neural inter-actions. It exists only as a function or process and not as a structure, property or loca-tion. A conscious visual experience does not exist only in visual system structures. As we have seen, frontal, parietal, and other areas participate. The pattern of activity may never be exactly the same on two occasions.

2. *Integration or unity*. A conscious experience cannot be broken down into separate components. If we took a functional cluster and removed any part of it, it would not be the same. Perception of a red car without the red obviously would be a different type of experience.

3. *Privateness*. Experience is always first person. It may not be possible for two people to have exactly the same visual experience even when they are looking at exactly the same thing. Even if they are having the same experience it is difficult to verify. The dynamic core in one individual for experience 1 may not be exactly the same as that of a second person due to differences in history and learning.

4. *Coherence of conscious states*. A person cannot be aware of two mutually incoherent scenes or objects simultaneously. The research on binocular rivalry and multi-stable figures shows that the brain prefers one percept or another but not both at the same time. Ostensibly, the reason for this is that it would be metaphysically confusing. One would perceive two possible realities but not know which one is real.

5. *Consciousness as a differentiated process*. Out of all the possible states one could perceive, only one is actually perceived. Consciousness at a fundamental level amounts to a "choice" between what one could experience and what one does. The visual system actively constructs a reality for the owner. Aspects of this process include filling-in and illusory contours. What we see at any moment is the product of these activities, and is not completely constrained by the visual input.

6. *The informativeness of consciousness*. The experienced state must be informative in some way to the organism, it must convey information that is useful. From an informa-tion theory perspective, the experience is a reduction of uncertainty. The resulting complexity of the dynamic core cannot be too ordered or too complex. Interestingly, if visual inputs are too simple, as in the Ganzfeld experiments or "white out" conditions, partial blindness results. If they are too complex as in a moving random dot pattern, there is also no information gained.

7. *Distribution of information, context-dependency, and global access*. Information in a functional cluster is distributed. There is no center where it all "comes together." This is in line with our understanding of vision being a massively parallel distributed process. Although there may be some be some convergence of information at certain points, no homunculus to date has been discovered.

8. *Flexibility and the ability to respond to and learn unexpected associations*. New or unusual information may be of value to the organism and as such should be attended to. Pop-out in visual search, salience maps and orienting all point to hard-wired attentional capture. Visual learning of new patterns is also possible.

9. *The limited capacity of consciousness*. We cannot keep in mind more than a few things at a time. Selective attention acts as a filter to reduce information overload from the

environment. Not more than a few (3–4?) objects can be held in awareness at one time. Illusory conjunctions demonstrate that the visual system has difficulty assigning features to the right objects if there are too many of them or they are viewed under limited durations.

10. *The serial nature of conscious experience.* Our conscious experience seems to present us with different information at different moments, but these are not experienced as categorical or discrete events with beginnings and endings. Consciousness is more like a continuous experience or stream, as William James first noticed so long ago. Saccadic suppression, apparent motion, and other phenomena show that our visual awareness does not unfold in real time but is taken in, edited, stitched together, and only then made available to awareness after some delay.

11. *Consciousness as a process that is continuous but continually changing.* Like a fountain, the dynamic core maintains a unity even though its components may be constantly changing. Functional imaging in recent years has done much to help us elucidate which brain areas activate and in what order during a visual task. This makes it much easier to construct neural information processing models as have been proposed by various researchers.

INTEGRATING MODELS

One way to learn more about a particular cognitive domain is to construct models to account for its performance. In this book we have described three of the major categories of attention models. Baars' (1997) global workspace theory (GWT) is a cognitive model of attention. It describes how items get into a workspace and how they are broadcast to other cognitive modules. Generally speaking, cognitive models specify the type and flow of information between processing units as well as the specific computations performed by those units. GWT is also a metaphorical model because it uses the analogy of a theater. Cognitive models provide a good overview of what needs to be done in order to carry out a process. The downside is that they do not capture the way these processes are carried out in biological organisms.

The second major type of model is neural. The Posner et al. (1987) component process model and the Mesulam (1981) distributed network model of attention are both examples. The dynamic core model just discussed is more of a hybrid neural/cognitive model as it addresses brain function but also describes mental processes in a very abstract way. There are a number of similarities between neural and cognitive models. Both specify computational centers, the pathways between them, and the types of computation performed. The difference is that the neural model must be based on actual nervous system anatomy and physiology. Each processing center must correspond to an actual such center in the brain, each pathway must correspond to actual fibers between them, and, most importantly, the computations performed by the centers must correspond to actual neural processing. So the advantage of a neural model is clear. It must describe how the process is instantiated in actual nervous systems. A disadvantage is that the neural models may not capture all aspects of how a process gets carried out, perhaps because these aspects aren't known or because they are in other brain areas.

The third and last major type of model is a computational one. The theory of visual attention (TVA) explicated in great detail by Bundesen and Habekost (2008) is an example. In these models, mathematical formulas are constructed that can be used to account for and to predict performance in real-world experiments. The advantage to these models is that they can be made very general and can account for a wide variety of different findings. Because they are quantitative, they also do a much better job at predicting these results. The downside to computational models is that they don't always explain how they are implemented, either at the information processing or neural levels (this is not a fault of TVA since it is accompanied by a cognitive process model).

So we have seen that each model has its advantages and disadvantages. One way to overcome this is to integrate across models. By this we mean an attempt to constrain one's own model based on information from the others. For instance, a cognitive modeler could attempt to map modules, pathways and computations onto those of a neural model. Alternatively a computational modeler could specify how equations are satisfied at the hardware or software level. In so doing, each model gets closer to the truth and can stimulate new theory and hypotheses.

Integration between models is difficult enough when we are talking about a particular cognitive subdomain such as attention or visual attention. This difficulty is magnified, however, when we attempt to compare models and ideas across two phenomena that are similar, but not identical, i.e., between visual attention and visual consciousness. We have seen that it is possible to attend to something but not be conscious of it and to be conscious of something without attending to it. We thus have not only different models to contend with but also different theories and phenomenon.

But the future is not that bleak. The domain of visual attention and consciousness is fairly restricted. We are not talking about cognition in general or even vision in general. Instead, we are referring to specific types of experiences that are limited to a single modality. Visual stimuli can be manipulated and controlled with a great degree of precision and the nervous system underlying sight is fairly well understood. What is more of a problem are the barriers that exist between disciplines. Researchers in each of these disciplines utilize different techniques and have varying theoretical approaches. Those with the greatest amount of interdisciplinary training will probably be the ones to make the greatest breakthroughs in consciousness research in the near future.

HOW WE DO IT: OVERCOMING OBSTACLES

Cognitive science has advanced a long way in the last few decades. This has been due to a number of factors. Prime among these is the development of new technologies. As technology can be expected to keep growing in the near future we can expect new findings that will add to our understanding of vision and consciousness. However, progress needs to take place on more than just the technological front. A change in thinking is also necessary. Below we outline a number of specific changes that we think are needed in order to rapidly advance our understanding.

ANATOMY

Although our understanding of brain anatomy at the gross level is fairly well understood, we are still lacking a structural description at smaller scales. Cognitive science desperately needs a completely cellular level map of the human brain. This map needs to be at least detailed enough to make out all the synaptic connections that each neuron has with its neighbors. The development of the knife-edge scanning microscope (KESM) will allow us to do this. The KESM sections tissue into very thin slices that are then imaged and used to construct a three-dimensional representation. This device is capable of digitizing a complete mouse brain, approximately one cubic centimeter at a 300 nm resolution within 100 hours (McCormick & Mayerich, 2004).

PHYSIOLOGY

Just as we need a spatial map of fine-level structure, we also need an understanding of the sorts of processes that are taking place within it. Currently we have single-cell recording techniques, but these are limited to a rather small number of neurons. Ideally we want to be able to measure neuron spiking activity across a broad section of tissue. There are computational problems to doing this. For each small increase in the volume of tissue measured there is an explosion in the number of cells to be recorded. This can be overcome by sampling methods. Recording across a random sample of tissue should at least provide us with a representative sample of the sort of activity that takes place there. Also, once we know the architecture and firing patterns that take place in one type of tissue, we can apply these findings to other areas that have a similar architecture or activity. The development of magnetoencephalography (MEG) is very promising in this regard. MEG measures small changes in magnetic fields that occur when neurons are active. The device has reasonably good spatial and temporal resolution equal to about one cubic millimeter and several milliseconds (Schwartz, Badier, Bihoue, & Bouliou, 1999).

CORRELATION AND MANIPULATION

One of the problems with measuring the NCC is that it provides only a correlation, not causation. That is, we can identify that a neuron population is doing thus and such during a task, but we cannot be certain that this is causing the observed behavior. Lesion studies in animals and victims of stroke in people can provide us with some causality since we can observe deficits with damage to particular areas. In the case of animals there is the question of generalization. We do not know whether the obtained results can generalize to people. In the case of human case studies, we can't control for the type of damage.

The use of TMS is a good start toward establishing causality effects in neuroscience. This device works by passing an electric current through a magnetic coil, inducing a magnetic field. When placed close to the surface of the skull the field disrupts neural action in that area. For instance, when placed over the parietal lobe, much of the activity in that lobe can be suppressed. One can observe behavioral changes when comparing TMS to normal conditions in order to assess the functional role that lobe plays (Walsh & Pascual-Leon, 2003). This procedure does not produce any long-term dysfunction and has even been used to treat disorders such as depression (Schutter, 2008).

CRACKING THE NEURAL CODE

There are a number of ways single neurons can code for information. In rate coding the average number of impulses over some time period is measured. Since this averages over time, it cannot be the way neurons represent fast changes. If synchrony takes place within 150 ms or less it is unlikely this code could be used. Another option is temporal coding in which the timing between impulses is measured. In burst coding neurons exhibit high frequency activity alternating with with lower or baseline level activity. The timing and frequency of these bursts and of the intervals between them can also represent information. Some cells have even shown fractal patterns over time in which the grouping of impulses over time demonstrate self-similarity, i.e., three groups of three, four groups of four, and so on.

There are other coding schemes involving groups of neurons. In specificity coding individual cells represent some attribute such as line orientation. If even a small collection of cells does this, then the ability would be lost when these cells died, so this is an unlikely format. In distributed coding, a stimulus is represented by the pattern of activity across a group of neurons (Ishai, Ungerleider, Martin, Schouten, & Haxby, 1999). The rate, temporal, or burst patterns for the collection could then code for more complex stimuli. This form is also more robust to damage.

Many alternative codes can also be possible. For instance, phase shifts where the firing of one cell relative to another varies are possible. One could also imagine ratios of firing rates where synchrony or alignment only occur at certain intervals such as 2:1 and 3:2. Perfect synchrony of every spike train seems the most basic and limiting form. Even changes in coding might code for information. A group of neurons could alternate between different codes or variations of a code. Neurons in different parts of the brain may have a special frequency "languages" governed by a syntax we have yet to fathom.

LEVELS OF ANALYSIS AND INTERDISCIPLINARY STUDY

The brain can be studied at many different levels of analysis. We can look at how large brain regions activate in response to stimuli and how these areas shuttle information back and forth between themselves. This is the level studied using EEG and fMRI that have limited resolution either in space or time. We can study at the level of the individual neuron using single cell recording techniques. Getting even smaller we can study what is happening at the synaptic level, measuring which neurotransmitters are released and how these amounts are regulated with learning and experience.

None of these levels are privileged. Each is important in its own way. In fact, it may not be possible to completely understand one level without understanding another. For instance the formation of links between neurons during learning cannot be explained without reference to synaptic changes like long-term potentiation and increased receptor density. What we need is an interdisciplinary effort to link levels. This could be achieved by having a biochemist work in collaboration with a neurophysiologist and a psychologist. This would cover the three levels we have already reviewed but there are obviously many more.

Another collaborative effort instead of spanning scale could span discipline. We have recently witnessed the merger of neuroscience and cognitive psychology to form cognitive neuroscience. Why not take this further to create evolutionary cognitive neuroscience? Comparative studies will also be very useful. What are the neural circuits that correspond to consciousness in different animal species? This will elucidate the selection pressures that drove the development of consciousness and help us understand its purpose better. Dynamical systems theory, network science, and other new paradigms have yet to be fully realized or applied to problems of cognition (Friedenberg, 2009).

ARTIFICIAL INTELLIGENCE AND ROBOTICS

We have not yet mentioned artificial intelligence (AI) and robotics. These two fields naturally complement the physical and social sciences, as they emphasize a constructive or "build it" approach in contrast to an exploratory and empirical one. It may be worth trying to create an artificial conscious entity. A software brain inserted into a robotic body and allowed to interact in a real-world environment could over time give rise to an emergent consciousness. At the very least, such an entity would need to be both embodied and situated (Brooks, 2003). Even if this endeavor fails it might point us in the right direction.

We should also not fail to discuss the role of computational modeling. Creating models that mimic real-world brains helps us not only to better understand brains, but to also build better computational models. An effective computational model of visual attention and consciousness can be implemented in systems such as security cameras or mobile robots. After all, machines that must move around and manipulate objects in the real world will need to pay attention and use vital information to make decisions. Model building is two-way: it helps us to understand the biology, while the biology helps us to understand the computational processes.

A New Science—Reprise

As explicated more fully at the end of the introduction chapter, we need a better science. This science will help bridge the explanatory gap. A first step towards this would be a scientific study of subjective report itself. Initially undertaken during psychology's early years by such figures as Wilhelm Wundt and Edward Titchener, introspective report was tried and ultimately abandoned. There were a number of reasons for this. For instance, introspection may not allow access to some mental processes. Thoughts may also change simply by thinking about them: a cognitive version of the Heisenberg uncertainty principle. Thoughts may also change prior to conscious access simply because some time has occurred between the formation of the thought and the subsequent report. Visual imaging techniques may help us untangle some of these issues by allowing us to measure the physical processes by which conscious decisions and responses are made.

Consciousness is self-evident. It can't be proven objectively but it exists as a subjective "fact" that may be irreducible to a neural or physical examination. This doesn't mean that we can't continue to learn more about it. One of the major future goals of cognitive science should be to provide a more complete picture of the relationship between subjective and objective measures of consciousness. The visual system is the logical starting point for such an endeavor since its biological and cognitive mechanisms are relatively well understood. There will undoubtedly be ongoing efforts to do this in other domains as well. This will raise all sorts of interesting questions. For example, does olfactory consciousness differ from visual consciousness? If so, in what ways? Does our awareness of a memory differ from an awareness of a percept or visual image? Does the conscious experience of any mental content always call on the same brain areas or are there unique patterns of activity for each type of conscious experience? Parallel research in these other areas should help us to piece together an understanding.

We may not know it yet, but we could be in a "golden age" of cognitive science. Technology has enabled us to map out most of the large-scale information processes that occur in the brain. There does not seem to be a limit at least in the near future of continuing to learn more about these processes at finer and finer scales of space and time. The knowledge gleaned from this future work will undoubtedly help us to make better sense of brains. What we consider to be the ultimate mystery today may in several decades end up to be considerably less puzzling.

References

Abrams, R. A., & Christ, S. E. (2003). Motion onset captures attention. *Psychological Science*, *14*(5), 427–432.

Addams, R. (1834). An account of peculiar optical phenomenon seen after having looked at a moving body. *London and Edinburgh Philosophical Magazine and Journal of Science*, *5*, 373–374.

Alais, D., & Blake, R. (1999). Neural strength of visual attention gauged by motion adaptation. *Nature Neuroscience*, *2*(11), 1015–1018.

Alais, D., & Blake, R. (2005). *Binocular rivalry*. Cambridge, MA: MIT Press.

Alais, D., O'Shea, R. P., Mesana-Alais, C., & Wilson, I. G. (2000). On binocular alternation. *Perception*, *29*, 1437–1445.

Albert, M. L. (1973). A simple test of visual neglect. *Neurology*, *23*, 658–664.

Albright, T. D., Desimone, R., & Gross, C. G. (1984). Columnar organization of directionally selective cells in visual area MT of the macaque. *Journal of Neurophysiology*, *51*, 16–31.

Allan, L.G, & Siegel, S. (1986). McCollough effects as conditioned responses: Reply to Skowbo. *Psychological Bulletin*, *100*, 388–393.

Allport, A. (1993). Attention and control: Have we been asking the wrong questions? A critical review of twenty-five years. In D. E. Meyer & S. Kornblum (Eds.), *Attention and performance XIV: Synergies in experimental psychology, artificial intelligence, and cognitive neuroscience* (pp. 183–219). Cambridge, MA: MIT Press.

Alperson, B. L. (1967). *The effect of semantic relatedness and practice on the color-word test.* Unpublished doctoral dissertation, Michigan State University, East Lansing.

Anders, S., Birbaumer, N., Sadowski, B., Erb, M., Mader, I., Grodd, W., & Lotze, M. (2004). Somatosensory association cortex mediates affective blindsight. *Nature Neuroscience*, *7*, 339–340.

Anderson, D. N., & Williams, E. (1994). The delusion of inanimate doubles. *Psychopathology*, *27*, 220–225.

Anllo-Vento, L., Schoenfeld, M. A., & Hillyard, S. A. (2004). Coritcal mechanisms of visual attention: Electrophysiological and neuroimaging studies. In M. I. Posner (Ed.), *Cognitive neuroscience of attention* (pp. 180–193). New York: Guilford Press.

Araragi, Y., & Nakamizo, S. (2003). Anisotropy of perceptual filling-in at the blind spot. *Japanese Journal of Psychonomic Science*, *22*(1), 45–46.

Araragi, Y., & Sunaga, S. (2009). Perceptual filling-in of a line segment presented on only one side of the blind spot. *Spatial Vision*, *22*(4), 339–353.

Armony, J. L., & Dolan, R. J. (2002). Modulation of spatial attention by fear-conditioned stimuli: An event-related MRI study. *Neuropsychologia*, *40*, 817–826.

Armstrong, I. T., & Mewhort, D. J. K. (1995). Repetition deficit in rapid-serial-visual-presentation displays: Encoding failure or retrieval failure? *Journal of Experimental Psychology: Human Perception and Performance*, *21*, 1044–1052.

Arnell, K. M., & Jolicoeur, P. (1997). Repetition blindness for pseudoobject pictures. *Journal of Experimental Psychology: Human Perception and Performance*, *23*, 999–1013.

Arrington, C. M., Carr, T. H., Mayer, A. R., & Rao, S. M. (2000). Neural mechanisms of visual attention: object-based selection of a region in space. *Journal of Cognitive Neuroscience*, *12*, 106–117.

Atchley, P., & Hoffman, L. (2004). Aging and visual masking: Sensory and attentional factors. *Psychology and Aging*, *19*, 57–67.

Awh, E., Serences, J., Laurey, P., Dhaliwal, H., van der Jagt, T., & Dassonville, P. (2004). Evidence against a central bottleneck during the attentional blink: Multiple channels for configural and featural processing. *Cognitive Psychology*, *48*(1), 95–126.

Baars, B. J. (1997). *In the theater of consciousness: The workspace of the mind.* Oxford: Oxford University Press.

Baars, B. J. (2002). The conscious access hypothesis: Origins and recent evidence. *Trends in Cognitive Sciences*, *6*(1), 47–52.

Baars, B. J. (2007). The global workspace theory of consciousness. In M. Velmans & S. Schneider (Eds.), *The Blackwell companion to consciousness* (pp. 236–246). Malden: Blackwell Publishing.

Babich, S., & Standing, L. (1981). Satiation effects with reversible figures. *Perceptual and Motor Skills*, *52*, 203–210.

Ballard, C. G., Saad, K., Patel, A., Gahir, M., Solis, M., Coope, B., & Wilcock, G. (1995). The prevalence and phenomenology of psychotic symptoms in dementia sufferers. *International Journal of Geriatric Psychiatry*, *10*, 477–485.

Ban, S., Lee, M., & Yang, H. (2004). A face detection using biologically motivated bottom-up saliency map model and top-down perception model. *Neurocomputing: An International Journal*, *56*, 475–480.

Banich, M.T. (2004). *Cognitive neuroscience and neuropsychology* (5th ed.). Boston, MA: Houghton-Mifflin.

Barbur, J. L., Watson, J. D. G., Frackowiak, R. D. G., & Zeki, S. (1993). Conscious visual perception without VI. *Brain*, *116*, 1293–1302.

Bargh, J. A., Chaiken, S., Raymond, P., & Hymes, C. (1996). The automatic evaluation effect: Unconditional automatic attitude activation with a pronunciation task. *Journal of Experimental Social Psychology*, *32*, 104–128.

Bartolomeo, P. (1997). Visual neglect. *Current Opinion in Neurology*, *20*, 381–386.

Bavelier, D., & Potter, M., C. (1992). Visual and phonological codes in repetition blindness. *Journal of Experimental Psychology: Human Perception and Performance*, *18*, 134–147.

Baylis, G. C. & Driver, J. (1992). Visual parsing and response competition: The effect of grouping factors. *Perception & Psychophysics*, *51*, 145–162.

Baylis, G. C., & Driver, J. (1993). Visual attention and objects: Evidence for hierarchical coding of location. *Journal of Experimental Psychology: Human Perception and Performance*, *19*, 451–470.

Baylis, G. C., Driver, J., Baylis, L. L., & Rafal, R. D. (1994). Readings of letters and words in a patient with Balint's syndrome. *Neuropsychologia*, *32*, 1273–1286.

Baylis, G. C., Driver, J., & Rafal, R. D. (1993). Visual extinction and stimulus repetition. *Journal of Cognitive Neuroscience*, *5*, 453–466.

Baylis, G. C., Gore, C. L., Rodriguez, P. D., & Shisler, R. J. (2001). Visual extinction and awareness: The importance of binding dorsal and ventral pathways. *Visual Cognition*, *8*(3), 359–379.

Beaver, J. D., Mogg, K., & Bradley, B. P. (2005). Emotional conditioning to masked stimuli and modulation of visuospatial attention. *Emotion*, *5*, 67–79.

Beck, D. M., Rees, G., Frith, C. D., & Lavie, N. (2001). Neural correlates of change detection and change blindness. *Nature Neuroscience*, *4*(6), 645–650.

Bednar, J. A., & Miikkulainen, R. (2000). Tilt aftereffects in self-organizing model of the primary visual cortex. *Neural Computation*, *12*, 1721–1740.

Beh, H. C., Wenderoth, P., & Purcell, A. T. (1971). The angular function of a rod-and-frame illusion. *Perception and Psychophysics*, *9*, 353–355.

Behrmann, M., Avidan, G., Marotta, J. J., & Kimchi, R. (2005). Detailed exploration of face-related processing in congenital prosopagnosia: 1. Behavioural findings. *Journal of Cognitive Neuroscience*, *17*, 1130–1149.

Berger, A., Henik, A., & Rafal, R. (2005). Competition between endogenous and exogenous orienting of visual attention. *Journal of Experimental Psychology: General*, *134*(2), 207–221.

Berkeley, M. A., Debruyn, B., & Orban, G. (1994). Illusory, motion and luminance-define contours interact in the human visual system. *Vision Research*, *34*, 209–216.

Bertamini, J., Friedenberg, L., & Argyle, L. (2002). No within-object advantage for detection of rotation. *Acta Psychologica*, *111*, 59–81.

Bertamini, M., Friedenberg, J., & Kubovy, M. (1997). Detection of symmetry and perceptual organization: The way a lock-and-key process works. *Acta Psychologia*, *95*(2), 119–140.

Bisiach, E. (1991). Extinction and neglect. In J. Paillard (Ed.), *Brain and space* (pp. 251–257). Oxford: Oxford University Press.

Bisiach, E., Geminiani, G., Berti, A., & Rusconi, M. L. (1990). Perceptual and premotor factors of unilateral neglect. *Neurology*, *40*, 1278–1281.

Blackmore, S. (2012). Turning on the light to see how the darkness looks. In S. Kreitler and O. Maimon (Eds.), *Consciousness: Its nature and functions* (pp. 1–22). New York: Nova.

Blake, R. (1989). A neural theory of binocular rivalry. *Psychological Review*, *96*, 145–167.

Blake, R., & Lema, S. A. (1978). Inhibitory effect of binocular rivalry suppression is independent of orientation. *Vision Research*, *18*, 541–544.

Blake, R. & Sekuler, R. (2006). *Sensation and perception* (5th ed.). New York: McGraw-Hill.

Blanke, O., Landis, T., Safran, A. B., & Seeck, M. (2002). Direction specific motion blindness induced by focal stimulation of human extrastriate cortex. *European Journal of Neuroscience, 15*, 2043–2048.

Block, N. (1995). On a confusion about a function of consciousness, *Behavioral and Brain Sciences, 18*, 227–247.

Block, N. (1996). How can we find the neural correlates of consciousness? *Trends in Neurosciences, 19*, 456–459.

Block, N. (2005). Two neural correlates of consciousness. *Trends in Cognitive Sciences, 9*, 46–52.

Bonneh, Y. S., Cooperman, A., & Sagi, D. (2001). Motion-induced blindness in normal observers. *Nature, 411*, 798–801.

Bornstein, R. F. (1989). Exposure and affect: Overview and meta-analysis of research, 1968–1987. *Psychological Bulletin, 106*, 265–289.

Bouvier, S. E., & Engel, S. A. (2006). Behavioral deficits and cortical damage loci in cerebral achromatopsia. *Cerebral Cortex, 16*(2), 183–191.

Bornstein, R. F., & d'Agostino, P. R. (1992). Stimulus recognition and the mere exposure effect. *Journal of Personality and Social Psychology, 63*, 542–552.

Bradley, B. P., Mogg, K., & Millar, N. H. (2000). Covert and overt orienting of attention to emotional faces in anxiety. *Cognition and Emotion, 14*(6), 789–808.

Brand, J. L., Holding, D.H., & Jones, P. D. (1987). Conditioning and blocking of the McCollough effects. *Perception and Psychophysics, 41*, 313–317.

Braun, J., Koch, C., & Davis, J. L. (2001). *Visual attention and cortical circuits.* Cambridge, MA: MIT Press.

Brefczynski, J. A., & DeYoe, E. A. (1999). A physiological correlate of the 'spotlight' of visual attention. *Nature Neuroscience, 2*(4), 370–374.

Breitmeyer, B. G. (1984). *Visual masking: An integrative approach.* New York: Oxford University Press.

Breitmeyer, B. G., & Ganz, L. (1976). Implications of sustained and transient channels for theories of visual pattern masking, saccadic suppression, and information processing. *Psychological Review, 87*, 1–36.

Breitmeyer, B. G., & Ogmen, H. (2000). Recent models and findings in visual backwards masking: A comparison, review, and update. *Perception and Psychophysics, 62*, 1572–1595.

Bressan, P., & Pizzighello, S. (2008). The attentional cost of inattentional blindness. *Cognition, 106*(1), 370–383.

Brighina, F., Ricci, R., Piazza, A., Scalia, S., Giglia, G., & Fierro, B. (2003). Illusory contours and specific regions of human extrastriate cortex: Evidence from rTMS. *European Journal of Neuroscience, 17*, 2469–2474.

Broadbent, D. E. (1958). *Perception and communication.* Oxford: Pergamon Press.

Broerse, J., & Grimbeek, P. (1994). Eye movements and the associative basis of contingent color aftereffects: A comment on Siegal, Allan, and Eissenberg. *Journal of Experimental Psychology: General, 123*, 83–85.

Brooks, R. A. (2003). *Flesh and machines: How robots will change us.* New York: Vintage.

Brouwer, W.H., Waterink, W., Van Wolfferlaar, P. C., & Rothengatter, T. (1991). Divided attention in experiences young and older drivers: Lane tracking and visual analysis in a dynamic driving simulator. *Human Factors, 33*(5), 572–582.

Brown, K. T. (1955). Rate of apparent change in a dynamic ambiguous figure as a function of observation time. *American Journal of Psychology, 68*, 358–371.

Bruce, C. J., Desimone, R., & Gross, C. G. (1981). Visual properties of neurons in a polysensory area in superior temporal sulcus of the macaque. *Journal of Neurophysiology, 46*, 369–384.

Bullier, J., & Henry, G. H. (1979). Neural path taken by afferent streams in striate cortex of the cat. *Journal of Neurophysiology, 42*, 1264–1270.

Bundesen, C. (1990). A theory of visual attention. *Psychological Review, 97*, 523–547.

Bundesen, C., & Habekost, T. (2008). *Principles of visual attention: Linking mind and brain.* Oxford: Oxford University Press.

Burns, A. (1985). The oldest patient with Capgras syndrome. *British Journal of Psychiatry, 147*, 719–720.

Burton, A. M., Young, A. W., Bruce, V., Johnston, R. A., & Ellis, A. W. (1991). Understanding covert recognition. *Cognition, 39*, 129–166.

Caldara, R., Schyns, P., Mayer, E., Smith, M. L., Gosselin, F., & Rossion, B. (2005). Does prosopagnosia take the eyes out face representations? Evidence for a defect in representing diagnostic facial information following brain damage. *Journal of Cognitive Neuroscience, 17*, 1652–1666.

Campion, J. (1987). Apperceptive agnosia: The specification and description of constructs. In G. W Humphreys & M. J. Riddoch (Eds.), *Visual object processing: A cognitive neuropsychological approach* (pp. 197–232). London: Erlbaum.

Carlson, J. M., & Reinke, K. S. (2008). Masked fearful faces modulate the orienting of covert special attention. *Emotion, 8*(4), 522–529.

Carpenter, R.H. S., & Blakemore, C. (1973). Interactions between orientations in human vision. *Experimental Brain Research, 18*, 287–303.

Carrasco, M., & Frieder, K. S. (1997). Cortical magnification neutralizes the eccentricity effects in visual search. *Vision Research, 37*, 63–82.

Carter, O. L., & Pettigrew, J. D. (2003). A common oscillator for perceptual rivalries? *Perception, 32*(3), 295–305.

Cavanagh, P. (1989). Multiple analysis of orientation in the visual system. In D. M. K. Lam & C. D. Gilbert (Eds.), *Neural mechanisms of visual perception* (pp. 261–280). Woodlands, TX: Portfolio Publishing,.

Cave, K. R. (1999). The FeatureGate model of visual selection. *Psychological Research, 62*, 182–194.

Cave, K. R., & Batty, M. J. (2006). From searching for features to searching for threat: Drawing the boundary between preattentive and attentive vision. *Visual Cognition, 14*, 629–646.

Cenec-Thaly, H., Frelot, C., Guinard, M., Triot, J. C., & Lacour, M. A. (1962). L'illusion des sosies. *Annales Medico-Psychologiques, 120*, 481–494.

Chalmers, D. J. (1996). *The conscious mind: In search of a fundamental theory.* New York: Oxford University Press.

Charnallet, A., Carbonnel, S., David, D., & Moreaud, O. (2008). Associative visual agnosia: A case study. *Behavioural Neurology, 19*, 41–44.

Chatterjee, A. (2002). Neglect: A disorder of spatial attention. In M. D'Esposito & M. S. Gazzaniga (Eds.), *Neurological foundations of cognitive neuroscience* (pp. 1–24). Cambridge, MA: MIT Press.

Chaudhuri, A. (1990). Modulation of the motion aftereffect by selective attention. *Nature, 344*(6261), 60–62.

Cheal, M., & Lyon, D. R. (1991). Central and peripheral precuing of forced-choice discrimination. *Quarterly Journal of Experimental Psychology: Human Experimental Psychology, 43A*, 859–880.

Chong, S. C., & Blake, R. (2006). Exogenous attention and endogenous attention influence initial dominance in binocular rivalry. *Vision Research, 46*(11), 1794–1803.

Chun, M. M., & Potter, M. C. (1995). A two-stage model for multiple target detection in rapid serial visual presentation. *Journal of Experimental Psychology: Human Perception and Performance, 21*, 109–127.

Churchland, P. S. (1996). The hornswaggle problem. *Journal of Consciousness Studies, 3*(4), 290–302.

Clark, V. P., Keil, K., Maisog, J. M., Courtney, S., Underleider, L. G., & Haxby, J. V. (1996). Functional magnetic resonance imaging of human visual cortex during face matching: A comparison with positron emission tomography. *Neuroimage, 4*, 1–15.

Cohen, A., Ivry, R., Rafal, R., & Kohn, C. (1995). Response code activation by stimuli in the neglected visual field. *Neuropsychology, 9*, 165–173.

Cohen, A., & Shoup, R. (1997). Perceptual dimensional constraints on response selection processes. *Cognitive Psychology, 32*, 128–181.

Cohen, J. D., Dunbar, K., & McClelland, J. L. (1990). On the control of automatic processes: A parallel distributed processing account of the Stroop effect. *Psychological Review, 97*, 332–361.

Cole, G. G., Heywood, C., Kentridge, R., Fairholm, I., & Cowey, A. (2003). Attentional capture by colour and motion in cerebral achromatopsia. *Neuropsychologia, 41*(13), 1837–1846.

Cole, G. G., Kuhn, G., & Liversedge, S. P. (2007). Onset of illusory figures attenuates change blindness. *Psychonomic Bulletin & Review, 14*(5), 939–943.

Coltheart, M. (1971). Visual feature-analyzers and aftereffects of tilt and curvature. *Psychological Review, 78*, 114–121.

Coltheart, V., Mondy, S., & Coltheart, M. (2005). Repetition blindness for novel objects. *Visual Cognition, 12*(3), 519–540.

Cooper, A. C. G., & Humphreys, G. W. (2000). Coding space within but not between objects: Evidence from Balint's syndrome. *Neuropsychologia, 38*, 723–733.

Corballis, P. M. (2003). Visuospatial processing and the right-hemisphere interpreter. *Brain and Cognition, 53*(2), 171–176.

Corballis, P. M., Fendrich, R., Shapley, R. M., & Gazzaniga, M. S. (1999). Illusory contour perception and amodal boundary completion: Evidence of a dissociation following callostomy. *Journal of Cognitive Neuroscience, 11*(4), 459–466.

Corballis, P. M., Funnell, M. G., & Gazzaniga, M. S. (1999). A dissociation between spatial and identity matching in callostomy patients. *NeuroReport: For Rapid Communication of Neuroscience Research, 10*(10), 2183–2187.

Corballis, M. C., & Sergent, J. (1988). Imagery in a commissurotomized patient. *Neuropsychologia, 26*(1), 13–26.

Corbetta, M., Kincade, J. M., Ollinger, J. M., McAvoy, M. P., Gordon, L., & Shulman, G. L. (2000). Voluntary orienting is dissociated from target detection in human posterior partietal cortex. *Nature Neuroscience, 3*, 292–297.

Corbetta, M., Miezin, F. M., Shulman, G. L., & Petersen, S. (1993). A PET study of visuospatial attention. *Journal of Neuroscience, 13*, 7426–7435.

Corbetta, M., & Schulman, G. L. (2002). Control of goal-directed and stimulus-driven attention in the brain. *Nature Reviews Neuroscience, 3*, 201–215.

Coren, S., Ward, L. M., & Enns, J. T. (2004). *Sensation & perception* (6th ed.). New York: Wiley.

Coslett, H. B., & Saffran, E. M. (1991). Simultanagnosia: To see but not two see. *Brain, 114*, 1523–1545.

Coull, J. T., & Nobre, A. C. (1998). Where and when to pay attention: The neural systems for directing attention to spatial locations and to time intervals as revealed by both PET and fMRI. *The Journal of Neuroscience, 18*(8), 7426–7435.

Cowey, A. (2010). The blindsight saga. *Experimental Brain Research, 200*, 3–24.

Cowey, A., & Heywood, C. A. (1997). Cerebral achromatopsia: Color blindness despite wavelength processing. *Trends in Cognitive Science, 1*, 133–139.

Cowey, A., Heywood, C. A., & Irving-Bell, L. (2001). The regional cortical basis of achromatopsia: A study on macaque monkeys and an achromatopsic patient. *European Journal of Neuroscience, 14*(9), 1555–1566.

Cowey, A., & Stoerig, P. (2003). Stimulus cueing in blindsight. *Progressive Brain Research, 144*, 261–267.

Cowey, A., & Walsh, V. (2000). Magentically induced phosphenes in sighted, blind, and blindsighted observers. *Neuroreport, 11*, 3269–3273.

Crick, F., & Koch, C. (1990). Towards a neurobiological theory of consciosness. *Seminar in the Neurosciences, 2*, 263–275.

Crick, F., & Koch, C. (1995). Are we aware of neural activity in primary visual cortex? *Nature, 375*, 121–123.

Crook, J. H. (1980). *The evolution of human consciousness*. Oxford: Clarendon Press.

Culham, J. C., Dukelow, S. P., Vilis, T., Hassard, F. A., Gati, J. S., Menon, R. S., & Goodale, M. A. (1999). Recovery of fMRI activation in motion area MT following storage of the motion aftereffect. *Journal of Neuropsychology, 81*(1), 388–393.

Cutting, J. (1991). Delusional misidentification and the role of right hemisphere in the appreciation of identity. *British Journal of Psychiatry, 159*, 70–75.

Cutting, J. (1994). Evidence for right hemisphere dysfunction in schizophrenia. In: A. S. David & J. Cutting (Eds.), *The neuropsychology of schizophrenia* (pp. 231–242). Oxford: Oxford University Press.

Czeisler, C. A., Shanahan, D. L., Klerman, E. B., Martens, H., Brotman, D. J., Emns, J. S., . . . Rizzo, J. F. (1995). Suppression of melatonin secretion in some blind patients by exposure to bright light. *New England Journal of Medicine, 322*, 6–11.

Dalrymple-Alford, E. (1972). Associative facilitation and interference in the Stroop color-word task. *Perception and Psychophysics, 11*, 274–276.

Damasio, A. R. (1999). *The feeling of what happens: Body and emotion in the making of consciousness*. New York: Harcourt Brace.

Damasio, A. R. (2000). A neurobiology for consciousness. In T. Metzinger (Ed.), *Neural correlates of consciousness: Empirical and conceptual questions* (pp. 111–120). Cambridge, MA: MIT Press.

Damasio, A. R., Damasio, H., & Van Hoesen, G. W. (1982). Prosopagnosiaa: Anatomic basis and behavioral mechanisms. *Neurology, 32*, 331–341.

Danckert, J., & Culham, J. C. (2010). Reflections on blindsight: Neuroimaging and behavioural explorations clarify a case of reversed localization in the blind field of a patient with hemianopia. *Canadian Journal of Experimental Psychology, 64*, 86–101.

Danckert, J., & Goodale, M. A. (2000). Blindsight: A conscious route to unconscious vision. *Current Biology, 10*(1), 31–43.

Danckert, J., & Rossetti, Y. (2005). Blindsight in action: What can the different sub-types of blindsight tell us about the control of visually guided actions. *Neuroscience and Biobehavioral Reviews, 29*(7), 1035–1046.

Davidoff, J. & Warrington, E. K. (1993). A dissociation of shape discrimination and figure–ground perception in a patient with normal acuity. *Neuropsychologia, 31*, 83–93.

Davis, G., & Driver, J. (1994). Parallel detection of Kanizsa subjective figures in the human visual system. *Nature, 371*, 791–793.

Davis, G., & Driver, J. (1998). Kanizsa subjective figures can act as occluding surfaces at parallel stages of visual search. *Journal of Experimental Psychology: Human Perception and Performance, 24*, 169–184.

Davis, G., & Holmes, A. (2005). Reversal of object-based benefits in visual attention. *Visual Cognition, 12*(5), 817–846.

Dawkins, R. (1976). *The selfish gene.* Oxford: Oxford University Press.

de Brecht, M., & Saiki, J. (2006). A neural network implementation of a saliency map model. *Neural Networks, 19*(10), 1467–1474.

De Haan, B., Morgan, P. S., & Rorden, C. (2008). Covert orienting of attention and overt eye movements activate identical brain regions. *Brain Research, 1204*, 102–111.

De Weerd, P., Desimone, R., & Ungerleider, L. G. (1998). Perceptual filling-in: A parametric study. *Vision Research, 38*, 2721–2734.

De Weerd, P., Smith, E., & Greenberg, P. (2006). Effects of selective attention on perceptual filling-in. *Journal of Cognitive Neuroscience, 18*(3), 335–347.

Dehaene, S., Kerszberg, M., & Changeux, J. P. (1998). A neuronal model of a global workspace in effortful cognitive tasks. *Proceedings of the National Academy of Sciences of the United States of America, 95*, 14529–14534.

Dehaene, S., Naccache, L., Cohen, L., Le Bihan, D., Mangin, J. F., Poline, J. B., & D. Rivière, D. (2001). Cerebral mechanisms of word masking and unconscious repetition priming. *Nature Neuroscience, 4*, 752–758.

Dehaene, S., Naccache, L., Le Clec'H, G., Koechlin, E., Mueller, M., Dehaene-Lambertz, G., . . . Le Bihan, D. (1998). Imaging unconscious semantic priming. *Nature, 395*, 597–600.

Dehaene, S., Sergent, C., & Changeux, J. P. (2003). A neuronal model linking subjective subjective reports and objective physiological data during conscious perception. *Proceedings of the National Academy of Sciences of the United States of America, 100*, 8520–8525.

Demb, J. B., Desmond, J. E., Gabrieli, J. D. E., Vaidya, C. J., Glover, G. H., & Gabrieli, J. D. (1995). Semantic encoding and retrieval in the left inferioro prefrontal cortex: A functional MRI study of task difficulty and process specificity. *Journal of Neuroscience, 15*(9), 5870–5878.

Dennett, D. C. (1991). *Consciousness explained.* Boston, MA: Little, Brown.

Desimone, R. (1999). Visual attention mediates by biased competition in extrastriate visual cortex. In G. W. Humphreys, J. Duncan, & A. M. Treisman (Eds.), *Attention, space, and action: Studies in cognitive neuroscience* (pp. 13–30). London: Oxford University Press.

Desimone, R., & Duncan, J. (1995). Neural mechanisms of selective visual attention. *Annual Review of Neuroscience, 18*, 193–222.

Deubel, H., & Schneider, W. X. (1996). Saccade target selection and object recognition: Evidence for a common attentional mechanism. *Vision Research, 36*, 1827–1837.

Deubel, H., Schneider, W. X., & Paprotta, I. (1998). Selective dorsal and ventral processing: Evidence for a common attentional mechanism in reaching and perception. *Visual Cognition, 5*(1/2), 81–107.

Deutsch, J. A., & Deutsch, D. (1963). Attention: Some theoretical considerations. *Psychological Review, 70*, 80–90.

Di Lollo, V., Enns, J. T., & Rensink, R. A. (2000). Competition for consciousness among visual events: The psychophysics of reentrant visual processes. *Journal of Experimental Psychology: General, 129*, 481–507.

Diedrichsen, J., Ivry, R. B., Cohen, A., & Danziger, S. (2000). Asymmetries in a unilateral flanker task depend on the direction of the response: The role of attentional shift and perceptual grouping. *Journal of Experimental Psychology: Human Perception and Performance, 26*(1), 113–126.

Diesfeldt, H. F., & Troost, D. (1995). Delusional misidentification and subsequent dementia: A clinical and neuropathological study. *Dementia, 6*, 94–98.

Dori, H., & Henik, A. (2006). Indications for two attentional graients in endogenous visual-spatial attention. *Visual Cognition, 13*(2), 166–201.

Dricot, L., Sorger, B., Schiltz, C., Goebel, R., & Rossion, B. (2008). Evidence for individual face discrimination in non-face selective areas of the visual cortex in acquired prosopagnosia. *Behavioural Neurology, 18*, 75–79.

Driver, J., & Baylis, G. C. (1989). Movement and visual attention: The spotlight metaphor breaks down. *Journal of Experimental Psychology: Human Perception and Performance, 15*, 448–456.

Driver, J., Davis, G., Ricciardelli, P., Kidd, P., Maxwell, E., & Baron-Cohen, S. (1999). Gaze perception triggers reflexive visuospatial orienting. *Visual Cognition, 6*, 509–540.

Duchaine, B. C., Yovel, G., Butterworth, E. J., & Nakayama, K. (2006). Prosopagnosia as an impairment to face-specific mechanisms: Elimination of alternative hypotheses in a developmental case. *Cognitive Neuropsychology, 23*, 714–747.

Duncan, J. (1980). The locus of interference in the perception of simultaneous stimuli. *Psychological Review, 87*, 272–300.

Duncan, J. (1984). Selective attention and the organization of visual information. *Journal of Experimental Psychology: General, 113*, 501–517.

Duncan, J. (1987). Attention and reading: Wholes and parts in shape recognition. In M. Coltheart (Ed.), *Attention and performance XII*. London: Lawrence Erlbaum Associates Ltd.

Duncan, J. (1996). Coordinated brain systems in selection perception and action. In T. Inui & J. L. McClelland (Eds.), *Attention and performance XVI* (pp. 549–578). Cambridge, MA: MIT Press.

Dyer, F. N. (1973). The Stroop phenomenon and its use in the study of perceptual, cognitive, and response processes. *Memory and Cognition, 1*, 106–120.

Easton, T. A. (1973). On the normal use of reflexes. *American Scientist, 60*, 591–599.

Edelman, G. M., & Tononi, G. (2000). *A universe of consciousness: How matter becomes imagination*. New York: Basic Books.

Edelstyn, N. M., & Oyebode, F. (1999). A review of the phenomenology and cognitive neuropsychological origin of the Capgras syndrome. *International Journal of Geriatric Psychiatry, 14*, 48–59.

Edelstyn, N. M. J., Oyebode, F., Booker, E., & Humphreys, G. W. (1998). Facial processing and the delusional misidentification syndromes. *Cognitive Neuropsychiatry, 3*(4), 299–314.

Egly, R., Driver, J., & Rafal, R. D. (1994). Shifting visual attention between objects and locations: Evidence from normal and parietal lesion subjects. *Journal of Experimental Psychology: General, 123*, 161–177.

Ehinger, K., Hidalgo-Sotelo, B., Torralba, A., & Oliva, A. (2009). Modeling search for people in 900 scenes: A combined source model of eye guidance. *Visual Cognition, 17*, 945–978.

Eimer, M. (1997). Attentional selection and attentional gradients: An alternative method for studying transient visual-spatial attention. *Psychophysiology, 34*, 365–376.

Eimer, M., & Schlaghecken, F. (2002). Links between conscious awareness and response inhibition: Evidence from masked priming. *Psychonomic Bulletin & Review, 9*, 514–520.

Eimer, M., Schubo, A.,& Schlaghecken, F. (2002). The locus of inhibition in the masked priming of response alternatives. *Journal of Motor Behavior, 34*, 3–10.

Einhauser, W., & Konig, P. (2003). Does luminance-contrast contribute to a saliency map for overt visual attention? *European Journal of Neuroscience, 17*, 1089–1097.

Einhauser, W., Martin, K. A. C., & Konig, P. (2004). Are switches in perception of the Necker cube related to eye position? *European Journal of Neuroscience, 20*, 2811–2818.

Ellis, A., Young, A. W., Quayle, A. H., & de Pauw, K. W. (1997). Reduced autonomic responses to faces in Capgras delusion. *Proceedings of the Royal Society of London, Series B: Biological Science, 264*(1384), 1085–1092.

Elsner, A. (1978). Hue difference contours can be used in processing orientation information. *Perception and Psychophysics, 24*, 451–456.

Engel, A. K., & Singer, W. (2001). Temporal binding and the neural correlates of sensory awareness. *Trends in Cognitive Sciences, 5*(1), 16–52.

Enns, J. T. (2004). Object substitution and its relation to other forms of visual masking. *Vision Research, 44*, 1321–1331.

Enns, J. T., & Di Lollo, V. (2000). What's new in visual masking? *Trends in Cognitive Sciences, 4*, 345–352.

Enns, J.T., Lleras, A., & Di Lollo, V. (2006). A reentrant view of visual masking, object substitution, and response priming. In H. Ogmen & B. G. Breitmeyer (Eds.), *The first half second: The microgenesis and temporal dynamics of unconscious and conscious visual processes* (pp. 127–147). Cambridge, MA: MIT Press.

Epstein, C. M., Verson, R., & Zangaladze, A. (1996). Magnetic coil suppression of visual perception at an extracalcarine site. *Journal of Clinical Neurophysiology, 13,* 247–252.

Eriksen, B. A., & Eriksen, C. W. (1974). Effects of noise letters upon the identification of a target letter in a nonsearch task. *Perception & Psychophysics, 16,* 143–149.

Eriksen, C. W. (1966). Independence of successive inputs and uncorrelated error in visual form perception. *Journal of Experimental Psychology, 72,* 26–35.

Eriksen, C. W., & Hoffman, J. E. (1972). Temporal and spatial characteristics of selective encoding from visual displays. *Perception and Psychophysics, 12,* 201–204.

Eriksen, C. W., Pan, K., & Botella, J. (1994). Attentional distribution in visual space. *Psychological Research, 56,* 5–13.

Eriksen, C. W., & Yeh, Y. Y. (1985). Allocation of attention in the visual field. *Journal of Experimental Psychology: Human Perception and Performance 11,* 583–597.

Esterman, M., McGlinchey-Berroth, R., & Milberg, W. (2000). Preattentive and attentive visual search in individuals with hemispatial neglect. *Neuropsychology, 14*(4), 599–611.

Fagot, C., & Pashler, H. (1995). Repetition blindness: Perception or memory failure? *Journal of Experimental Psychology: Human Perception and Performance, 21,* 275–292.

Fahle, M. (1983). Binocular rivalry: Suppression depends on orientation and spatial frequency. *Vision Research, 22*(7), 787–800.

Fan, J., McCandliss, B. D., Sommer, T., Raz, A., & Posner, M. I. (2002). Testing the efficiency and independence of attentional networks. *Journal of Cognitive Neuroscience, 14,* 340–347.

Fang, F., & He, S. (2005). Cortical responses to invisible objects in the human dorsal and ventral pathways. *Nature Neuroscience, 8*(10), 1380–1385.

Farah, M. J. (1990). *Visual agnosia.* Cambridge, MA: MIT Press.

Farah, M. J., Monheit, M. A., & Wallace, M. A. (1991). Unconscious perception of "extinguished" visual stimuli: Reassessing the evidence. *Neuropsychologia, 29,* 949–958.

Faubert, J., Diaconu, V., Ptito, M., & Ptito, A. (1999). Residual vision in the blind field of hemidecorticated humans predicted by a diffusion scatter model and selective spectral absorption of the human eye. *Vision Research, 39*(1), 149–157.

Fei-Fei, L., Iyer, A., Koch, C., & Perona, P. (2007). What do we perceive in a glance of a real-world scene? *Journal of Vision, 7*(1), 1–29.

Feinberg, T. E. (2001). *Altered egos.* New York: Oxford University Press.

Feinberg, T. E., & Keenan, J. P. (2005). *The lost self: Pathologies of the brain and identity.* Oxford: Oxford University Press.

Feinberg, T. E., Roane, D. M., & Ali, J. (2000). Illusory limb movements in anosognosia for hemiplegia. *Journal of Neurology, Neurosurgery, and Psychiatry, 68,* 511–513.

Feinberg, T. E., Schindler, R. J., Ochoa, E., Kwan, P. C., & Farah, M. J. (1994). Associative visual agnosia and alexia without prosopagnosia. *Cortex: A Journal Devoted to the Study of the Nervous System and Behavior, 30*(3), 395–412.

Felleman, D. J., & van Essen, D. C. (1991). Distributed hierarchical processing in the primate cerebral cortex. *Cerebral Cortex, 1,* 1–47.

Fendrich, R., Wessinger, C. M., & Gazzaniga, M. S. (1992). Residual vision in a scotoma: Implications for blindsight. *Science, 258,* 1489–1491.

Fenske, M. J., & Eastwood, J. D. (2003). Modulation of focused attention by faces expressing emotion: evidence from flanker tasks. *Emotion, 3*(4), 327–343.

Findlay, J. M., & Walker, R. (1999). A model of saccade generation based on parallel processing and competitive inhibition. *Behavioral and Brain Sciences, 4,* 661–721.

Forster, B., Corballis, P. M., & Corballis, M. C. (2000). Effect of luminance on successive discrimination in the absence of the corpus callosum. *Neuropsychologia, 38*(4), 441–450.

Forstl, H., Almeida, O. P., & Iacoponi, E. (1991). Capgras delusion in the elderly: The evidence for a possible organic origin. *International Journal of Geriatric Psychiatry, 6,* 845–852.

Forstl, H., Almeida, O. P., Owen, A. M., Burns, A., & Howard, R. (1991). Psychiatric, neurological and medical aspects of misidentification syndromes: A review of 260 cases. *Psychological Medicine, 21,* 905–910.

Fotopoulou, A., Pernigo, S., Maeda, R., Rudd, A., & Kopelman, M. A. (2010). Implicit awareness in anosognosia for hemiplegia: Unconscious interference without conscious representation. *Brain: A Journal of Neurology, 133*(12), 3564–3577.

Fotopoulou, A., Rudd, A., Holmes, P., & Kopelman, M. (2009). Self-observation reinstates motor awareness in anosognosia for hemiplegia. *Neuropsychologia, 47*(5), 1256–1260.

Fox, E. (2002). Processing emotional facial expressions: The role of anxiety and awareness. *Cognitive, Affective, & Behavioral Neuroscience, 2*, 52–63.

Fox, M. D., Corbetta, M., Snyder, A. Z., Vincent, J. L., & Raichle, M. E. (2006). Spontaneous neuronal activity distinguishes human dorsal and ventral attention systems. *Proceedings of the National Academy of Arts and Sciences of the United States of America, 103*, 10046–10051.

Fox, M. D., Snyder, M. Z., Vincent, J. L., Corbetta, M., Van Essen, D. C., & Raichle, M. E. (2005). The human brain is intrinsically organized into dynamic, anticorrelated functional networks. *Proceedings for the National Academy of Sciences of the United States of America, 102*, 9673–9678.

Francis, G., & Cho, Y. S. (2006). Computational models of visual masking. In H. Ogmen & B. G. Breitmeyer (Eds.), *The first half second: The microgenesis and temporal dynamics of unconscious and conscious visual processes* (pp. 111–126). Cambridge, MA: MIT Press.

Francis, G., & Herzog, M. (2004). Testing quantitative models of backward masking. *Psychonomic Bulleting & Review, 11*, 104–112.

Franconeri , S. L., & Simons, D. J. (2003). Moving and looming stimuli capture attention. *Perception & Psychophysics, 65*, 999–1000.

Frazer, S. J., & Roberts, J. M. (1994). Three cases of Cagras' syndrome. *British Journal of Psychiatry, 164*, 557–559.

Friedenberg, J. (2008). *Artificial psychology: The quest for what it means to be human.* New York: Psychology Press.

Friedenberg, J. (2009). *Complexity, self-organization, and mind.* Litchfield Park, AZ: ISCE Publishing.

Friedenberg, J., & Bertamini, M. (2000). Contour symmetry detection: The influence of axis orientation and number of objects. *Psychologia, 105*(1), 107–118.

Friedman-Hill, S. R., Robertson, L. C., & Treisman, A. (1995). Parietal contributions to visual feature binding: Evidence from a patient with bilateral lesions. *Science, 269*, 853–855.

Friesen, C. K., & Kingstone, A. (1998). The eyes have it! Reflexive orienting is triggered by nonpredictive gaze. *Psychonomic Bulletin & Review, 5*, 490–495.

Frith, C., Perry, R., & Lumer, E. (1999). The neural correlates of conscious experience: An experimental framework. *Trends in Cognitive Sciences, 3*(3), 105–114.

Fu, S., Caggiano, D. M., Greenwood, P. M., & Parasuraman, R. (2005). Event-related potential reveal dissociable mechanisms for orienting and focusing visuospatial attention. *Cognitive Brain Research, 23*, 341–353.

Fuentes, L. J. (2004). Inhibitory processing in the attentional networks. In M. I. Posner (Ed.), *Cognitive neuroscience of attention* (pp. 45–55). New York: Guilford Press.

Fuentes, L. J., & Campoy, G. (2008). The time course of alerting effect over orienting in the attention network test. *Experimental Brain Research, 185*, 667–672.

Funnell, M. G., Corballis, P. M., & Gazzaniga, M. S. (1999). A deficit in perceptual matching in the left hemisphere of a callostomy patient. *Neuropsychologia, 37*(10), 1143–1154.

Fuster, J. M. (2003). *Cortex and mind.* Oxford: Oxford University Press.

Gabrieli, J. D. E., Poldrack, R. A., & Desmond, J. E. (1998). The role of left prefrontal cortex in language and memory. *Proceedings of the National Academy of Sciences of the United States of America, 95*, 906–913.

Gazzaniga, M. S., & Miller, M. B. (2009). The left hemisphere does not miss the right hemisphere. In S. Laureys & G. Tononi (Eds.), *The neurobiology of consciousness* (pp. 261–270). Amsterdam: Elsevier.

Geng, J. J., & Mangun, G. R. (2009). Anterior intraparietal sulcus is sensitive to bottom-up attention drive by stimulus salience. *Journal of Cognitive Neuroscience, 21*(8), 1584–1601.

Gerrits, H. J., de Haan, B., & Vendrik, A. J. (1966). Experiments with retinal stabilized images. Relations between the observations and neural data. *Vision Research, 6*, 427–440.

Gibson, J. J., & Radner, M. (1937). Adaptation, after- effect and contrast in the perception of tilted lines: I. Quantitative studies. *Journal of Experimental Psychology, 20*, 453–467.

Giesbrecht, B., Woldorff, M. G., Song, A. W., & Mangun, G. R. (2003). Neural mechanisms of top-down control during spatial and feature attention. *Neuroimage, 19*, 496–512.

Gitelman, D., Nobre, A., Parish, T., LaBar, K., Kim, Y. H., Meyer, J., & Mesalum, M. M. (1999). Large-scale distributed network for covert spatial attention: Further anatomical delineation based on stringent behavioral and cognitive controls. *Brain, 122*, 1093–1106.

Givre, S. J., Schroeder, C. E., & Arezzo, J. C. (1994). Contribution of extrastriate area V4 to the surface-recorded flash VEP in the awake macaque. *Vision Research, 34*, 415–428.

Goldsmith, M., & Yeari, M. (2003). Modulation of object-base attention by spatial focus under endogenous and exogenous orienting. *Journal of Experimental Psychology: Human Perception and Performance, 29*, 897–918.

Goldstein, E. B. (2010). *Sensation and perception* (8th ed.). Belmont, CA: Wadsworth.

Golla, H., Their, P., & Haarmeier, T. (2005). Disturbed overt but normal covert shifts of attention in adult cerebellar patients. *Brain, 128*, 1525–1535.

Goodale, M. A., & Milner, A. D. (1992). Separate visual pathways for perception and action. *Trends in Neuroscences, 15*, 20–25.

Goodale, M. A., & Milner, A. D. (1995). *The visual brain in action*. Oxford: Oxford University Press.

Goodale, M. A., Pelisson, D., & Prablanc, C. (1986). Large adjustments in visually guided reaching do not depend of vision of the hand of perception of target displacement. *Nature, 320*, 748–750.

Goolkasian, P., & Tarantino, M. (1999). Covert and overt attention and the processing of cues for location and target identification. *The Journal of General Psychology, 126*(3), 235–260.

Gray, J. A. (2004). *Consciousness: Creeping up on the hard problem*. New York: Oxford University Press.

Gregory, R. (1972). Cognitive contours. *Nature, 238*, 51–52.

Grossberg, S. (1987). Cortical dynamics of three-dimensional form, color, and brightness perception: I. Monocular theory. *Perception & Psychophysics, 41*, 87–116.

Grossberg, S., & Mingolla, E. (1985). Neural dynamics of form perception: Boundary completion, illusory figures, and neon color spreading. *Psychological Review, 92*, 173–211.

Gur, M., & Snodderly, D. M. (1997). Visual receptive fields of neurons in primary visual cortex (V1) move in space with the eye movements of fixation. *Vision Research, 37*(3), 257–265.

Gyulai, E. (2007). Motion-induced illusory contours: Priority of global aspects on motion perception. *Perceptual and Motor Skills, 105*, 1059–1074.

Haber, R. N. (1969). *Information processing approaches to visual perception and cognition*. New York: Holt, Rinehart, & Winston.

Hamm, A. O., Weike, A. I., Schupp, H. T., Treig, T., Dressel, A., & Kessler, C. (2003). Affective blindsight: Intact fear conditioning to a visual cue in a cortically blind patient. *Brain: A Journal of Neurology, 126*(2), 267–275.

Harms, L., & Bundesen, C. (1983). Color segregation and selective attention in a nonsearch task. *Perception & Psychophysics, 33*, 11–19.

Harris, A. L., & Morris, C. L. (2004). Repetition blindness: Out of sight or out of mind? *Journal of Experimental Psychology: Human Perception and Performance, 30*(5), 913–922.

Haynes, J. D., Deichmann, R., & Rees, G. (2005). Eye-specific effects of binocular rivalry in the human lateral geniculate nucleus. *Nature, 438*, 469–499.

Haynes, J. D., Driver, J., & Rees, G. (2005). Visibility reflects dynamic changes of effective connectivity between V1 and fusiform cortex. *Neuron, 46*, 811–821.

Hayward, W. G., Man, W., Zhou, G., and Harris, I. M. (2010). Repetition blindness for rotated objects. *Journal of Experimental Psychology: Human Perception and Performance, 36*(1), 57–73.

He, S., Cohen, E. R., & Hu, X. (1998). Close correlation between activity in brain area MT/V5 and the perception of a visual motion aftereffect. *Current Biology, 8*(22), 1215–1218.

He, X., Fan, S., Zhou, K., and Chen, L. (2004). Cue validity and object-based attention. *Journal of Cognitive Neuroscience, 16*(6), 1085–1097.

Heilman, K. M. (1979). Neglect and related disorders. In K. M. H. Valenstein (Ed.), *Clinical neuropsychology* (pp. 268–307). New York: Oxford University Press.

Heilman, K. M., Barrett, A. M., & Adair, J. C. (1998). Possible mechanisms of anosognosia: A defect in self-awareness. *Philosophical Transactions of the Royal Society of London B: Biological Sciences, 353*, 1903–1909.

Heilman, K. M., & Van Den Abell, T. (1980). Right hemisphere dominance for attention: The mechanisms underlying hemispheric asymmetries of inattention (neglect). *Neurology, 30*, 327–330.

Heiner, D., Schneider, W. X., & Paprotta, I. (1998). Selective dorsal and ventral processing: Evidence for a common attentional mechanism in reaching and perception. *Visual Cognition, 5*, 81–107.

Heinze, H. J., Mangun, G. R., Burchert, W., Hinrichs, H., Münte, T. E., Scholz, M., . . .

Henderson, J., & Macquistan, A. (1993). The spatial distribution of attention following an exogenous cue. *Perception & Psychophysics, 53*, 221–230.

Henderson, J. M., Weeks, P. A., & Hollingworth, A. (1999). The effects of semantic consistency on eye movements during complex scene viewing. *Journal of Experimental Psychology: Human Perception and Performance, 25*, 210–228.

Herculano-Houzel, S., Munk, M. H., Neuenschwander, S., & Singer, W. (1999). Precisely synchronized oscillatory firing patterns require electroencephalographic activation. *Journal of Neuroscience, 19*, 3992–4010.

Heywood, C. A., Gadotti, A., & Cowey, A. (1992). Cortical area V4 and its role in the perception of color. *Journal of Neuroscience, 12*, 4056–4065.

Hier, D. B., Davis, K. R., Richardson, E. P., & Mohr, J. P. (1977). Hypertensive putaminal hemorrhage. *Annals of Neurology, 1*, 189–207.

Hildebrandt, H., Schutze, C., Ebke, M., & Spang, K. (2004). Differential impact of parvocellular and magnocellular pathways on visual impairment in apperceptive agnosia? *Neurocase, 10*(3), 207–214.

Hillyard, S. A. (1994). Combined spatial and temporal imaging of brain activity during visual selective attention in humans. *Nature, 372*, 543–546.

Hillyard, S. A., Hink, R. F., Schwent, V. L., & Picton, T. W. (1973). Electric signs of selective attention in the human brain. *Science, 182*, 177–179.

Hillyard, S. A., Vogel, E. K., & Luck, S. J. (1999). Sensory gain control (amplification) as a mechanism of selective attention: Electrophysiological and neuroimaging evidence. In G. W. Humphreys, J. Duncan, & A. Treisman (Eds.), *Attention, Space, and Action: Studies in Neuroscience* (pp. 31–53). Oxford: Oxford University Press.

Hinton, G. E. (1981). A parallel computation that assigns canonical object-based frames of reference. In *Proceedings of the Seventh International Joint Conference on Artificial Intelligence* (pp. 683–685). Los Altos, CA: Morgan Kaufmann.

Hirose, N., & Osaka, N. (2010). Asymmetry in object substitution masking occurs relative to the direction of spatial attention shift. *Journal of Experimental Psychology: Human Perception and Performance, 36*(1), 25–37.

Hirstein, W., & Ramachandran, V. S. (1997). Capgras syndrome: A novel probe for understanding the neural representation of the identity and familiarity of persons. *Proceedings of the Royal Society of London, Series B: Biological Science, 264*(1380), 437–444.

Ho, M. C., & Atchley, P. (2009). Perceptual load modulates object-based attention. *Journal of Experimental Psychology: Human Perception and Performance, 35*(6), 1661–1669.

Hochberg, J. (1968). In the mind's eye. In R. N. Haber (Ed.), *Contemporary theory and research in visual perception* (pp. 309–331). New York: Holt, Rinehart, & Winston.

Hochberg, J. (1971). Perception I: Color and shape. In J. W. Kling & L. A. Riggs (Eds.), *Woodworth and Schlossberg's experimental psychology* (pp. 395–474). New York: Holt, Rinehart & Winston.

Hochberg, J. (1978). *Perception*. Englewood Cliffs, NJ: Prentice-Hall.

Hochberg, J., & Peterson, M. A. (1987). Piecemeal organization and cognitive components in object perception: Perceptually coupled responses to moving objects. *Journal of Experimental Psychology: General, 116*, 370–380.

Hochstein, S., & Ahissar, M. (2002). View from the top: Hierarchies and reverse hierarchies in the visual system. *Neuron, 36*, 791–804.

Hock, H. S., & Egeth, H. (1970). Verbal interference with encoding in a perceptual classification task. *Journal of Experimental Psychology, 83*, 209–303.

Hoffman, J. E., & Nelson, B. (1981). Spatial selectivity in visual search. *Perception and Psychophysics, 30*(3), 283–290.

Holcombe, A. O., & Cavanagh, P. (2001). Early binding of feature pairs for visual perception. *Nature Neuroscience, 4*, 127–128.

Holland, P. C. (1998). Temporal control in Pavlovian occasion setting. *Behavioural Processes, 44*(2), 225–236.

Hollingworth, A., & Henderson, J. M. (2002). Accurate visual memory for previously attended objects in natural scenes. *Journal of Experimental Psychology: Human Perception and Performance, 28,* 113–136.

Hommel, B., Kessler, K., Schmitz, F., Gross, J., Akyurek, E., Shapiro, K., & Schnitzler, A. (2006). How the brain blinks: towards a neurocognitive model of the attentional blink. *Psychological Research, 70,* 425–435.

Hood, B. M., Willen, J. D., & Driver, J. (1998). Adult's eyes trigger shifts of visual attention in human infants. *Psychological Science, 9*(2), 131–134.

Hopf, J. M., & Mangun, G. R. (2000). Shifting visual attention in space: An electrophysiological analysis using high spatial resolution mapping. *Clinical Neurophysiology, 111,* 1241–1257.

Horstmann, G. (2007). Preattentive face processing: What do visual search experiments with schematic faces tell us? *Visual Cognition, 15*(7), 799–833.

Horstmann, G., Borgstedt, K., & Heumann, M. (2006). Flanker effects with faces may depend on perceptual rather than emotional differences. *Emotion, 6,* 28–39.

Hotson, J., Braun, D., Herberg, W., & Boman, D. (1994). Transcranial magnetic stimulation extrastriate cortex degrades human motion direction discrimination. *Vision Research, 34,* 2215–2123.

Houck, M. R., & Hoffman, J. E. (1986). Conjunction of color and form without attention: Evidence from an orientation-contingent color aftereffect. *Journal of Experimental Psychology: Human Perception and Performance, 12*(2), 186–199.

Houghton, R. J., Macken, W. J., & Jones, D. M. (2003). Attention modulation of the visual motion aftereffect has a central cognitive locus: Evidence of interference by the postcategorical on the precategorical. *Journal of Experimental Psychology: Human Perception and Performance, 29*(4), 731–740.

Hubner, R., & Lehle, C. (2007). Strategies of flanker coprocessing in single and dual tasks. *Journal of Experimental Psychology: Human Perception and Performance, 33*(1), 103–123.

Humphrey, N. (2002). *The mind made flesh: Consciousness and the physical world.* Oxford: Oxford University Press.

Humphrey, N. (2006). *Seeing red: A study in consciousness.* Cambridge, MA: Belknap Press.

Humphreys, G. W. (1998). The neural representation of objects in space: A dual coding account. *Philosophical Transactions of the Royal Society, B353,* 1341–1351.

Humphreys, G. W., & Riddoch, M. J. (1987). The fractionation of visual agnosia. In G. W. Humphreys & M. J. Riddoch (Eds.), *Visual object processing: A cognitive neuropsychological approach* (pp. 281–306). Hove, UK: Erlbaum.

Hunt, C., Keogh, E., & French, C. C. (2006). Anxiety sensitivity: The role of conscious awareness and selective attentional bias to physical threat. *Emotion, 6,* 418–428.

Husain, M., & Kennard, C. (1996). Visual neglect associated with frontal lobe infraction. *Journal of Neurology, 243,* 652–657.

Husain, M., & Stein, J. (1988). Rezso Balint and his most celebrated case. *Archives of Neurology, 45,* 89–93.

Ignashchenkova, A., Dicke, P. W., Haarmeir, T., & Their, P. (2004). Neuro-specific contribution of the superior colliculus to overt and covert shifts of attention. *Nature Neuroscience, 7*(1), 56–64.

Ingle, D. (1973). Evolutionary perspectives on the function of the optic tectum. *Brain Behavior and Evolution, 8,* 211–237.

Iorio, C., Falanga, A., Fragassi, N. A., & Grossi, D. (1992). Visual associative agnosia and optic aphasia: A single case study and a review of the syndromes. *Cortex: A Journal Devoted to the Study of the Nervous System and Behavior, 28*(1), 23–37.

Ishai, A., Ungerleider, L. G., Martin, A., Schouten, J. L., & Haxby, J. V. (1999). Distributed representation of objects in the human ventral visual pathway. *Proceedings of the National Academy of Sciences of the United States of America, 96,* 9379–9384.

Itti, L., & Koch, C. (2000). A saliency-based search mechanisms for overt and covert shifts of visual attention. *Vision Research, 40,* 1489–1506.

Itti, L., & Koch, C. (2001). Computational modeling of visual attention. *Nature Reviews Neuroscience, 2*(3), 194–203.

Jackson, F. (1982). Epiphenomenal qualia. *Philosophical Quarterly, 32,* 127–136.

Jackson, G. M., Swainson, R., Mort, D., Husain, M., & Jackson, S. R. (2009). Attention, competition, and the parietal lobes: Insights from Balint's syndrome. *Psychological Research, 73,* 263–270.

James, W. (1890). *The principles of psychology.* New York: Dover Publications.

Janssen, E., Everaerd, W., Spiering, M., & Janssen, J. (2000). Automatic processes and the appraisal of sexual stimuli: Toward in information processing model of sexual arousal. *Journal of Sex Research, 37*, 8–23.

Jeannerod, M. (1994). The representing brain: Neural correlates of motor intention and imagery. *Brain and Behavioral Sciences, 17*, 187–245.

Jenkinson, P., & Fotopoulou, A. (2010). Motor awareness in anosognosia for hemiplegia: Experiments at last! *Experimental Brain Research, 204*(3), 295–304.

Jiang, Y., & Chun, M. M. (2001). Asymmetric object substitution masking. *Journal of Experimental Psychology: Human Perception and Performance, 27*, 895–918.

Johnston, J. C., Hochaus, L., & Ruthruff, E. (2002). Repetition blindness has a perceptual locus: Evidence from online processing of targets in RSVP streams. *Journal of Experimental Psychology: Human Perception and Performance, 28*, 477–489.

Johnston, W., & Heinz, S. P. (1978). Flexibility and the capacity demands of attention. *Journal of Experimental Psychology: General, 107*, 420–435.

Jolicoeur, P., Dell'Acqua, R., & Crebolder, J. (2000). Multitasking performance deficits: forging links between the attentional blink and the psychological refractory period. In S. Monsell & J. Driver (Eds.), *Control of cognitive processes: Attention and performance* (pp. 309–330). Cambridge, MA: MIT Press.

Jonides, J. (1981). Voluntary vs. automatic control over the mind's eye's movement. In J. B. Long & A. D. Baddeley (Eds.), *Attention and performance IX* (pp. 187–203). Hillsdale, NJ: Erlbaum.

Joseph, A. (1986). Cotard's syndrome in a patient with coexistent Capgras' syndrome, syndrome of subjective doubles, and palinopsia. *Journal of Clinical Psychiatry, 47*, 605–606.

Joseph, A., O'Leary, D. H., & Wheeler, H. G. (1990). Bilateral atrophy in Fregoli syndrome. *Journal of Clinical Psychiatry, 51*, 322–325.

Joubert, S., Felician, O., Barbeau, E., Sontheimer, A., Barton, J. J., Ceccaldi, M., & Poncet, M. (2003). Impaired configurational processing in a case of progressive prosopagnosia associated with predominant right temporal lobe atrophy. *Brain, 126*, 2537–2550.

Joung, W., & Latimer, C. (2003). Tilt aftereffects generated by symmetrical dot patterns with two or four axes of symmetry. *Spatial Vision, 16*(2), 155–182.

Joung, W., van der Zwan, R., & Latimer, C. (2000). Tilt aftereffects generated by bilaterally symmetrical patters. *Spatial Visions, 13*, 107–128.

Juola, J. F., Bouwhuis, D. G., Cooper, E. E., & Warner, C. B. (1991). Control of attention around the fovea. *Journal of Experimental Psychology: Human Perception and Performance, 17*(1), 125–141.

Juola, J. F., Koshino, H., & Warner, C. B. (1995). Tradeoffs between attentional effects of spatial cues and abrupt onsets. *Perception and Psychophysics, 37*, 333–342.

Kahneman, D. (1973). *Attention and effort*. Englewood Cliffs, NJ: Prentice-Hall.

Kamitani, Y., & Shimojo, S. (1999). Manifestation of scotomas created by transcranial magnetic stimulation of human visual cortex. *Nature Neuroscience, 2*(8), 767–771.

Kanizsa, G. (1955). Margini quasi-percettivi in campi con stimolazione omogenea. *Rivista di Psicologia, 49*, 7–20.

Kanizsa, G. (1975). The role of regularity in perceptual organization. In G. Flores d'Arcais (Ed.), *Studies in perception* (pp. 48–66). Florence, Italy: Martello.

Kanizsa, G. (1979). *Organization of vision: Essays in Gestalt perception*. New York: Praefer Press.

Kanizsa, G., & Gerbino, W. (1982). Amodal completion: Seeing or thinking? In J. Beck (Ed.), *Organization and representation in perception* (pp.167–190). Hillside, NJ: Erlbaum.

Kanwisher, N. (1987). Repetition blindness: Type recognition without token individuation. *Cognition, 27*, 117–143.

Kanwisher, N. (1991). Repetition blindness and illusory conjunctions: Errors in binding visual types with visual tokens. *Journal of Experimental Psychology: Human Perception and Performance, 17*, 404–421.

Kanwisher, N., McDermott, J., & Chum, M. M. (1997). The fusiform face area: A module in the human extrastriate cortex specialized for face perception. *Journal of Cognitive Neuroscience, 17*, 4302–4311.

Kanwisher, N., Yin, C., & Wojciulik, E. (1999). Repetition blindness for pictures: Evidence for the rapid computation of abstract visual descriptions. In V. Coltheart (Ed.), *Fleeting memories* (pp. 119–150). Cambridge, MA: MIT Press.

Kapadia, M. K., Westhimer, G., & Gilbert, C. D. (1999). Dynamics of spatial summation in primary visual cortex of alert monkeys. *Proceedings of National Academy of Sciences of the United States of America, 96,* 12073–12078.

Kaplan-Solms, K. L., & Solms, M. (2000). *Clinical studies in neuropsychoanalysis: Introduction of a depth neuropsychology.* London: Karnac Books.

Karnath, H. O. (1988). Deficits of attention in acute and recovered visual hemi-neglect. *Neuropsychologia, 26,* 27–43.

Kasamatsu, T., Polat, U., Pettet, M. W., & Norcia, A. M. (2001). Colinear facilitation promotes reliability of single-cell responses in cat striate cortex. *Experimental Brain Research, 138,* 163–172.

Kastner, S., De Weerd, P., Desimone, R., & Underleider, L. G. (1998). Mechanisms of directed attention in human extrastriate cortex during as revealed by functional MRI. *Science, 282,* 108–111.

Kellman, P. J., Guttman, S. E., & Wickens, T. D. (2001). Geometric and neural models of object perception. In T. F. Shipley & P. J. Kellman (Eds.), *From fragments to objects: Segmentation and grouping in vision* (pp. 183–245). New York: Elsevier.

Kellman, P. J., & Shipley, T. F. (1991). A theory of visual interpolation in object perception. *Cognitive Psychology, 23,* 141–221.

Kelly, D. H. (1983). Spatiotemporal variation of chromatic and achromatic contrast thresholds. *Journal of the Optical Society of America, 73,* 742–750.

Kelso, J.A.S. (1995). *Dynamic patterns: The self-organization of brain and behavior.* Cambridge, MA: MIT Press.

Kentridge, R. W., Heywood, C. A., & Weiskrantz, L. (1997). Residual vision in multiple retinal locations within a scotoma: Implications for blindsight. *Journal of Cognitive Neuroscience, 9,* 191–202.

Kentridge, R. W., Heywood, C. A., & Weiskrantz, L. (1999). Attention without awareness in blindsight. *Proceedings of the Royal Society of London Series B: Biological Sciences, 266,* 1805–1811.

Kim, Y. H., Gitelman, D. R., Nobre, A. C., Parrish, T. B., LaBar, K. S., & Mesulam, M. M. (1999). The large-scale neural network for special attention displays multifunctional overlap but differential asymmetry. *Neuroimage, 9,* 269–277.

Kimchi, R., & Peterson, M. A. (2008). Figment–ground segmentation can occur without attention. *Psychological Science, 19*(7), 660–668.

Kimura, M., & Katayama, J. (2005). Neural correlates of preattentive and attentive processing of visual changes. *NeuroReport: For Rapid Communication of Neuroscience Research, 16*(18), 2061–2064.

Kimura, S. (1986). Review of 106 cases with the syndrome of Capgras. *Bibliotheca Psychiatrica, 164,* 121–130.

Kincade, J. M., Abrams, R. A., Astafiev, S. V., Shulman, G. L., & Corbetta, M. (2005). An event-related functional magnetic resonance imaging study of voluntary and stimulus-driven orienting of attention. *The Journal of Neuroscience, 25*(18), 4593–4604.

King, S. M., Azzopardi, P., Cowey, A., Oxbury, J., & Oxbury, S. (1996). The role of light scatter in the residual visual sensitivity of patients with complete cerebral hemispherectomy. *Visual Neuroscience, 13,* 1–13.

Kinsbourne, M. (1987). Mechanisms of unilateral neglect. In M. Jeannerod (Ed.), *Neurophysiological and neuropsychological aspects of spatial neglect* (pp. 69–86). New York: North-Holland.

Kirov, G., Jones, P., & Lewis, S. W. (1994). Prevalence of delusional misidentification syndromes. *Psychopathology, 27,* 148–149.

Kitterle, F. L., & Thomas, J. (1980). The effects of spatial frequency, orientation and color upon binocular rivalry and monocular pattern alternation. *Bulletin of the Psychonomic Society, 16,* 406–407.

Kitzis, S. N. (2002). *Mind and meaning: A flight of imagination, a voyage of discovery.* Pacific Grove, CA: Wadsworth Thompson.

Kjaer, T. W., Nowak, M., Kjaer, K. W., Lou, A. R., & Lou, H. C. (2001). Precuneus-prefrontal activity during awareness of visual verbal stimuli. *Consciousness and Cognition: An International Journal, 10*(3), 356–365.

Koch, C. (2004). *The quest for consciousness: A neurobiological approach.* Englewood, CO: Roberts.

Koch, C., & Ullman, S. (1985). Shifts in selective visual attention: Towards the underlying neural circuitry. *Human Neurobiology, 4,* 219–227.

Kohler, W., & Wallach, H. (1944). Figural after-effects: An investigation of visual processes. *Proceedings of the American Philosophical Society, 88,* 269–357.

Knierim, J. J., & van Essen, D. C. (1992). Neuronal responses to static texture patterns ion area V1 of the alert macaque monkeys. *Journal of Neurophysiology, 67,* 961–980.

Komatsu, H. (2006). The neural mechanisms of perceptual filling-in. *Neuroscience, 7*, 220–231.

Koivisto, M., Hyona, J., & Revonsuo, A. (2004). The effects of eye movements, spatial attention, and stimulus features on inattentional blindness. *Vision Research, 44*(27), 3211–3221.

Komatsu, H., Kinoshita, M., & Murakami, I. (2000). Neural responses in the retinotopic representation of the blind spot in the macaque V1 to stimuli for perceptual filling-in. *The Journal of Neuroscience, 20*(24), 9310–9319.

Komatsu, H., Kinoshita, M., & Murakami, I. (2002). Neural responses in the primary visual cortex of the monkey during perceptual filling-in at the blind spot. *Neuroscience Research, 44*(3), 231–236.

Kornblum, S., Hasbroucq, T., & Osman, A. (1990). Dimensional overlap: Cognitive basis for stimulus–response compatibility—A model and taxonomy. *Psychological Review, 97*, 253–270.

Kornmeier, J., & Bach, M. (2004). Early neural activity in Necker-cube reversal: Evidence for low-level processing of gestalt phenomenon. *Psychophysiology, 41*, 1–8.

Koster, E. H., Crombez, G., Verschuere, B., & De Houwer, J. (2004). Selective attention to threat in the dot probe paradigm: Differentiating vigilance and difficulty to disengage. *Behaviour Research and Therapy, 42*, 1183–1192.

Kramer, A, F., & Jacobson, A. (1991). Perceptual organization and focused attention: The role of objects and proximity in visual processing. *Perception and Psychophysics, 50*, 267–284.

Kramer, A. F., & Watson, S. E. (1995). Object-based visual selection and the principle of uniform correctedness. In A. F. Kramer, M. G. H. Coles, & G. D. Logan (Eds.), *Converging operations in the study of visual selective attention* (pp. 395–414). Washington, D.C.: American Psychological Assoication.

Kravitz, D. J., & Behrmann, M. (2008). The space of an object: Attention alters the spatial gradient in the surround. *Journal of Experimental Psychology: Human Perception and Performance, 34*(2), 298–309.

Kress, T., & Daum, I. (2003). Developmental prosopagnosia: A review. *Behavioural Neurology, 14*, 109–121.

Krieger, G., Rentschler, I., Hauske, G., Schill, K., & Zetzsche, C. (2000). Object and scene analysis by saccadic eye-movements: An investigation with higher-order statistics. *Spatial Vision, 13*, 201–214.

Kroustallis, B. (2005). Blindsight. *Philosophical Psychology, 18*(1), 31–43.

Krubitzer, L. A. (1998). What can monotremes tell us about brain evolution? *Philosophical Transactions of the Royal Society of London, 353*, 1127–1146.

Kuhn, G., & Findlay, J. M. (2010). Misdirection, attention, and awareness: Inattentional blindness reveals temporal relationship between eye movements and visual awareness. *The Quarterly Journal of Experimental Psychology, 63*(1), 136–146.

Kusunoki, M., Gottlieb, J., & Goldberg, M. E. (2000). The lateral intraparietal area as a salience map: The representation of abrupt onset, stimulus motion, and task relevance. *Vision Research, 40*, 1459–1468.

Kwak, H., Dagenbach, D., & Egeth, H. (1991). Further evidence for a time-independent shift of the focus of attention. *Perception & Psychophysics, 49*(5), 473–480.

LaBerge, D., & Brown, V. (1989). Theory of attentional operations in shape identification. *Psychological Review, 96*(1), 101–124.

LaBerge, D., Brown, V., Carter, M., Bash, D., & Hatley, A. (1991). Reducing the effects of adjacent distractors by narrowing attention. *Journal of Experimental Psychology: Human Perception and Performance, 17*(1), 65–76.

Lamme, V. A. (2003). Why visual attention and awareness are different. *Trends in Cognitive Science, 7*, 12–18.

Lamme, V. A. F., & Roelfsema, P. R. (2000). The distinct modes of vision offered by feed-forward and recurrent processing. *Trends in Neurosciences, 23*, 571–579.

Lang, P. J. (1995). The emotion probe. *American Psychologist, 50*, 372–385.

Larsson, J., Amunts, K., Gulyas, B., Malikovic, A., Ziles, K., & Roland, P. E. (1999). Neuronal correlates of real and illusory contour perception: Functional anatomy with PET. *European Journal of Neuroscience, 11*, 4024–4036.

Lauwereyns, J. (1998). Exogenous/endogenous control of space-based/object-based attention: Four types of visual selection? *European Journal of Cognitive Psychology, 10*(1), 41–74.

LeDoux, J. E. (1996). *The emotional brain.* New York: Simon and Schuster.

LeDoux, J. E. (1998). *The emotional brain: The mysterious underpinnings of emotional life.* New York: Simon & Schuster.

Lee, H. L., & Vecera, S. P. (2005). Visual cognition influences early vision. The role of short-term memory in amodal completion. *Psychological Science, 16*(10), 763–768.

Lee, T. S., & Nguyen, M. (2001). Dynamics of subjective contour formation in the early visual cortex. *Proceedings of National Academy of Sciences of the United States of America, 98*, 1907–1911.

Leibovitch, F. S., Black, S. E., Caldwell, C. B., Ebert, P. L., Ehrlich, I. E., & Szalai, J. P. (1998). Brain–behavior correlations in hemispheral neglect using CT and SPECT. *Neurology, 50*, 901–908.

Levine, D. N., & Calvanio, R. (1989). Prosopagnosia: A defect in visual configural processing. *Brain and Cognition, 10*(2), 149–170.

Levy, J., Trevarthen, C., & Sperry, R. W. (1972). Perception of bilateral chimeric figures following hemispheric deconnexion. *Brain: A Journal of Neurology, 95*(1), 61–78.

Lewis, T. G. (2009). *Network science: Theory and practice.* Hoboken, NJ: Wiley.

Li, Z. (2002). A saliency map in primary visual cortex. *Trends in Cognitive Science, 6*, 9–16.

Likova, L. T., & Tyler, C. W. (2008). Occipital network for figure/ground organization. *Experimental Brain Research, 189*, 257–267.

Liu, G. T., Bolton, A. K., Price, B. H., & Weintraub, S. (1992). Dissociated perceptual-sensory and exploratory-motor neglect. *Journal of Neurology, Neurosurgery, and Psychiatry, 55*, 701–706.

Lleras, A., & Enns, J. T. (2004). Negative compatibility or object updating? A cautionary tale of mask-dependent priming. *Journal of Experimental Psychology: General, 133*, 475–493.

Lleras, A., & Enns, J. T. (2006). How much like a target can a mask be? Geometric, spatial, and temporal similarity in priming: A reply to Schlaghecken and Eimer (2006). *Journal of Experimental Psychology: General, 135*(3), 495–500.

Logan, G. D. (1980). Attention and automaticity in Stroop and priming tasks: Theory and data. *Cognitive Psychology, 12*, 523–553.

Logothetis, N. K. (1998). Single untis and conscious vision. *Philosophical Transactions of the Royal Society of London Series B, 353*, 1801–1818.

Logothetis, N. K., Leopold, D. A., & Sheinberg, D. L. (1996). What is rivaling during binocular rivalry? *Nature, 380*, 621–624.

Long, G. M., & Toppino, T. C. (1981). Multiple representations of the same reversible figure: Implications for cognitive decisional interpretations. *Perceptions, 10*, 231–234.

Long, G. M., Toppino, T. C., & Kostenbauder, J. F. (1983). As the cube turns: Evidence for two processes in the perception of a dynamic reversible figure. *Perception & Psychophysics, 34*, 29–38.

Lu, Z., & Dosher, B. A. (1998). External noise distinguishes attention mechanisms. *Vision Research, 38*(9), 1183–1198.

Luck, S. J., & Hillyard, S. A. (1994). Electrophysical correlates of feature analysis during visual search. *Psychophysiology, 31*, 291–308.

Luck, S. J., Hillyard, S. A., Mangun, G. R., & Gazzaniga, M. S. (1989). Independent hemispheric attentional systems mediate visual search in split-brain patients. *Nature, 342*, 543–545.

Luck, S. J., Hillyard, S. A., Mangun, G. R., & Gazzaniga, M. S. (1994). Independent attentional scanning in the separated hemispheres of split-brain patients. *Journal of Cognitive Neuroscience, 6*, 84–91.

Luiga, I., & Bachmann, T. (2007). Different effects of the two types of spatial pre-cueing: What precisely is 'attention' in Di Lollo's and Enns' substitution masking theory? *Psychological Research, 71*, 634–640.

Luria, A. R. (1959). Disorders of "simultaneous perception" in a case of bilateral occipito-parietal brain injury. *Brain, 83*, 437–449.

Mack, A. (2003). Inattentional blindness: Looking without seeing. *Current Directions in Psychological Science, 12*(5), 180–184.

Mack, A., & Rock, I. (1998). *Inattentional blindness.* Cambridge, MA: MIT Press.

Macknik, S. L., & Livingstone, M. S. (1998). Neuronal correlates of visibility and invisibility in the primate visual system. *Nature Neuroscience, 1*, 144–149.

MacLeod, C., & Hagan, R. (1992). Individual differences in the selective processing of threatening information, and emotional responses to a stressful life event. *Behaviour Research and Therapy, 30*, 151–161.

MacLeod, C., & Matthews, A. (1988). Anxiety and the allocation of attention to threat. *Quarterly Journal of Experimental Psychology, 40*, 653–670.

MacLeod, C., & Rutherford, E. M. (1992). Anxiety and the selective processing of emotional information: Mediating roles of awareness, trait and state variables, and personal relevance of stimulus materials. *Behaviour Research and Therapy, 30*, 479–491.

MacLeod, C. M. (1991). Half a century of research on the Stroop effect: An integrative review. *Psychological Bulletin, 109*(2), 163–203.

Madden, D. J., Turkington, T. G., Provenzale, J. M., Hawk, T. G., Hoffman, J. M., & Coleman, R. E. (1997). Selective and divided visual attention: Age-related changes in regional cerebral flow measured by $H_2^{15}O$ PET. *Human Brain Mapping, 5*(6), 389–409.

Maertens, M., & Pollmann, S. (2005). fMRI reveals a common neural substrate of illusory and real contours in V1 after perceptual learning. *Journal of Cognitive Neuroscience, 17*, 1553–1564.

Magnussen, S., & Mathiesen, T. (1989). Detection of moving and stationary gratings in the absence of the striate cortex. *Neuropsychologia, 27*, 725–728.

Mak, K. Y., Wong, C. W., & Lo, W. H. (1985). The Capgras syndrome in the Chinese. *Journal of the Hong Kong Psychiatric Association, 5*, 14–17.

Mangun, G. R., Hillyard, S. A., & Luck, S. J. (1993). Electrocortical substrates of visual selective attention. In: D. Meyer & S. Kornblum (Eds.), *Attention and Performance XIV* (pp. 219–243). Cambridge, MA: MIT Press.

Marcel, A. J. (1998). Blindsight and shape perception: Deficit of visual consciousness or of visual function? *Brain, 121*, 1565–1588.

Mark, V. (1996). Conflicting communicative behavior in a split-brain patient: Support for dual consciousness. In S. R. Hameroff (Ed.), *Towards a science of consciousness* (pp. 189–196). Cambridge, MA: MIT Press.

Mark, V. W., & Heilman, K. M. (1997). Diagonal neglect on cancellation. *Neuropsychologia, 35*, 1425–1436.

Marois, R., Chun, M. M., & Gore, J. C. (2000). Neural correlates of the attentional blink. *Neuron, 28*, 299–809.

Marr, D. (1982). *Vision*. San Francisco, CA: Freeman.

Martens, U., Ansorge, U., & Kiefer, M. (2011). Controlling the unconscious: attention task sets modulate subliminal semantic and visuomotor processes differentially. *Psychological Science, 22*(2), 282–291.

Marshall, J. C., & Halligan, P. W. (1993). Visuo-spatial neglect: A new copying test to assess perceptual parsing. *Journal of Neurology, 240*, 37–40.

Martinez-Conde, S., Macknik, S. L., & Hubel, D. H. (2004). The role of fixational eye movements in visual perception. *Nature Reviews Neuroscience, 5*, 229–240.

Marzi, C. A., Smania, N., Martini, M. C., Gambina, G., Tomelleri, G., Palmara, A., . . . Prior, M. (1996). Implicit redundant-targets' effect in visual extinction. *Neuropsychologia, 34*, 9–22.

Matchock, R. L., & Mordkoff, J. T. (2009). Chronotype and time-of-day influences on the alerting, orienting, and executive components of attention. *Experimental Brain Research, 192*, 189–198.

Mather, G., & Harris, J. (1998). Theoretical models of the motion after- effect. In G. Mather, F. A. J. Verstraten, & S. Anstis (Eds.), *The motion aftereffect: A modern perspective* (pp. 157–185). Cambridge, MA: MIT Press.

Mattingley, J. B., Pisella, L., Rossetti, Y., Rode, G., Tiliket, C., Boisson, D., & Vighetto, A. (2000). Visual extinction in oculocentric coordinates: A selective bias in dividing attention between hemifields. *Neurocase, 6*(6), 465–475.

Mattingley, J. B., Davis, G., & Driver, J. (1997). Preattentive filling-in of visual surfaces in parietal extinction. *Science, 275*, 671–674.

Mazoyer, B., Zago, L., & Mellet, E. (2001). Cortical networks for working memory and executive functions sustain the conscious resting state in man. *Brain Research Bulletin, 54*(3), 287–298.

McCollough, C. (1965). Color adaptation of edge-detectors in the human visual system. *Science, 149*, 1115–1116.

McCormick, B. H., & Mayerich, D. M. (2004). Three-dimensional imaging using knife-edge scanning microscope. *Microscopy and Microanalysis, 10*, 1466–1467.

Mcmains, S. A. (2006). Mechanisms for attending to multiple spatial locations: fMRI of divided visual attention. *Dissertation Abstracts International, 66*, 6306.

Melloni, L., Molina, C., Pena, M., Torres, D., Singer, W., & Rodriguez, E. (2007). Synchronization of neural activity across cortical areas correlates with conscious perception. *Journal of Neuroscience, 27*, 2858–2865.

Memmert, D. (2006). The effects of eye movements, age, and expertise on inattentional blindness. *Consciousness and Cognition: An International Journal, 15*(3), 620–627.

Mendola, J. D., Conner, I. P., Sharma, S., Bahekar, A., & Lemieux, S. (2006). fMRI measures of perceptual filling-in in the human visual cortex. *Journal of Cognitive Neuroscience, 18*(3), 363–375.

Meng, M., Remus, D. A., & Tong, F. (2005). Filling-in of visual phantoms in the human brain. *Nature Neuroscience, 8*, 1248–1254.

Meng, M., & Tong, F. (2004). Can attention selectively bias bistable perception? Differences between binocular rivalry and ambiguous figures. *Journal of Vision, 4*, 539–551.

Mentis M. J., Weinstein E. A., Horwitz B., McIntosh A. R., Pietrini P., Alexander G. E., . . . Murphy, D. G. M. (1995). Abnormal brain glucose metabolism in the delusional misidentification syndromes: a positron emission tomography study in Alzheimer disease. *Biological Psychiatry, 38*, 438–449.

Merigan, W. H., & Maunsell, J. H. R. (1993). How parallel are the primate visual pathways? *Annual Review of Neuroscience, 16*, 369–402.

Mesulam, M. M. (1981). A cortical network for directed attention and unilateral neglect. *Annals of Neurology 10*, 309–325.

Mesulam, M. M. (1990). Large-scale neuro-cognitive networks and distributed processing for attention, language, and memory. *Annals of Neurology, 28*, 597–613.

Meyer, D. E., & Schvaneveldt, R. W. (1971). Facilitation in recognizing pairs of words: Evidence of a dependence between retrieval operations. *Journal of Experimental Psychology, 90*, 227–234.

Michotte, A., Thines, G., Costall, A., & Butterworth, G. (1991). *Michotte's experimental phenomenology of perception*. Hillsdale, NJ: Erlbaum.

Miller, G. A. (1962). *Psychology: The science of mental life*. New York: Harper & Row.

Miller, J. (1991). The flanker compatibility effect as a function of visual angle, attentional focus, visual transients, and perceptual load: A search for boundary conditions. *Perception & Psychophysics, 49*, 270–288.

Miller, M. B., & Valsangkar-Smyth, M. (2005). Probability matching in the right hemisphere. *Brain & Cognition, 57*(2), 165–167.

Milner, B. (1962). Les troubles de la memoire accompagnant des lesions hippocampiques bilaterales [Memory impairment accompanying bilateral hippocampal lesions]. In *Psychologie de l'hippocampe*. Paris: Centre National de la Recherche Scientifique.

Milner, A. D. (1998). Insights in blindsight. *Trends in Cognitive Science, 7*, 237–238.

Milner, A. D., & Goodale, M. A. (1995). *The visual brain in action*. New York: Oxford University Press.

Milner, A. D., Perrett, D. I., Johnston, R. S., Benson, P. J., Jordan, T. R., Heeley, D. W., . . . Davidson, D. L. W. (1991). Perception and action in "visual form agnosie". *Brain, 114*, 405–428.

Mitroff, S. R., Simons, D. J., & Levin, D. T. (2004). Nothing compares 2 views: Change blindness can occur despite preserved access to changed information. *Perception and Psychophysics, 66*, 1268–1281.

Mogg, K., & Bradley, B. P. (2002). Selective orienting of attention to masked threat faces in social anxiety. *Behaviour Research and Therapy, 40*, 1403–1414.

Moldakarimov, S., Bazhenov, M., & Sejnowski, T. (2010). Representation sharpening can explain perceptual priming. *Neural Computation, 22*(5), 1312–1322.

Montaser-Kouhsari, L., Landy, M. S., Heeger, D. J., & Larsson, J. (2007). Orientation-selective adaptation to illusory contours in human visual cortex. *Journal of Neuroscience, 27*, 2186–2195.

Moody, T. C. (1994). Conversations with zombies. *Journal of Consciousness Studies, 1*(2), 196–200.

Moore, C., & Corkum, V. (1998). Infant gaze following based on eye direction. *British Journal of Developmental Psychology, 16*, 495–503.

Moore, C. M., & Egeth, H. (1997). Perception without attention: Evidence of grouping under conditions of inattention. *Journal of Experimental Psychology: Human Perception and Performance, 23*(2), 339–352.

Moore, C. M., & Lleras, A. (2005). On the role of object representation in substitution masking. *Journal of Experimental Psychology: Human Perception and Performance, 29*, 106–120.

Morland, A. B., Jones, S. R., Finlay, A. L., Deyzac, E., Le, S., & Kemps, S. (1999). Visual perception of motion, luminance, and colour in a human hemianope. *Brain, 122*(6), 1183–1198.

Morris, A. L., & Still, M. L. (2008). Now you see it, now you don't: Repetition blindness for nonwords. *Journal of Experimental Psychology: Learning, Memory, and Cognition, 34*(1), 146–166.

Morton, J., & Chambers, S. M. (1973). Selective attention to words and colours. *Quarterly Journal of Experimental Psychology, 25*, 387–397.

Most, S. B., Simons, D. J., Scholl, B. J., Jimanez, R., Clifford, E., & Chabris, C. F. (2001). How not to be seen: The contribution of similarity and selective ignoring to sustained inattentional blindness. *Psychological Science, 12*(1), 9–17.

Moutoussis, K., & Zeki, S. (2002). The relationship between cortical activation and perception investigated with invisible stimuli. *Proceedings of the National Academy of Sciences of the United States of America, 99*, 99527–9532.

Munk, M. H. J., Roelfsema, P. R., Konig, P., Engel, A. K., & Singer, W. (1996). Roles of reticular activation in the modulation of intracortical synchronization. *Science, 272*, 271–274.

Murphy, S. T., Monahan, J. L., & Zajonc, R. B. (1995). Additivity of nonconscious affect: Combined effects of priming and exposure. *Journal of Personality and Social Psychology, 69*, 589–602.

Murphy, S. T., & Zajonc, R. B. (1993). Affect, cognition, and awareness: Affective priming and suboptimal stimulus exposure. *Journal of Personality and Social Psychology, 64*, 723–739.

Naccache, L., Blandin, E., & Dehaene, S. (2002). Unconscious masked priming depends on temporal attention. *Psychological Science, 13*, 416–424.

Nagel, T. (1974). What is it like to be a bat? *Philosophical Review, 83*, 435–450.

Nawrot, M. (2003). Disorders of motion and depth. *Neurologic Clinics, 21*(3), 609–629.

Nebes, R. D. (1972). Dominance of the minor hemisphere in commissurotomized man on a test of figural unification. *Brain: A Journal of Neurology, 95*(3), 633–638.

Nebes, R. D. (1973). Perception of spatial relationships by the right and left hemispheres in commissurotomized man. *Neuropsychologia, 11*(3), 285–289.

Neisser, U. (1967). *Cognitive psychology*. New York: Appleton-Century-Crofts.

Neumann, H., Pessoa, L., & Hansen, T. (2001). Visual filling-in for computing perceptual surface properties. *Biological Cybernetics, 85*, 355–369.

Nguyen, V. A., Freeman, A. W., & Alais, D. (2003). Increasing depth of binocular rivalry suppression along two visual pathways. *Vision Research, 43*, 2003–2008.

Nilsson, R., & Perris, C. (1971). The Capgras Syndrome: A case report. *Acta Psychiatrica Scandinavica, 47*, 53–58.

Noguchi, Y., Inui, K., & Kakigi, R. (2004). Temporal dynamics of neural adaptation effect in the human visual ventral stream. *The Journal of Neuroscience, 24(28)*, 6283–6290.

Norman, D. A. (1968). Toward a theory of memory and attention. *Psychological Review, 75*, 522–536.

Norretranders, T. (1999). *The user illusion*. New York: Penguin.

Nothdurft, H. C. (1993). Faces and facial expressions do not pop out. *Perception, 22*, 1287–1298.

Nothdurft, H. C. (2000). Salience from feature contrast: Additivity across dimensions. *Vision Research, 40*, 1183–1202.

Odom-White, A., de Leon, J., Stanilla, J., Cloud, B. S., & Simpson, G. M. (1995). Misidentification syndromes in schizophrenia: Case reviews with implications for classification and prevalence. *Austria New Zealand Journal of Psychiatry, 29*, 63–68.

Ohman, A., Lunqvist, D., & Esteves, F. (2001). The face in the crowd revisited: A threat advantage to schematic stimuli. *Journal of Personality and Social Psychology, 80*, 381–396.

Oliva, A., & Schyns, P. G. (1997). Coarse blobs or fine edges? Evidence that information diagnosticity changes the perception of complex visual stimuli. *Cognitive Psychology, 34*(1), 72–107.

Olivers, N. L., & Nieuwenhuis, S. (2005). The beneficial effect of concurrent task-irrelevant mental activity on temporal attention. *Psychological Science, 16*(4), 265–269.

Orbach, J., Zucker, E., & Olson, R. (1966). Reversibility of the Necker cube: VII. Reversal rate as a function of figure-on and figure-off durations. *Perceptual and Motor Skills, 22*, 615–618.

Oyebode, F., & Sargeant, R. (1996). Delusional misidentification syndromes: A descriptive study. *Psychopathology, 29*, 209–214.

Paffen, L. E., Alais, D., & Verstraten, F. A. J. (2006). Attention speeds binocular rivalry. *Psychological Science, 17*(9), 753–756.

Paillere-Martinot, M. L., Dao-Castellana, M. H., Masure, M. C., Pillong, B., & Martinot, J. L. (1994). Delusional misidentification: A clinical, neuropsychological and brain imaging case study. *Psychopathology, 27*, 200–210.

Palmer, S., & Rock, I. (1994). Rethinking perceptual organization: The role of uniform connectedness. *Psychonomic Bulletin and Review, 1*, 29–55.

Palmer, S. E., Neff, J., & Beck, D. (1996). Late influences on perceptual grouping: Amodal completion. *Psychonomic Bulletin & Review, 3*, 75–80.

Paquet, L., & Lortie, C. (1990). Evidence for early selection: Precuing target location reduces interferences from same-category distractors. *Perception & Psychophysics, 48*, 382–388.

Paradiso, M. A., & Nakayama, K. (1991). Brightness perception and filling-in. *Vision Research, 31*, 1221–1236.

Paradiso, M. A., Shimojo, S., & Nakayama, K. (1989). Subjective contour, tilt aftereffects and visual cortical organization. *Vision Research, 29*(9), 1205–1213.

Parkhurst, D., Law, K., & Niebur, E. (2002). Modelling the role salience in the allocation of overt visual attention. *Vision Research, 42*, 107–123.

Parkin, A. J. (1996). *Explorations in cognitive neuropsychology*. London: Psychology Press.

Pascual-Leone, A., & Walsh, V. (2001). Fast backprojections from the motion to the primary visual area necessary for visual awareness. *Science, 292*, 510–512.

Pashler, H. (1995). Attention and visual perception: Analyzing divided attention. In S. M. Kosslyn & D. N. Osherson (Eds.), *An invitation to cognitive science* (pp. 71–100). Cambridge, MA: MIT Press.

Pashler, H. E. (1998). *The psychology of attention*. Cambridge, MA: MIT Press.

Pashler, H., & Badgio, P. C. (1985). Visual attention and stimulus identification. *Journal of Experimental Psychology: Human Perception and Performance, 10*, 429–448.

Pashler, H., & Badgio, P. C. (1987). Attentional issues in the identification of alphanumeric characters. In M. Coltheart (Ed.), *Attention and performance XI: The psychology of reading* (pp. 63–81). Hillsdale, NJ: Erlbaum.

Pasternak, T., & Merigan, W. H. (1994). Motion perception following lesions of the superior temporal sulcus in the monkey. *Cerebral Cortex, 4*, 247–259.

Peterhans, E., & von der Heydt, R. (1989). Subjective contours—bridging the gap between psychophysics and physiology. *Trends in Neuroscience, 14*, 112–119.

Peterson, M. A., & Hochberg, J. (1983). Opposed-set measurement procedure: A quantitative analysis of the roles of local cues and intention in form perception. *Journal of Experimental Psychology: Human Perception and Performance, 9*, 183–193.

Polonsky, A., Blake, R., Braun, J., & Heeger, D. J. (2000). Neuronal activity in human primary visual cortex correlates with perception during binocular rivalry. *Nature Neuroscience, 3*, 1153–1159.

Polat, U., Mizobe, K., Pettet, M. W., Kasamatsu, T., & Norcia, A. M. (1998). Collinear stimuli regulate visual responses depending on cell's contrast threshold. *Nature, 391*, 580–584.

Posner, M. I. (1978). *Chronometric explorations of mind*. Hillsdale, NJ: Erlbaum.

Posner, M. I. (1980a). Attention and detection of signals. *Journal of Experimental Psychology: General, 109*(2), 160–174.

Posner, M. I. (1980b). Orienting of attention. *Quarterly Journal of Experimental Psychology, 32*, 3–25.

Posner, M. I. (1994). Attention: The mechanisms of consciousness. *Procedures of the National Academy of Science, 91*, 7398–7403.

Posner, M. I., & Dehaene, S. (1994). Attentional networks. *Trends in Neuroscience, 17*, 75–79.

Posner, M. I., Inhoff, A. W., Friedrich, F. J., & Cohen, A. (1987). Isolating attentional systems: A cognitive-anatomical analysis. *Psychobiology, 15*(2), 107–121.

Posner, M. I., & Petersen, S. E. (1990). The attention system of the human brain. *Annual Review of Neuroscience, 13*, 25–42.

Posner, M. I., & Snyder, C. R. R. (1975). Facilitation and inhibition in the processing of signals. In P. M. A. Rabbitt & S. Dormic (Eds.), *Attention and performance V*. New York: Academic Press.

Posner, M. I., Snyder, C. R. R., & Davidson, B. (1980). Attention and the detection of signals. *Journal of Experimental Psychology: General, 109*, 160–174.

Potter, M. C. (1999). Understanding sentences and scenes: The role of conceptual short term memory. In V. Coltheart (Ed.), *Fleeting memories: Cognition of brief visual stimuli* (pp. 13–46). Cambridge, MA: MIT Press.

Pribram, K. H. (1999). Brain and the composition of conscious experience. *Journal of Consciousness Studies, 6*, 19–42.

Puce, A., Allison, T., Gore, J. C., & McCarthy, G. (1995). Face-sensitive regions in human extrastriate cortex studied by functional MRI. *Journal of Neurophysiology, 74*, 1192–1199.

Purmann, S., Badde, S., Luna-Rodriguez, A., & Wendt, M. (2011). Adaptation to frequent conflict in the Eriksen Flanker task: An ERP study. *Journal of Psychophysiology, 25*(2), 50–59.

Qiu, F. T., Sugihara, T., & von der Heydt, R. (2007). Figure–ground mechanisms provide structure for selective attention. *Nature Neuroscience, 10*(11), 1493–1499.

Rafal, R. (2002). Control of visuomotor reflexes. In D. T. Studd & R. T. Knight (Eds.), *Principles of frontal lobe function* (pp. 149–158). New York: Oxford University Press.

Rafal, R., Danziger, S., Grossi, G., Machado, L., & Ward, R. (2002). Visual attention is gated by attending for action: Evidence from hemispatial neglect. Proceedings of the National Academy of Sciences of the United States of America, *99(25)*, 16371–16375.

Ramachandran, V. S. (1992). Filling in gaps in perception: Part I. *Current Directions in Psychological Science, 1*, 199–205.

Ramachandran, V. S. (1993). Filling in gaps in perception: Part II. Scotomas and phantom limbs. *Current Directions in Psychological Science, 2*(2), 56–65.

Ramachandran, V. S. (1995). Anosognosia in parietal lobe syndrome. *Consciousness and Cognition, 4*, 22–51.

Ramachandran, V. S., & Blakeslee, S. (1998). *Phantoms in the brain: Human nature and the architecture of the mind.* London: Fourth Estate.

Ramachandran, V. S., & Cobb, S. (1995). Visual attention modulates metacontrast masking. *Nature, 373*, 66–68.

Ramachandran, V. S., Gregory, R. L., & Aiken, W. (1993). Perceptual fading of visual texture borders. *Vision Research, 33*, 717–721.

Ramsden, B. M., Hung, C. P., & Roe, A. W. (2001). Real and illusory contour processing in area V1 of the primate: A cortical balancing act. *Cerebral Cortex, 11*, 648–665.

Rees, G. (2008). The anatomy of blindsight. *Brain, 131*(6), 1414–1415.

Rees, G. (2009). Visual awareness. In M. S. Gazzaniga, E. Bizzi, L. M. Chalupa, S. T. Grafton, T. F. Heatherton, C. Koch, & B. A. Wandell (Eds.), *The cognitive neurosciences*, (4th ed., pp. 1151–1163). Cambridge, MA: MIT Press.

Rees, G., & Heeger, D. J. (2003). Neuronal correlates of perception in early visual cortex. *Nature Neuroscience, 6*, 414–420.

Reinagel, P., & Zador, A. M. (1999). Natural scene statistics at the center of gaze. *Network: Computation in Neural Systems, 10*, 341–350.

Reisberg, D., & O'Shaughnessy, M. (1984). Diverting subjects' concentration slows figural reversals. *Percption, 13*, 461–468.

Rensink, R. A. (2004). Visual sensing without seeing. *Psychological Science, 15*, 27–32.

Rensink, R. A., & Enns, J. T. (1998). Early completion of occluded objects. *Vision Research, 38*, 2498–2505.

Rensink, R. A., O'Regan, K., & Clark, J. (1997). To see or not to see: The need for attention to perceive changes in scenes. *Psychological Science, 8*(5), 368–373.

Riddoch, M. J., Johnston, R. A., Bracewell, R. M., Boutsen, L., Humphreys, G. W. (2008). Are faces special? A case of pure prosopagnosia. *Cognitive Neuropsychology, 25*(1), 3–26.

Riggs, L. A., & Day, R. H. (1980). Visual aftereffects derived from inspection of orthogonally moving patterns. *Science, 208*, 416–418.

Rizzolatti, G., Riggio, L., & Sheliga, B. M. (1994). Space and selective attention. In C. Umilta & M. Moscovitch (Eds.), *Attention and performance XV: Conscious and nonconscious information processing* (pp. 231–265). Cambridge, MA: MIT Press.

Ro, T. M., Kanwisher, L., Rafal, N., & Robert, D. (2002). Covert orienting to the location of targets and distractors: Effects on response channel activation in a flanker task. *The Quarterly Journal of Experimental Psychology A: Human Experimental Psychology, 55A*(3), 917–936.

Rock, I., & Anson, R. (1979). Illusory contours as the solution to a problem. *Perception, 8*, 665–681.

Roelfsema, P. R., Engel, A. K., Konig, P., & Singer, W. (1997). Visuomotor integration is associated with zero time-lag synchronization among cortical areas. *Nature, 385*, 157–161.

Rolls, E. T. (2006). Consciousness absent and present: A neurophysiological exploration of masking. In H. Ogmen & B. G. Breitmeyer (Eds.), *The first half second: The microgenesis and temporal dynamics of unconscious and conscious visual processes* (pp. 89–108). Cambridge: MIT Press.

Rolls, E. T., & Tovee, M. J. (1994). Processing speed in the cerebral cortex, and the neurophysiology of visual masking. *Proceedings of the Royal Society of London, B, 257*, 9–15.

Rolls, E. T., Tovee, M. J., & Panzeri, S. (1999). The neurophysiology of backward visual masking: Information analysis. *Journal of Cognitive Neuroscience, 11*(3), 300–311.

Rolls, E. T., Tovee, M. J., Purcell, D. G., Stewart, A. L., & Azzopardi, P. (1994). The responses of neurons in the temporal cortex of primates and face identification and detection. *Experimental Brain Research, 101*, 473–484.

Roser, M. E., Fugelsang, J. A., Dunbar, K. N., Corballis, P. M., & Gazzaniga, M. S. (2005). Dissociating processes supporting causal perception and causal inference in the brain. *Neuropsychologia, 19*(5), 591–602.

Rotteveel, M., de Groot, P., Geutskens, A., & Hans Phaf, R. (2001). Stronger suboptimal than optimal affective priming? *Emotion, 1*(4), 348–364.

Rubin, E. (1958). Figure and ground. In D. C. Beardsless & M. Wertheimer (Eds.), *Readings in perception* (pp. 194–203). Princeton, NJ: Van Nostrand. (Original work published 1915.)

Rudolph, K., & Pasternak, T. (1999). Transient and permanent deficits in motion perception after lesions of cortical areas MT and MST in the macaque monkey. *Cerebral Cortex, 9*, 90–100.

Sacks, O. (1985). *The man who mistook his wife for a hat.* New York: Harper & Row.

Sacks, O. (1996). *An anthropologist on Mars: Seven paradoxical tales.* New York: Knopf.

Sakaguchi, Y. (2001). Target/surround asymmetry in perceptual filling-in. *Vision Research, 41*, 2065–2077.

Sary, G., Koteles, K., Kaposvari, P., Lenti, L., Csifcsak, G., Franko, E., . . . Tompa, T. (2008). The representation of Kanizsa illusory contours in the monkey inferior temporal cortex. *European Journal of Neuroscience, 28*, 2137–2146.

Sasaki, Y., & Watanabe, T. (2004). The primary visual cortex fills in color. *Proceedings of the National Academy of Sciences, 101*, 18251–18256.

Sautter, S. W., Briscoe, L., & Farkas, K. (1991). A neuropsychological profile of Capgras syndrome. *Neuropsychology, 5*(3), 139–150.

Schacter, D. L. (1990). Toward a cognitive neuropsychology of awareness: Implicit knowledge and anosognosia. *Journal of Clinical and Experimental Neuropsychology, 12*, 155–178.

Schacter, D. L. (1992). Implicit knowledge: New perspectives on unconscious processes. *Proceedings of the National Academy of Sciences of the United States of America, 89*, 11113–11117.

Scharli, H., Brugger, P., Regard, M., Mohr, C., & Landis, T. (2003). Localisation of "unseen" visual stimuli: Blindsight in normal observers? *Swiss Journal of Psychology, 62*(3), 159–165.

Schenk, T., Mai, N., Ditterich, J., & Zihi, J. (2000). Can a motion-blind patient reach for moving objects? *Journal of Neuroscience, 12*, 3351–3360.

Schenk, T., & Zihl, J. (1997). Visual motion perception after brain damage: II. Deficits in global motion perception. *Neuropsychologia, 35*, 1289–1297.

Schlaghecken, F., & Eimer, M. (2006). Active masks and active inhibition: A comment on Lleras and Enns (2004) and on Verleger, Jaskowski, Aydemir, van der Lubbe, and Groen (2004). *Journal of Experimental Psychology: General, 135*(3), 484–494.

Schmalzl, L., Palermo, R., Harris, I. M., & Coltheart, M. (2009). Face inversion superiority in a case of prosopagnosia following congenital brain abnormalities: What can it tell us about the specificity and origin of face-processing mechanisms? *Cognitive Neurophysiology, 26*(3), 286–306.

Schneider, W. X. (1995). VAM: A neuro-cognitive model for visual attention control of segmentation, object recognition, and space-based motor action. *Visual Cognition, 2*, 231–375.

Schutter, D. (2008). Antidepressant efficacy of high-frequency transcranial magnetic stimulation over the left dorsolateral prefrontal cortex in double-blind sham-controlled designs: a meta-analysis. *Psychological Medicine, 39*(1), 65–75.

Schwartz, D. P., Badier, J. M., Bihoue, P., & Bouliou, A. (1999). Evaluation of a new MEG–EEG spatio-temporal localization approach using a realistic source model. *Brain Topography, 11*, 279–289.

Seiss, E., & Praamstra, P. (2004). The basal ganglia and inhibitory mechanisms in response selection: Evidence from subliminal priming of motor responses in Parkinson's disease. *Brain, 127*, 330–339.

Sejnowski, T. J., & Hinton, G. E. (1987). Separating figure from ground with a Boltzmann machine. In M. A. Arbib & A. R. Hanson (Eds.), *Vision, brain, and cooperative computation* (pp. 703–724). Cambridge, MA: MIT Press.

Seki, K., & Ishii, S. (1996). Diverse patterns of performance in copying and severity of unilateral spatial neglect. *Journal of Neurology, 243*, 1–8.

Sergent, J. (1988). An investigation into perceptual completion in blind areas of the visual field. *Brain, 111*, 347–373.

Sergent, C., Baillet, S., & Dehaene, S. (2005). Timing of the brain events underlying access to consciousness during the attentional blink. *Nature Neuroscience, 8*(10), 1391–1400.

Sergent, C., & Dehaene, S. (2004). Is consciousness a gradual phenomenon? Evidence for an all-or-none bifurcation during the attentional blink. *Psychological Science, 15*(11), 720–728.

Shapiro, K. L. (1994). The attentional blink: The brain's "eyeblink." *Psychological Science 3*(3), 86–89.

Shapiro, K. L., Raymond, J. E., & Arnell, K. A. (1994). Attention to visual pattern information produces the attentional blink in RSVP. *Journal of Experimental Psychology: Human Perception and Performance, 20*, 357–371.

Shelley-Tremblay, J., & Mack, A. (1999). Metacontrast masking and attention. *Psychological Science, 10*(6), 508–515.

Shelton, P. A., Bowers, D., Duara, R., & Heilman, K. M. (1994). Apperceptive visual agnosia: A case study. *Brain and Cognition, 25*(1), 1–23.

Shepherd, M., & Muller, H. J. (1989). Movement versus focusing of visual attention. *Perception & Psychophysics, 46*, 146–154.

Sheth, B. R., Sharma, J., Rao, S. C., & Sur, M. (1996). Orientation maps of subjective contours in visual cortex 18. *Science, 274*, 2110–2115.

Shiffrin, R. A., & Gardner, G. T. (1972). Visual processing capacity and attentional control. *Journal of Experimental Psychology, 93*(1), 72–82.

Shipp, S. (2004). The brain circuitry of attention. *Trends in Cognitive Science, 8*(5), 223–230.

Shulman, G. L., & Wilson, J. (1987a). Spatial frequency and selective attention to local and global information. *Perception, 16*, 89–101.

Shulman, G. L., & Wilson, J. (1987b). Spatial frequency and selective attention. *Perception, 16*, 103–111.

Siegel S., Allan, L. G., & Eissenberg, T. (1992). The associative basis of contingent color aftereffects. *Journal of Experimental Psychology: General, 121*(1), 79–94.

Siegel, S., Allan, L. G., & Eissenberg, T. (1994). Scanning and form-contingent color aftereffects. *Journal of Experimental Psychology: General, 123*(1), 91–94.

Sieroff, E., Decaix, C., Chokron, S., & Bartolomeo, P. (2007). Impaired orienting of attention in left unilateral neglect: A componential analysis. *Neuropsycholgy, 21*(1), 94–113.

Signer, S. F. (1994). Localization and lateralization in the delusion of substitution. Capgras syndrome and its variants. *Psychopathology, 27*, 168–176.

Silberstein, M. (2002). Reduction, emergence and explanation. In P. Machamer & M. Silberstein (Eds.), *The Blackwell Guide to the Philosophy of Science* (pp. 80–107). New York: Blackwell.

Silva, J. A., & Leong, G. B. (1995). A case of inanimate doubles syndrome. *Canadian Journal of Psychiatry, 40*, 277.

Silva, J. A., Leong, G. B., Weinstock, R., & Penny, G. (1995). Dangerous delusions of misidentification of the self. *Journal of Forensic Science, 40*, 570–573.

Silva, A, Leong, G. B., & Wine, D. B. (1993). Misidentification delusions, facial misrecognition and right brain injury. *Canadian Journal of Psychiatry, 38*, 239–241.

Silvanto, J., Cowey, A., Lavie, N., & Walsh, V. (2005). Making the blindsighted see. *Neuropsychologia, 45*, 3346–3350.

Sims, A., & White, J. (1973). Coexistence of Capgras and de Clerambault syndromes: A case history. *British Journal of Psychiatry, 123*, 635–637.

Simons, D. J. (1996). In sight, out of mind: When object representation fails. *Psychological Science, 7*, 301–305.

Simons, D. J. (2000). Current approaches to change blindness. *Visual Cognition, 7*, 1–15.

Simons, D. J., & Ambinder, M. S. (2005). Change blindness: Theory and consequences. *Current Directions in Psychological Science, 14*(1), 44–48.

Simons, D. J., & Chabris, C. F. (1999). Gorillas in our midst: Sustained inattentional blindness for dynamic events. *Perception, 28*, 1059–1074.

Simons, D. J., & Levin, D. T. (1997). Change blindness. *Trends in Cognitive Science, 1*(7), 261–267.

Sincinch, L. C., Park, K. F., Wohlgemuth, M. J., & Horton, J. C. (2004). Bypassing V1: A direct geniculate input area to MT. *Nature Neuroscience, 7*(10), 1123–1135.

Singer, J., & Kreiman, G. (2009). Toward unmasking the dynamics of visual perception. *Neuron, 64*, 446–447.

Singer, W. (1999). Neuronal synchrony: A versatile code for the definition of relations? *Neuron, 24*, 49–65.

Sinnett, S., Snyder, J. J., & Kingstone, A. (2009). Role of the lateral prefrontal cortex in visual object-based selective attention. *Experimental Brain Research, 194*, 191–196.

Skowbo, D., Timney, B., Gentry, T. A., & Morant, R. B. (1975). McCollough effects: Experimental findings and theoretical accounts. *Psychological Bulletin, 82*, 497–510.

Snow, J. C., & Mattingley, J. B. (2006). Stimulus- and goal-driven biases of selective attention following unilateral brain damage: Implications for rehabilitation of spatial neglect and extinction. *Restorative Neurology and Neuroscience, 24*, 233–245.

Smania, N., Martini, M. C., Gambina, G., Tomelleri, G., Palamara, A, Natale, E., & Marzi, C. A. (1998). The spatial distribution of visual attention in hemineglect and extinction patients. *Brain, 121*, 1759–1770.

Sperling, G., & Weichselgartner, E. (1995). Episodic theory of the dynamics of spatial attention. *Psychological Review, 102*(3), 503–532.

Sperry, R. W. (1961). Cerebral organization and behavior. *Science, 133*, 1749–1757.

Spillmann, L., & Kurtenbach, A. (1992). Dynamic noise backgrounds facilitate target fading. *Vision Research, 32*, 1941–1946.

Spillman, L., Otte, T., Hamburger, K., & Magnussen, S. (2006). Perceptual filling-in from the edge of the blind spot. *Vision Research, 46*(25), 4252–4257.

Staton, R. D., Brumback, R. A., & Wilson, H. (1982). Reduplicative paramnesia: A disconnection syndrome of memory. *Cortex: A Journal Devoted to the Study of the Nervous System and Behavior, 18*, 23–36.

Sterzer, P., & Rees, G. (2008). A neural basis for percept stabilization in binocular rivalry. *Journal of Cognitive Neuroscience, 20*(3), 389–399.

Stoerig, P. (1996). Varieties of vision: From blind responses to conscious recognition. *Trends in Neuroscience, 19*, 401–406.

Stoerig, P. (2002). Neural correlates of consciousness as state and trait. In L. Nadel (Ed.), *Encyclopedia of cognitive neuroscience* (pp. 232–240). London: Macmillan.

Stoerig, P., & Cowey, A. (1997). Blindsight in man and monkey. *Brain, 120*, 535–559.

Stromeyer, C. F., & Mansfield, R. (1970). Colored after-effects produced with moving edges. *Perception and Psychophysics, 7*, 108–114.

Stroop, J. R. (1935). The basis of Ligon's theory. *American Journal of Psychology, 47*, 499–504.

Struber, D., Basar-Eroglu, C., Miener, M., & Stadler, M. (2001). EEG gamma-band response during the perception of Necker cube reversals. *Visual Cognition, 8*, 609–621.

Stuerzel, F., & Spillmann, L. (2001). Texture-fading correlates with stimulus salience. *Vision Research, 41*, 2969–2977.

Summerfield, C., Jack, A., & Burges, I. (2002). Induced gamma activity is associated with conscious awareness of pattern masked nouns. *International Journal of Psychophysiology, 44*(2), 93–100.

Super, H., Spekreijse, H., & Lamme, V. A. (2001). Two distinct modes of sensory processing observed in monkey primary visual cortex (V1). *Nature Neuroscience, 4*, 304–310.

Sverd J. (1995). Comorbid Capgras syndrome. *Journal of the American Academy of Child and Adolescent Psychiatry, 34*, 538–539.

Sy, J. L., & Giesbrecht, B. (2009). Target–target similarity and the attentional blink: task relevance matters! *Visual Cognition, 17*(3), 307–317.

Takeichi, H., Nakazawa, H., Murakami, I., & Shimojo, S. (1995). The theory of curvature-constraint line for amodal completion. *Perception, 24*, 373–389.

Tatler, B. W. (2007). The central fixation bias in scene viewing: Selecting an optimal viewing position independently of motor biases and image feature distributions. *Journal of Vision, 7*, 1–17.

Tatler, B.W., & Vincent, B. T. (2009). The prominence of behavioural biases in eye guidance. *Visual Cognition, 17*, 1029–1054.

Theeuwes, J. (1994). The effects of location cuing on redundant-target processing. *Psychological Research, 57*(1), 15–19.

Theeuwes, J. (1995). Abrupt luminance change pops out; abrupt color change does not. *Perception and Psychophysics, 57*(5), 637–644.

Thomas, J. (1980). Binocular rivalry: The effects of orientation and patter color arrangement. *Perception & Psychophysics, 23*(4), 360–362.

Tipper, S. P., Lortie, C., & Baylis, G. C. (1992). Selective reaching: Evidence for action-centered attention. *Journal of Experimental Psychology: Human Perception and Performance, 18*, 891–905.

Todd, J., Dewhurst, K., & Wallis, G. (1981). The syndrome of Capgras. *British Journal of Psychiatry, 131*, 922–924.

Tolhurst, D. J., & Thompson, P. G. (1975). Orientation illusions and aftereffects: Inhibition between channels. *Visual Research, 15*, 967–972.

Tong, F., & Engel, S. A. (2001). Interocular rivalry revealed in the human cortical blind-spot representation. *Nature*, *411*, 195–199.

Tootell, R. B. H., & Hadjikhani, N. (2000). Attention—brains at work! *Nature Neuroscience*, *3*, 206–208.

Tootell, R. H. B., Reppas, J. B., Dale, A. M., Look, R. B., Sereno, I.B., Brady, T. J., & Rosen, B. R. (1995). Functional MRI evidence for a visual motion aftereffect in human cortical area MT/V5. *Nature*, *375*, 139–141.

Treisman, A. M. (1964). Verbal cues, language, and meaning in selective attention. *American Journal of Psychology*, *77*, 206–219.

Treisman, A. M. (1969). Strategies and models of selective attention. *Psychological Review*, *76*, 282–299.

Treisman, A. M. (1986). Features and objects in visual processing. *Scientific American*, *255*, 114–125.

Triesman, A. M. (1988). Features and objects: The Fourteenth Bartlett Memorial Lecture. *The Quarterly Journal of Experimental Psychology A: Human Experimental Psychology*, *40*(2), 201–237.

Treisman, A. M., & Gelade, G. (1980). A feature-integration theory of attention. *Cognitive Psychology*, *12*, 97–136.

Treu, S., & Trujillo, J. C. M. (1999). Feature-based attention influences motion processing gain in macaque visual cortex. *Nature*, *399*, 575–579.

Tsuchiya, N., & Koch, C. (2009). The relationship between consciousness and attention. In S. Laureys & G. Tononi (Eds.), *The neurology of consciousness* (pp.63–77). Amsterdam: Elsevier, Academic Press.

Tyler, C. W. (1975). Stereoscopic tilt and size aftereffects. *Perception*, *4*, 187–192.

Umilta, C., Castiello, U., Fontana, M., & Vestri, A. (1995). Object-centered orienting of attention. *Visual Cognition*, *2*, 165–181.

Underwood, G., Foulsham, T., & Humphrey, K. (2009). Saliency and scan patterns in the inspection of real-world scenes: Eye movements during encoding and recognition. *Visual Cognition*, *17*, 812–834.

Underwood, G., Foulsham, T., van Loon, E., Humphreys, L., & Bloyce, J. (2006). Eye movements during scene inspection: A test of the saliency map hypothesis. *European Journal of Cognitive Psychology*, *18*(3), 321–342.

Ungerleider, I. G., & Mishkin, M. (1982). Two cortical visual systems: In D. J. Ingle, M. A. Goodale, & R. J. W. Mansfield (Eds.), *Analysis of visual behavior* (pp. 549–586). Cambridge, MA: MIT Press.

Vaina, L. M., Cowey, A., Eskew, R. T., LeMay, M., & Kemper, T. (2001). Regional cerebral correlates of global motion perception: evidence from unilateral cerebral brain damage. *Brain*, *124*, 310–321.

Valentine, T. (1988). Upside-down faces: A review of the effect of inversion upon face recognition. *British Journal of Psychology*, *79*, 471–491.

Vallar, G., Daini, R., & Antonucci, G. (2000). Processing of illusion of length in spatial hemineglect: A study of line bisection. *Neuropsychologia*, *11*, 30–43.

Vallar, G., Rusconi, M. L., Bignamini, L., Geminiani, G., & Perani, D. (1994). Anatomical correlates of visual and tactile extinction in humans. A clinical CT scan study. *Journal of Neurology, Neurosurgery, and Psychiatry*, *57*, 464–470.

Van den Bussche, E., Hughes, G., Van Humbeeck, N., & Reynvoet, B. (2010). The relation between consciousness and attention: An empirical study using the priming paradigm. *Consciousness and Cognition: An International Journal*, *19*(1), 86–97.

Van den Bussche, E., Segers, G., & Reynvoet, B. (2008). Conscious and unconscious proportion effects in masked priming. *Consciousness and Cognition: An International Journal*, *17*(4), 1345–1358.

van Ee, R. (2005). Dynamics of perceptual bi-stability for stereoscopic slant rivalry and a comparison with grating, house-face, and Necker cube rivalry. *Vision Research*, *45*, 29–40.

Van Essen, D. C., Anderson, C. H., & Felleman, D. J. (1992). Information processing in the primate visual system: An integration systems perspective. *Science*, *255*, 419–423.

van Koningsbruggen, M. G., Gabay, S., Sapir, A., Henik, A., & Rafal, R. D. (2010). Hemispheric asymmetry in the remapping and maintenance of visual saliency maps: A TMS study. *Journal of Cognitive Neuroscience*, *22*(8), 1730–1738.

van Lier, R., van der Helm P., & Leeuwenberg, E. (1995). Integrating global and local aspects in visual occlusion. *Perception*, *23*, 883–903.

Vanni, S., Revonsuo, A., & Hari, R. (1997). Modulation of the parieto-occipital alpha rhythm during object detection. *The Journal of Neuroscience*, *17*(18), 7141–7147.

Vecera, S. P., & Farah, M. J. (1994). Does visual attention select objects or locations? *Journal of Experimental Psychology: General*, *123*, 146–160.

Vecera, S. P., Flevaris, A. V., & Filapek, J. C. (2004). Exogenous spatial attention influences figure-ground assignment. *Psychological Science, 15,* 20–26.

Vecera, S. P., & Gilds, K. S. (1998). What processing is impaired in apperceptive agnosia? Evidence from normal subjects. *Journal of Cognitive Neuroscience, 10*(5), 568–580.

Vecera, S. P., Vogel, E. K., & Woodman, G. F. (2002). Lower region: A new cue for figure-ground assignment. *Journal of Experimental Psychology: General, 131,* 194–205.

Venneri, A., & Shanks, M. F. (2004). Belief and awareness: Reflections on a case of persistent anosognosia. *Neuropsychologia, 42*(2), 230–238.

Verfaellie, M., Rapcsak, S. Z., & Heilman, K. M. (1990). Impaired shifting of attention in Balint's syndrome. *Brain and Cognition, 12*(2), 195–204.

Verleger, R., Jaskowski, P., Aydemir, A., van der Lubbe, R. H. J, & Groen, M. (2004). Qualitative differences between conscious and nonconscious processing on inverse priming induced by masked arrows. *Journal of Experimental Psychology: General. 133*(4), 494–515.

Verstraten, R. E., Fredericksen, F. A. J., & van de Grind, W. A. (1994). An analysis of the temporal integration mechanism in human motion perception. *Vision Research, 34*(23), 3153–3170.

Visser, T. A., Merikle, P. M., & Di Lollo, V. (2005). Priming in the attentional blink: Perception without awareness? *Visual Cognition, 12*(7), 1362–1372.

Vogeley, K., Kurthen, M., Falkai, P., & Maier, W. (1999). The prefrontal cortex generates the basic constituents of the self. *Consciousness and Cognition, 8,* 343–363.

Vogels, R., & Orban, G. A. (1987). Illusory contour orientation discrimination. *Vision Research, 27,* 453–467.

Vuilleumier, P., & Rafal, R. (2000). A systematic study of visual extinction. Between- and within-field deficits of attention in hemispatial neglect. *Brain, 123,* 1263–1279.

Vul, E., & Macleod, D. I. A. (2006). Contingent aftereffects distinguish conscious and preconscious color processing. *Nature Neuroscience, 7*(9), 873–874.

Wachsmuth, E., Oram, M. W., & Perret, D. I. (1994). Recognition of objects and their component parts: Responses of single units in the temporal cortex of the macaque. *Cerebral Cortex, 4*(5), 509–522.

Walker, P., & Powell, D. J. (1979). The sensitivity of binocular rivalry to changes in the nondominant stimulus. *Vision Research, 19,* 247–249.

Walker, R., & Mattingly, J. B. (1997). Ghosts in the machine? Pathological visual compltion phenomena in the damaged brain. *Neurocase, 3*(5), 313–315.

Walsh, V. and Pascual-Leone, A. (2003). Transcranial magnetic stimulation: A neurochronometics of mind. Cambridge, MA: MIT Press.

Washburn, M. F., Mallat, H., & Naylor, A. (1931). The influence of the size of an outline cube on the fluctuations of its perspective. *American Journal of Psychology, 43,* 484–489.

Watson, R. T., Heilman, K. M., Cauthen, J. C., & King, F. A. (1973). Neglect after cingulectomy. *Neurology, 23,* 1003–1007.

Watson, R. T., Valenstein, E., & Heilman, K. M. (1981). Thalamic neglect. *Archives of Neurology, 38,* 501–506.

Weichman, A. E., & Harris, J. M. (2001). Filling-in the details on perceptual fading. *Vision Research, 21,* 2107–2117.

Weiskrantz, L. (1980). Varieties of residual experience. *Quarterly Journal of Experimental Psychology, 32,* 365–386.

Weiskrantz, L. (1995). Blindsight: Not an island unto itself. *Current directions in Psychological Science. 4,* 146–151.

Weiskranz, L. (2009). Is blindsight just degraded normal vision? *Experimental Brain Research, 192,* 413–416.

Weiskranz, L., Warrington, E. K., Sanders, M., & Marshall, J. (1974). Visual capacity in the hemianopic field following a restricted cortical ablation. *Brain, 97,* 709–728.

Whittlesea, B. W. A., Dorken, M. D., & Podrouzek, K. W. (1995). Repeated events in rapid lists. Part 1: Encoding and representation. *Journal of Experimental Psychology: Learning, Memory, and Cognition, 21,* 1670–1688.

Whittlesea, B. W. A., & Masson, M. E. J. (2005). Repetition blindness in rapid lists: Activation and inhibition versus construction and attribution. *Journal of Experimental Psychology: Learning, Memory, and Cognition, 31,* 54–67.

Whitwell, R. L., Striemer, C. L., Nicolle, D. A., & Goodale, M. A. (2011). Grasping the non-conscious: Preserved grip scaling to unseen objects for immediate but not delayed grasping following a unilateral lesion to primary visual cortex. *Vision Research, 51*(8), 908–924.

Wilson, H. R. (2003). Computational evidence for a rivalry hierarchy in vision. *Proceedings of the National Academy of Sciences of the United States of America, 100*, 14499–14503.

Willemssen, R., Hoormann, J., Hohnsbein, J., & Falkenstein, M. (2004). Central and parietal event-related lateralizations in a flanker task. *Psychophysiology, 41*, 762–771.

Winawer, J., Huk, A. C., & Boroditsky, L. (2008). A motion aftereffect from still photographs depicting motion. *Psychological Science, 19*(3), 276–282.

Wisowaty, J. J. (1981). Estimate for the temporal response characteristics of chromatic pathways. *Journal of the Optical Society of America, 71*(8), 970–977.

Wojciulik, E., & Kanwisher, N. (1999). The generality of parietal involvement in visual attention. *Neuron, 23*, 747–764.

Wolfe, J. M., Kluender, K. R., Levi, D. M., Bartoskuk, L. M., Herz, R. S., Klatzky, R. L., & Lederman, S. (2010). *Sensation and perception* (2nd ed.). Sunderland, MA: Sinauer Associates.

Womelsdorf, T., Fries, P., Mitra, P. P., & Desimone, R. (2006). Gamma-band synchronization in visual cortex predicts speed for change detection. *Nature, 439*, 733–736.

Wong, E., & Weisstein, N. (1982). A new perceptual context-superiority effect: Line segments are more visible against a figure than against a ground. *Science, 218*(4572), 587–589.

Wong, E., & Weisstein, N. (1983). Sharp targets are detected better against a figure, and blurred targets are detected better against a background. *Journal of Experimental Psychology: Human Perception and Performance, 9*(2), 194–202.

Wunderlich, K., Schneider, K. A., & Kastner, S. (2005). Neural correlates of binocular rivalry in the human lateral geniculate nucleus. *Nature Neuroscience, 8*, 1595–1602.

Yantis, S. (1992). Multielement visual tracking: Attention and perceptual organization. *Cognitive Psychology, 24*, 295–340.

Yantis, S., & Hillstrom, A. P. (1994). Stimulus-driven attentional capture: Evidence from equiluminant visual objects. *Journal of Experimental Psychology: Human Perception and Performance, 20*(1), 95–107.

Yeari, M., & Goldsmith, M. (2010). Attention mandatory? Strategic control over mode of attention. *Journal of Experimental Psychology: Human Perception and Performance, 36*(3), 565–579.

Yeshurun, Y., & Carrasco, M. (1998). Attention improves or impairs visual performance by enhancing spatial resolution. *Nature, 396*, 72–75.

Young, A. W. (1994). Recognition and reality. In E. M. R. Critchley (Ed.), *Neurological boundaries of reality*. London: Farrand Press.

Yovel, G., & Duchaine, B. (2006). Specialized face perception mechanisms extract both part and spacing information: Evidence from developmental prosopagnosia. *Journal of Cognitive Neuroscience, 18*, 580–593.

Zeki, S. (1991). Cerebral akinetopsia (visual motion blindness). A review. *Brain, 114*, 811–824.

Zeki, S. (1993). *A vision of the brain*. Oxford: Blackwell Scientific.

Zeki, S. (1998). Parallel processing, asynchronous perception and a distributed system of consciousness in vision. *Neuroscientist, 4*, 365–372.

Zhaoping, L., & Snowden, R. J. (2006). A theory of a saliency map in primary visual cortex (V1) tested by psychophysics of colour- orientation interference in texture segmentation. *Visual Cognition, 14*, 911–933.

Index